THE WAR ON NEIGHBORHOODS

POLICING, PRISON, AND PUNISHMENT IN A DIVIDED CITY

RYAN LUGALIA-HOLLON and DANIEL COOPER

BEACON PRESS, BOSTON

BEACON PRESS
Boston, Massachusetts
www.beacon.org

Beacon Press books
are published under the auspices of
the Unitarian Universalist Association of Congregations.

21 20 19 18   8 7 6 5 4 3 2 1

This book is printed on acid-free paper that meets the uncoated paper
ANSI/NISO specifications for permanence as revised in 1992.

Text design and composition by Kim Arney

Many names and identifying characteristics of people mentioned
in this work have been changed to protect their identities.

Library of Congress cataloging information is available for this title.
LOC Cataloging in Publication Control Number: 2017040386

Without the will required to see that which is obscured,
we will continue to produce and reproduce human beings and
social relationships rooted in inequality and captivity.

—CHARLES MILLS, *The Racial Contract*

CONTENTS

THE HEROIN HIGHWAY

AT ANY TIME OF DAY, on any day of the year, you can see cars zooming down Chicago's Eisenhower Expressway. The bulk of drivers head to downtown jobs in the morning, rushing to desks with coffee in hand. In the evening, they drive out into the sunset, a pink and orange sky that appears for twenty or so fleeting minutes, a temporary horizon equally accessible to all. Those drivers head back to subdivisions and cul-de-sac homes, communities that might have made President Eisenhower smile. Going the opposite way, city dwellers head out to suburban jobs in the morning. They make the reverse commute at night, many of them heading back to friends, partners, and kids of their own.

Each day the expressway is filled with cautious motorists and careless lane switchers focused on the views directly in front of them. Windshields discipline their gaze and frame their focus. Through their radios, the world speaks many tongues: Talk shows and soft rock. R&B and throwback hip-hop. Classical music and country. Each car its own listening booth en route to its destination. While each vehicle makes its own journey, the larger patterns are clear—a predictable flow of traffic, rising to intense peaks on weekday mornings and evenings. The flow bridges downtown Chicago, the region's western suburbs, and the half-dozen neighborhoods that stand in between. Drivers within this traffic all share the same asphalt trade line. For the length of their commute, they are bound by the same lanes, speed limit, and rules of the road. But each and every day, they enter and exit diverging worlds, where the rules differ wildly.

Every few off-ramps, a new world begins. Depending on where you get off, the housing stock changes: from the high-rise condos at the heart of the city, to brick homes near Little Italy, to West Side graystones, to the charming mini-mansions of inner-ring suburbs, and, finally, the sprawling newer construction deep in suburbia. Employment levels vary dramatically. Chicago, where race and geography are commonly linked, has one of the largest racial employment gaps in the county. The employment rate for whites is about 73 percent among twenty- to twenty-four-year-olds, compared to 47 percent for blacks in the same age range.[1] Across these differing landscapes, violence plagues some communities, while others are affected much less directly.[2] Incarceration rates also vary dramatically, with some neighborhoods having the highest levels of imprisonment in the world while others are far below the global average.[3]

The Eisenhower Expressway begins in the city's center. Downtown Chicago is home to skyscrapers, theaters, hidden restaurants, and universities. It is also home to city hall's fifth floor, where Chicago's mayors have chosen, with surprisingly few exceptions, to pour their greatest resources into a vibrant central business district and a robust police force.[4] These mayors, like the city councils they've controlled, have labored under the delusion that a rising downtown might lift all boats and that neighborhoods left behind could simply be policed. Meanwhile, the undercurrents of violence and addiction have never ceased, drowning thousands and thousands of Chicagoans each year with waves that constantly pound on much of the city's West and South Sides. These same mayors have struggled to keep reporters at bay when these waves are detected by national media outlets, when outbreaks in shootings confirm, yet again, the limits of their theories on how to make a city great.

Head west from downtown and you'll reach the Morgan Street exit, where you'll find the University of Illinois at Chicago, a large state school. The campus, composed of concrete buildings, is organized around a large riot-proof tower, built in an era in which fear of racial unrest was translated into defensive architectural design. Erected roughly a decade after the expressway was opened, the tower hovers quietly, looking over the daily traffic, a reminder of a time when vast racial inequality was not so well disguised. The remnants of Greek Town and Little Italy are near the campus, each with its own ethnic restaurants and small stores, carryovers from a time before the university and the expressway displaced tens of thousands of white immigrant families.[5]

Drive farther away from downtown and you will pass through the Near West Side, North and South Lawndale, East and West Garfield Park. If you exit at Central Avenue, you will be in Austin, the most western part of Chicago's West Side. This area is the focus of our story. Like much of the West Side, Austin's economic bottom started to fall out after World War II, with the onslaught of deindustrialization. Once a mecca for the production of goods as diverse as candy and telephones, boarded-up factories are now strewn across its major thoroughfares.[6]

While billions in tax subsidies have gone into the development of Chicago's downtown from the 1980s through the present, the West Side economy has been heavily neglected. Businesses still line Austin's commercial corridors, but shoppers are fewer and farther between, and prices must be kept low enough to stay relevant in a neighborhood where living-wage jobs are all but an urban legend. Disposable income is rare. Often, unbudgeted purchases cannot be afforded, without risking the rent, diapers, or groceries. The parks are gorgeous and abundant, but the programs and sports leagues that should fill them up are too few. Meanwhile, imprisonment has been used to obscure the deeper needs of the neighborhood: the need for jobs, more stable housing, well-resourced schools, and a higher quality of life. Though it has failed to uproot gang violence or drug sales, the criminal justice system has been the dominant approach to neighborhood governance since the 1980s.[7]

Riding westward, the next exit leads to Oak Park, the first suburb past Chicago's western city limit and a common congestion point for traffic. The census reads very differently here, as does the institutional landscape and the approach to governance. Oak Park is a land of great schools and vibrant businesses. On lunch breaks, evenings, weekends, or anytime in their retirement, Oak Parkers can choose from a wealth of bars, ice cream shops, and restaurants. Many of them have the income available to do so regularly, a benefit accumulated from years of great-paying jobs, from family wealth passed down the generational bloodline, from investment strategies now paying dividends, or from a little bit of all three. Here, double-income households are the norm. The median household income of $80,196 is more than double that of neighboring Austin's $33,800.[8] An inner-ring suburb, Oak Park is full of unique character and historic buildings. It is home to many biracial families and was once voted one of the "sexiest suburbs in America."[9] Its buildings are deemed beautiful, and lovers of architecture pass through regularly to see the Prairie houses designed by Frank Lloyd Wright, a Midwestern point of pride. Here, imprisonment is a rare occurrence, with the criminal justice system playing a relatively minor role in community life.

The impacts of racism on these diverging landscapes is often hard to perceive. From the expressway, drivers cannot see the legislative histories, tax codes, and public-spending patterns that shape the terrain. There are no road signs explaining that redlining prevented banks from investing in West Side neighborhoods in the 1960s and '70s, using artificial geographical lines to refuse loans to people because of their race and class. Nor are there markers of the inverse strategy that targeted households in these areas for subprime loans in the 2000s. Drivers cannot see the white flight that persisted throughout the closing decades of the twentieth century, the ways that fear of black neighbors helped to drive the fast sales of homes and that real estate agents exploited the atmosphere for personal profit.[10] They cannot see how the residents in some communities are much more likely to be punished, to be removed from their homes, taken away from families and neighbors for years at a time.

These historical forces are not detectable when traveling at fifty or sixty miles an hour, but their influence is extraordinary, shaping the odds of success and stability, one generation after the next.[11] As these forces make clear, racism is not marked merely by Confederate flags and monuments. It goes far beyond individual hate or bigotry, far beyond even the violence that hateful individuals may commit. Racism is also structural. It shapes places themselves, the very environments in which life unfolds.[12] Without a willingness to look deeply, to cross boundaries of social comfort and convenience, you will miss these shaping effects. To see structural racism, it is not enough to stay behind your windshield, to peer only into your social media feed and immediate surroundings. You won't see how antiblack attitudes act upon institutions, upon budgets and laws, and then ultimately upon entire communities. You won't pierce the myth of punishment, the false idea that everyone is equally likely to be held accountable for their actions. You won't see the ways certain segments of society have been kept vulnerable, one of the rare constants in the more than sixty years since the Eisenhower Expressway opened.[13] All of that will remain hidden in plain sight. And because of this blind spot, you will also miss how the vulnerability of some endangers us all.

EXITS ON THE HIGHWAY: MICHAEL'S AND HAROLD'S STORIES

Though most drivers on the Eisenhower Expressway rarely take exits that are not part of their home, work, or school routine, there are exceptions. Some travelers, driven by addiction, have entered into underground trade lines. For them, the expressway has a different name: *the Heroin Highway*. They come at all hours. En route to the office, on their way back to their houses or apartments, and amid late-night urges, they pull over at streetside stores in hopes of finding something pure, a product that can help the blood flow faster through their veins.

For decades, Michael was one of those drivers. It took him years before he could comfortably drive along the expressway again. The memories of his drug addiction were too fresh. Michael would get off at the Central Avenue exit, drive into Austin, and purchase his drug of choice. He made that trip thousands of times, throughout his decades-long addiction, sometimes staying in the neighborhood to use his drugs as well. Years into his successful recovery, Michael explains that the urge to fall back into that habit is still present. He recalls, "For a long time just driving down the Eisenhower made me real nervous. It would just start spinning in my head, but when I crossed Central Avenue I'd be okay. But now I'm good, I can do it."

Michael, now in his forties, is a lifelong Chicagoland suburbanite with pale white skin who survived a long-running addiction to heroin. He is one of thousands of Chicagoland residents who became hooked on the drug in the 1990s. Since then, the epidemic has only grown, both in Illinois and across the country. Between 1999 and 2014, heroin-related deaths in the United States rose by more than 400 percent, with an estimated 10,574 lives lost in 2014.[14] This rise has been part of a larger trend of opioid-related deaths in the country. Overdoses from heroin and prescription drugs now take more lives every year than car crashes or shootings.[15] By 2017, drug deaths were the leading cause of death for Americans under age fifty, and the drug death rate has climbed faster than ever in recent years.[16]

Michael's substance abuse issues began to develop when he was seventeen years old. He says, "That's when I started drinking every day. And marijuana, of course, and a little acid, a little coke, then I got into crack. I didn't start using heroin until I was twenty-five. Once I started that, everything else went to the side. I didn't want anything else."

During the eight years that Michael had a daily heroin habit, he was spending a hundred dollars a day on the drug, a practice that he estimates cost him more than $100,000. Explaining this calculation, he says, "I couldn't go every day, but even if I went three hundred days in a year, that's $30,000 right there." He pulled the money to support his habit from anywhere he could. "I lived with my grandma for three years and she had a lot of money. . . . My grandma had to file bankruptcy because of what I did. I think she gave me $25,000 over three years." Sharing other financing strategies, Michael says, "Every morning I was just, like, making a beeline and doing all the things you do to get money, scamming and stealing and shit." He recalls blowing a $12,000 disability check from Social Security and a $2,000 settlement from a car accident. Michael explains, "The day the settlement check came, I went to the currency exchange. They took $37 to cash my $2,000 check. I was down in Austin for thirty hours—I came home with $150. I spent $1,800 in, like, thirty hours."

Money was only one of Michael's many problems. Throughout his years of addiction, he lost countless jobs, close friends, and romantic interests. And most devastatingly to him, he lost the trust of beloved family members. The downward spiral continued until 2001, when he had his first truly successful rehab experience. Today, Michael says, "It's been twenty years since I first started using heroin. It messed up my life, big time. Jail time, legal problems, health problems, overdoses. I got robbed several times at gunpoint."

During his long stretches of heavy use, Michael believes he was arrested thirty times, with charges ranging from possession of cocaine to car theft to burglary. He says, "I was in jail multiple times, nothing longer than ten or eleven days. . . . I've been in Cook County Jail five times. I've been in DuPage County Jail; I've been in the Will County Adult Detention Facility. I've been locked up in Lombard, Oak Brook Terrace, Elmhurst. I don't even know how many times I've been held in the precincts; I couldn't even tell you. In Orland Park, I was in jail many times, and Tinley Park." With the exception of Cook County, all the jails he names are in relatively affluent suburbs surrounding the city.

Despite years of illegal activity, Michael never went to prison. From his thirty arrests, Michael made over one hundred court appearances and skipped court on many occasions. In every single one of his cases, he recalls, "I got off." Describing one of those instances, Michael explains, "My grandma got me a lawyer and they threw [the case] out for illegal search and seizure because they had no reason to stop me." With the help of private lawyers he walked away from decades of illegal behavior without spending a single day in a penitentiary. He says, "Cook County Jail, that's as far as I went." Michael's experience is no anomaly. Many white users and sellers of drugs never even face arrest. White drug users are 2.5 times less likely to be arrested for drug use than blacks, despite using them at equal rates, and 3.6 times less likely to be arrested for selling drugs, despite distributing them at a rate 45 percent greater than blacks.[17]

Whether through his own resources or his family's, in almost all of his cases Michael was able to secure a private lawyer. Summarizing these experiences, he says, "If you go to court and you have a lawyer, you're going to do way better than if you go in by yourself. I stole a car and got arrested once and had a public defender, then I got two years' probation for that." That was the harshest punishment Michael ever received. Describing one of his lawyers, he says, "For $5,500, he knows everyone. Plus, if you have a [private] lawyer, the judge knows you have put out some bucks."

Michael's ability to navigate the criminal justice system without any prison time is striking. Amid all of his contact with judges, the most severe sanction he ever received was probation. During his painful and treacherous years of addiction, Michael's race, suburban background, and family finances functioned as clear protective factors against imprisonment. The benefits were even surprising to him; he says, "Sometimes I was like, 'Damn, they let me out on that?'"

If you take the Eisenhower until its western edge and then keep going, you can wind your way to the Sheridan Correctional Center. A ninety-minute drive from downtown Chicago, in the village of Sheridan, the prison houses over 1,700 inmates a year. It was first built as a juvenile facility in 1941 and now has seventy-five buildings, spread across 270 acres. This is where Harold was confined for many years of his life.

Like Michael, Harold also had a decades-long struggle with heroin and many encounters with the law. Unlike Michael, Harold is black, from Austin, and could never afford a private attorney. His race, geography, and class all greatly multiplied his likelihood of being incarcerated.[18] Also unlike Michael, Harold was both a user and a seller of drugs, a dual identity that reveals the fragility of many of the young men drawn into the illegal street economy. Growing up in a family where several relatives sold drugs, Harold's social world surrounded him with abundant opportunities to get involved. After many years of this exposure, Harold started using heroin and cocaine at the age of twenty-six. In his words, "I was around it so much that I wanted to try." Throughout his addiction, Harold was drawn into distributing drugs, a type of offense that disproportionately leads to long prison sentences for African American men.[19]

At the time of our interview, Harold had been imprisoned four times in his life for drug-related offenses, for a total of twenty-one years and nearly half a million taxpayer dollars. "My first conviction I had to do three [years], my second one I had to do six, my third one I had to do six, and my fourth one I had to do six." Those were all lost years, spent mostly in maximum-security prisons far from the city. Harold was isolated from his family and children. He missed life outside during much of the 1980s, 1990s, and 2000s. And for large swaths of time while he was imprisoned, Harold's addiction only deepened. He describes how he and other users got their drugs in prison: "The officers were bringing it in or the [inmates] got away with their girlfriends sneaking it in. You know, certain ways." His story highlights how basic mental and physical needs not only go unaddressed in "correctional" institutions, but are frequently made worse.

During his third imprisonment, Harold finally "got clean, and has been clean ever since." He recalls, "They had offered the inmates a drug program. And I signed up for the drug program about the second year of [that] incarceration and they stuck me down there." Describing the program, he says, "It was all right. I had a counselor that evaluated me. Within six months they made me a team leader to talk to the young guys when they come in, to let them know what the drugs will do to you. They saw me as more of a leader than a follower, so they put me in the forefront to be someone they can talk to about it and see that ain't the path they need to take. That's how I got clean." Harold's recovery happened through the drug treatment program at Sheridan Correctional Center, the very prison where he was first incarcerated years earlier. As he recalls, "Sheridan didn't have the drug program in place then"; it was not launched until 2004.

In the meantime, Harold lost precious years with his first son. Today they are still working to rebuild a relationship. "We get along. He comes by and sees me, we talk. I try to stress to him about how important it is he get a job." He tells his son, "You've got five kids; you've got to try to take care of them."

But Harold has a limited ability to intervene in his son's life trajectory. Though he may change for a short while after conversations with his father, "a month later he is doing the same thing." Harold's years of addiction and absence all happened during formative stages for this child, a pattern that is repeating itself as his grandchildren now watch the struggles of their father. Stories like Harold's show why the experience of imprisonment—which is supposed to operate as a deterrent from future crime—has become a near inevitability for many Austin residents.[20]

CONCENTRATING PUNISHMENT

Where you live along the Heroin Highway heavily influences how you'll be treated by the law. For decades, both Michael and Harold struggled with addiction before they were able to get clean, a fact that speaks to a universal need for better recovery options. Taking very different routes to their freedom, both men ultimately overcame painful addictions before those addictions took their lives. But that is where their parallels end. Their stories illustrate that race and class—so often fused with residential geography—are determining forces at nearly every level of the criminal justice system. Whereas Michael's story shows how white skin, ample finances, and influential networks can serve as protective factors for those breaking the law, Harold's experience shows what happens in the absence of those protections—and in the presence of the temptations facing youth and young adults on the West Side to enter the business of illegal drugs. As their stories illustrate, a vast disparity exists between the experiences of low-income African American dealers and their customers who come to them from outside suburbs and towns.[21]

The differences between Michael's and Harold's journeys are indicative of much larger patterns. According to Robert Sampson, a leading sociologist on urban neighborhood trends, the incarceration rate for parts of Chicago's predominantly black West Side are hundreds of times higher than Chicago's highest-incarceration white community. The incarceration rate in West Garfield Park, a neighborhood adjacent to Austin, is "forty-two times higher than the highest-ranked white community on incarceration (4,226 vs. 103 per 100,000)."[22] As Sampson declares, "This is a staggering differential even for community-level comparisons," one that suggests entirely different social realities exist within the same city, created by policies and systems that are poles apart.

In the West Side's 60644 zip code, between 2005 and 2009, there were 6,700 residents who were convicted and sentenced to prison. In neighboring Oak Park, just 311 residents were sentenced to prison in this period.[23] The former number points to tens of thousands of years lost by Austin residents. Every prison sentence marks a forced migration trail, spanning living rooms, courtrooms, and prison cells, where punitive policies actively remake city blocks, disrupting households and shifting the ways many neighborhood residents experience time.

As these numbers show, mass incarceration feeds on the punishment of people in places like Austin. In fact, Sampson and his colleague Charles Loeffler have said the very term "mass incarceration" is a misnomer. According to them, the United States' unparalleled rates of imprisonment are really the result of "concentrated incarceration," meaning that a relatively small pool of neighborhoods accounts for the great majority of those imprisoned. In these predominantly black areas, poverty is high and risky survival strategies are abundant. Residents of these areas are more likely to be arrested, tried, and convicted of felony charges. Because of legislative shifts starting in the 1980s, once convicted these residents are more likely to be sent to prison and to stay there for years on end. Furthermore, once a prisoner is released, no matter where they might have lived prior, they are more likely to return to an area like Austin, thereby fueling a "revolving door" effect that further strains limited community resources.[24]

Not only is incarceration itself geographically concentrated, so are the ripple effects of the punishment it carries, increasing depression and anxiety among *all* residents, regardless of their history with the criminal justice system.[25] We use the term "concentrated punishment" to describe how the effects of mass incarceration are experienced in places like Austin, where prison sentences are felt not just by the person behind bars but also by their neighbors, loved ones, and communities at large. However, the phrase "mass incarceration" is still helpful in describing a national criminal justice infrastructure that locks up nearly 25 percent of the world's prisoners.[26] We use this phrase when referring to the laws, prison buildings, criminal justice professionals, and varied private interests that comprise this infrastructure. They are what gives incarceration its mass. And when describing how some places bear the brunt of this mass, we use the term concentrated punishment.

Globally, there is little precedent for the United States' incredible reliance on prisons. At any given time, Chicago's Austin area has more people behind bars than several small countries combined. Incarceration rates on Chicago's West Side are ten times that of Russia (442 per 100,000), which is among the other top jailers on earth. Meanwhile, the incarceration rates of even the most impacted white areas are nothing extraordinary. The rate of Chicago's most affected white neighborhood is roughly the same as South Korea's (104 per 100,000), which is very close to the global average (100 per 100,000). These numbers make clear that some areas endure concentrated punishment, while many others are largely immune.[27]

If you live in one of the most affected areas, it would be normal for you to know many people with felony convictions, or to have a record yourself. One of the residents we interviewed explains, "Out of the people that I know from Austin, about 60 to 70 percent of people have felony convictions. I know hundreds of people. Out of 300 people, probably about 180 would have felony convictions." Tragically, this resident's estimate is well aligned with West Side averages for African American males in their age group.[28] These convictions have profound implications in the larger world, often determining who can get job interviews, access educational loans, or secure subsidized housing.

Though mass incarceration affects regions across the country, it is especially bad in Midwestern states like Illinois and Wisconsin, where more than one in three black men will serve time in state prisons and where black men have a higher cumulative risk of imprisonment than in any other region.[29] What enables these rates of conviction and imprisonment?

In theory, high incarceration rates in areas like Austin can simply be explained away by levels of crime. But, as the stories of Michael and Harold illustrate, no such simple correlation exists. Crime is not a pure predictor for levels of imprisonment. "Punishment's Place: The Local Concentration of Mass Incarceration," Sampson and Loeffler's pioneering 2010 study of how incarceration concentrates in certain urban areas, details how neighborhoods with high levels of both crime and other markers of disadvantage—such as low education levels and sparse capital investments—have much higher incarceration rates than high-crime areas with few markers of disadvantage.[30] In the words of these scholars, "Communities that experienced high disadvantage experienced incarceration rates more than three times higher than communities with a similar crime rate." As their work implies, you cannot understand incarceration without also looking at social forces beyond crime.[31]

SEEING THE WAR

Just between the years of 2005 and 2009, roughly 322,000 people were sentenced to the Illinois Department of Corrections from Cook County. The boom in mass incarceration began more than twenty-five years earlier, meaning hundreds of thousands more were sent to prison before and after that time period. And that is in just one county.[32] Though community leaders of all stripes have never stopped doing the vital labor of neighborhood building—from creating opportunities for youth to providing healing resources for those who need them—even their most successful efforts have struggled to receive the investments needed to be brought to scale. Instead, one conviction at a time, massive amounts of money have been poured into the punishment of African American residents from low-income neighborhoods.

This concentrated punishment is one of the most sophisticated operations of structural racism the world has ever seen. Rather than uproot poverty and disadvantage in urban areas, it has been a perverse attempt to manage it, which in turn has led to an extreme overreliance on the criminal justice system.[33] In so doing, concentrated punishment extends a long legacy of antiblack policies and practices, one of the few true constants in US history.[34]

But despite the evidence, the idea that punishment is concentrated is not a widely accepted truth. There is a pervasive and persistent myth that says people are equally likely to be arrested, prosecuted, and convicted for their actions no matter where they live, how they look, or what conditions they may be striving to overcome. There is an equally persistent myth that punishment creates public safety. These myths sustain society's heavy investments in incarceration, which is justified by one of four basic rationales: retribution, incapacitation, deterrence, and rehabilitation, each of which is based on a different set of assumptions about how change will happen given a particular series of rules and enforcement mechanisms.[35]

Retribution is based on the idea that people who break society's laws inherently deserve to receive some measure of harm in return. Incapacitation says that those who break laws should be removed from their social contexts for a designated period of time to prevent them from breaking further laws. Deterrence asserts that by damaging those who damage others and their property, we send an important social message that wrongdoing is not acceptable and triggers substantive consequences, which thereby discourages others from engaging in it. Finally, the rehabilitative theory of incarceration says that isolation from society can help people to improve themselves, creating space to change whatever characteristics led them to their acts of wrongdoing.[36]

Under each of these justifications, prisons are a way to govern disorderly people who cause significant harm to others. Separation from the rest of society is presented as a form of individual-level population management, where the law is enforced, interpreted, and applied on an individual basis as a way of assessing the degree of past harm and future risk. Based on due process and the weighing of evidence, the idea of individual-level application of the law is foundational to the American legal system. In the minds of many Americans, the behavior of police officers and judges is consistent across geography, punishing only people who are guilty beyond reasonable doubt. In reality, the definitions of both guilt and doubt are directly influenced by the geography in question and the poverty and skin color of the people living in that geography.[37] What police officers see as suspicious behavior depends largely on the areas they are patrolling, just as the ways judges conceive of threat often hinges on the lawyers presenting the case to them. For these reasons, actual crime is only one predictor of the incarceration rates of an area, with levels of poverty and structural disadvantage being a close and inextricable second.[38]

Consequently, in high-incarceration neighborhoods the law is not just applied individually. It has become a vehicle for collective punishment, used as a basic public policy response to the struggles of marginalized African American communities, not only in Chicago but also in New York City, New Orleans, Baltimore, Detroit, Los Angeles, Dallas, Houston, Louisville, Memphis, and dozens of other US cities suffering from deindustrialization and selective community divestment.[39] In New York City, for example, just five neighborhoods—the South Bronx, Brownsville, East New York, Harlem, and Bedford-Stuyvesant—felt the brunt of this policy response, and as a result make up over a third of the entire state's prison population.[40] Within these areas, there is now a major gap between the logics of the law and the actual, on-the-ground reality of the law. Only by interrogating that gap is it possible to see how the law is experienced by residents of these communities, where police officers have lost much of their public respect, deterrence has lost its power, children and families frequently become incapacitated, and rehabilitation often isn't even a consideration.

Despite these failings, the law remains the primary force for social intervention among the most disadvantaged communities in the United States. Policymakers have leaned heavily on the criminal justice system to hide, rather than solve, many of society's most entrenched challenges. But penal institutions have limited power to heal the traumas that drive so many offenders. Nor can they uproot the pain that often torments survivors and the loved ones of victims. Incarceration does nothing to change the dilemmas and difficulties faced by residents of high-incarceration neighborhoods. It makes them no less dependent upon survival strategies like selling drugs or their own bodies. It neither removes the abundant stressors they face nor expands the limited opportunities they can claim in the face of those stressors. Rather, arrests, felony trials, and prison time all become the basis for society to further condemn these residents, to pile upon the stressors, removing them from existing supports and further narrowing any redemptive opportunities.[41]

When prisons go unquestioned, they complete a tidy but dangerous story line for how society creates safety on the streets. But when we take a critical look at imprisonment patterns in areas like Austin, a more difficult story emerges. What has so often been called a "war on drugs" is really part of a larger war on neighborhoods, a prolonged and costly period of conflict that has destabilized low-income African Americans and the communities they call home. Fueled by concentrated punishment, this war is waged every time society attempts to make the world safer simply through punitive measures. Such measures have only left communities more isolated and cities more divided. The war is carried out through both the broken logics and the broken tools of the law, propelled by policies that respond to economic isolation and trauma with confinement, which has only produced missing parents and the further fragmentation of families. As we show throughout this book, the war on neighborhoods amounts to a legally codified attack on pain and dysfunction, through which high rates of conviction and imprisonment have become a self-fulfilling prophecy.

OUTSIDE LOOKING IN

When driving on the Eisenhower Expressway, you pass places with very different relationships to the war on neighborhoods. When you drive into Oak Park, you are unlikely to see arrests on the street or people selling drugs on the corners. Walk into the homes of this suburb and very few parents will have been removed and put into prison. Young people on the streets are likely to be wearing gear from their sports team or after-school programs. In stark contrast, if you take the exit at Central Avenue and drive through Austin, evidence of the prison system and its effects are abundant. Police cars are more likely to be flashing their lights, and their back seats are often occupied. Surveillance cameras adorn many street corners. Young people typically navigate life after school without the backing of formal programs or sports clubs and instead are often left alone to occupy those hours.

We first learned of these differences as graduate students, eager to sharpen our understanding of the Chicago we called home. Long before meeting Michael or Harold, we met at the College of Urban Planning and Public Administration, in a modest building just on the other side of the expressway from the University of Illinois at Chicago's main campus. As we sat at cafeteria-style tables beneath fluorescent lighting, our professors lectured about community histories, plans gone awry, and the profound gap that exists between the visions of policymakers and the realities of those whom their policies will impact most. They also taught us about the limits of any research project, starting with the limits among the researchers themselves.

Neither of us has ever been to jail. While we've been handcuffed, we've never been taken to a police station. Though we have broken the law, we've largely been left to deal with our own consciences and, on some occasions, our parents' wrath. We do not personally know what it's like to be forcibly removed from our homes, or to be harassed while walking down our own blocks. Though we acted up in school, we were never expelled. Our relationships with friends were never treated as a threat to society, even when we were sneaking out of our homes in the middle of the night to meet them.

We have been trusted and protected in ways that millions of young Americans never experience. From a young age, powerful institutions— from local community centers to summer camps to prestigious universities—have invested in us. We have been surrounded by loving and caring responses, even when we were the most disruptive forces in a room. Countless times we have been deemed funny or spirited rather than dangerous. Our energy and imaginations have consistently been accepted as assets instead of challenges to the social order. Our parents and siblings have been treated similarly, despite their own deviances, allowing them to always be within reach when we needed them.[42] Law and order has never worked against us.

Just as we have never felt the force of cell doors locking us out from the world, we have also been protected from other dangers. We were rebellious, buying drugs from friends, smoking and drinking in parks and on school grounds. But our drug use was "recreational" and rarely policed. While some friends did lose years of their lives to serious addictions, they had the supports they needed to recover. Guns were never in the picture. We were not pressured by peers to carry them and we never once thought they were necessary for our safety. We did not grow up in the middle of contested turfs, never had to dodge bullets, and never buried a teenage friend. As a result, it has been relatively easy for us to adjust to challenging yet rewarding lives, with meaningful work and lasting friendships.

We have written *The War on Neighborhoods* as witnesses—white, male scholars largely immune to the types of government actions we describe. Our insights stem from years of work on Chicago's West Side as well as formal research in one community area, Austin, where over $100 million has been spent annually on adult incarceration costs, not including any other criminal justice expenses.[43] We draw upon over fifty individual interviews with residents and officials of that area, as well as hundreds of community meetings and observations. We studied the lives of formerly incarcerated residents, police officers, grassroots leaders, juvenile justice officials, local politicians, and a wide array of community members. We also draw from secondary data on public-safety systems, ranging from the Chicago Police Department and the Cook County State's Attorney's Office to the Illinois Department of Corrections.

But we have no direct personal experience with mass incarceration, and neither do our immediate families. Because this book was written from our vantage points, we lift up the stories of our interviewees at every turn, providing key context for their realities. However, though we strive to paint a balanced picture of Austin, there are millions of stories that we never even heard, let alone retold in this book.

As with any place, Austin is full of intricacies that we do not fully capture. This limitation is evident in our definition and use of the term "neighborhood." Strictly speaking, Austin is not a single neighborhood. It is a collection of them, bundled together as the largest of Chicago's seventy-seven community areas. Like each of these areas, Austin is an invented parcel of space, a carving of a made-up whole, bound by artificial borders that occasionally make concrete sense.

Whereas a neighborhood is something you can often feel when you walk out your front door, a community area must be seen on a map to be understood. They carry great weight for planners, real estate agents, and bankers, but sometimes hold little meaning for actual residents, who navigate smaller borders on a day-to-day basis. We use both terms throughout the book. "Community area" is used to refer to Austin at large, while "neighborhood" is used to refer to main subsections within Austin. We privilege the term "neighborhoods" in our title and central framework because it is familiar to readers and is a more transferrable unit of analysis across other cities.[44]

Chicago's original seventy-five community areas were defined by the University of Chicago Social Science Research Committee in the late 1920s, based largely on "statistical areas" that were developed early in the century to help understand problems of crime.[45] Though the remaining two areas were added decades later, these original demarcations have gone relatively unchanged for the better part of a century. Each of

these areas is large, comparable to the size of many towns and munici-
palities. And none is larger or more populous than Austin. More than
seven square miles in size, it has nearly fourteen thousand people per
square mile, with over ninety-eight thousand people in total. Across this
terrain, Austin has five distinct neighborhoods: Galewood, the Island,
L-Town, North Austin, and South Austin.[46]

Of Austin's neighborhoods, Galewood is the most unlike the others.
It is on the far northwestern edge of the community area, bordered to the
north by the Metra rail line. The area was originally a 320-acre farm in
1938. The founding farmer, Abraham Gale, sold an interest in the property to the Chicago & Pacific Railroad, after which it was dubbed Galewood. As more and more residences were built on the property, lots sold
for between five and twenty-five dollars. In the twentieth century, it became home to Italian residents who left areas closer to downtown. With
long-standing residents and businesses, Galewood experienced relatively
low levels of blockbusting, a practice whereby real estate agents propa-
gated fear of "racial transition" to white homeowners in order to buy
their houses at cheap prices. Galewood did not have the same levels of
"white flight"—white families fleeing in fear of this transition—as other
neighborhoods within Austin. To this day, Galewood stands as the most
diverse of Austin's predominantly African American neighborhoods.

The Island is the smallest and most well-defined of Austin's neighborhoods. Found in the area's far southwest corner, it is surrounded by
industry, the Eisenhower Expressway, and two neighboring suburbs. As
its name suggests, the Island is largely isolated from the rest of the city.
Today it is home to about 1,700 diverse residents. But that diversity was
hard fought. In the mid-1980s, the neighborhood became infamous for
its bigotry, when an African American family was attacked with bricks
and bottles when attempting to move in.[47] The Island's industrial zone
has had a rotating cast of businesses over time, including Chicago Studio
City, a hundred-thousand-square-foot filmmaking studio that has produced movies and TV shows like *Ali*, *Ocean's Eleven*, *Batman Begins*, and
Transformers 3.[48]

In contrast to the Island, L-Town may be the most porous of Austin's
neighborhoods. To the north and south, it has few clear borders. It is
named after an accumulation of streets starting with the letter L. There

Figure 1: Austin Community Map

are fifteen such streets in all: La Crosse, Lamon, Laporte, Lavergne, Law-
ler, Leclaire, Leamington, Laramie, Latrobe, Lockwood, Lorel, Long,
Lotus, Linder, and Luna. While these avenues are clearly bound on the
east and west, many of them extend far north of Austin, reaching high
into Chicago's Northwest Side. To the south, they find their ends at two
junctures, some concluding at Madison Avenue, others stopping at the
Eisenhower. Only Laramie extends beyond Austin to the south, cutting
through the suburb of Cicero. But then, all fifteen L streets reemerge on
Chicago's Southwest Side, just north of Midway Airport.

North Austin is an expansion of a 280-acre subdivision developed
by Henry W. Austin in 1865.[49] After twenty-five years working for hard-
ware manufacturers, Austin invested his profits into real estate and
eventually into this subdivision, which was a part of the nearby town-
ship of Cicero until it was annexed to Chicago in 1899. Located below
Galewood, it is more affluent than South Austin. A famous subsection
of the neighborhood is Midway Park, a small and stunning section of
nineteenth-century homes that was made a National Register historic
district in the mid-1980s. Frederick Schock, Frank Lloyd Wright, and
Wright's students were among the architects who gave the area its neo-
classical and Queen Anne–style housing stock.

South Austin is the largest neighborhood in the area, spanning from
Roosevelt to Division Street and from Austin Boulevard to Cicero Avenue. Once a mecca for jobs, home to vibrant commercial and industrial
corridors, South Austin was heavily impacted by deindustrialization. It
was also the first of Austin's neighborhoods to be affected by the rise
of the drug trade and the concentrated punishment that followed. One
former resident recalls, "Right before the '80s, South Austin just fizzled
away. You saw a lot of positive activity disappear. I still had family that
lived over in the area and I saw the difference in my family members, in
my cousins. We were all very athletic and creative; [my cousins] would
draw and were artistic. But I saw nothing come of their talents."[50]

Each of these Austin neighborhoods has its unique history and characteristics. But they have all developed in a shared political and economic
climate. They've been home to redlining, mortgage discrimination, and
racially restrictive covenants, where African Americans were denied access to homes because of their race. They've been sites of blockbusting
and white flight. And they've witnessed decades of general divestment,

where basic infrastructure was allowed to decay without routine maintenance.[51] L-Town, North Austin, and South Austin have been the most affected by these practices. They have also been the most affected by drugs,
violence, policing, and the prison system. Today, they form the core of
the highest-incarceration community area in Chicago. Most of the dynamics explored in this book refer to these parts of Austin.

Another major limitation of this study is our neglect of the ways that
other communities of color across US cities are impacted by structural
racism and forced removal. Many low-income Latino neighborhoods
face disproportionately high incarceration levels, as well as routine surveillance of their legal-documentation status from the Immigration and
Customs Enforcement agency. As happens with African American areas
like Austin, this patrol and surveillance is propped up by disparaging
narratives about individual residents, while being disconnected from
real root-cause analysis of the conditions those residents must navigate.
Similarly, neighborhoods with large South Asian and Middle Eastern
populations can experience extreme discrimination under the banner of
anti-Muslim rhetoric and actions. These are profoundly important issues
and worth the full attention of every reader of this book. While they
fall outside the scope of our focus on the country's highest-incarceration
neighborhoods, they are no less important.

Our study is restricted to those places where the criminal justice
system has become the commanding approach to neighborhood governance and investment. These are predominantly African American
areas. They range from Chicago's far West Side to Ferguson, Missouri,
Houston's Fifth Ward, and Miami's Liberty City. Within these places,
generations of neighborhood citizens have been robbed of a future under the guise of a war on drugs and "tough on crime" policies.[52]

The War on Neighborhoods goes beyond a policy-only lens of mass
incarceration. We analyze the legislative reforms of the 1980s and
1990s alongside the neighborhood conditions where these regressive
reforms took root. Throughout the book, we demonstrate that the on-
the-ground conditions of neighborhoods like Austin made residents
uniquely vulnerable to the punitive logics of law enforcement. We walk
you through the impact that deindustrialization had on Austin and its
trajectory, the maddening persistence of addiction and violence, and the
failures of modern policing efforts to uproot these destructive forces. We

then tally up the cumulative effect these dynamics have had on Austin's children and youth, highlighting the systemic absence of protective factors that would prevent the entrance of another generation of residents into the prison system.

Recognizing the above dangers, the book's final chapters advance an alternative vision for how public safety should work, while also describing the interdependence of urban African American communities most impacted by the triple threat of violence, lethal drugs, and incarceration, and white rural communities, where prisons are a major driver of employment. We argue that efforts to end mass incarceration must go beyond reforming legislation or police practices; they must also help rebuild those neighborhoods that have been most devastated by incarceration's ill and concentrated effects. To move forward, we must create a future where money is invested to undo the damage punishment has caused, where outside officials are not the only leaders empowered to create safety, where 911 is only one of several numbers residents can call for help, and where young people no longer feel like they have to pick up the cold steel of a gun and take matters of justice into their own hands.

CHAPTER 1

HISTORY OF THE WAR

IN CHICAGO, a notoriously flat city, it is hard to find even a small hill that is not artificial. But when it comes to the distribution of opportunity, Chicago looks a lot more like the Swiss Alps. Some areas have incredible views while others struggle to get daylight. In terms of opportunity, Austin is a valley town sitting at the western edge of the city, far from the towering peaks of downtown but just steps away from the great cliffs that surround Oak Park.[1] Though Austin has ample land and space, many of its residents struggle for basic sustenance, often lacking access to even minimum-wage jobs. And like other valley dwellers, residents of Austin are under routine surveillance. Just across Austin Boulevard, in Oak Park, living-wage jobs are the norm and there is little police oversight. Though the two communities are a stone's throw from each other, Austin and Oak Park feel like separate realities.

Across Chicago, the value of white homes is twelve times greater than that of those owned by people of color. Further, median household income of black families is less than half of that for white families, and roughly three out of every five households are rent-burdened, meaning they are spending more than 30 percent of their income on housing costs.[2] Life on the edge keeps Austin residents keenly aware of the gaps between their circumstances and those of their neighbors. In the words of one resident, "You're very close to affluent lifestyles. Being that close to Oak Park, seeing big cars, nice houses, that's not far away for you. You are literally blocks away if you wanted to go and see that. You see fancy cars go through Chicago Avenue." This inequality can have a subconscious effect on residents, especially younger ones who are working to make sense of their place in the broader world.[3] But the effects are not just mental. Life expectancy in Cook County varies by more than thirty years depending on where a person lives.[4]

The unequal terrains we describe are not unique to Chicagoland. Much of America is shaped by similar divides. And, not coincidentally, the most economically segregated cities in the United States have their own high-incarceration areas. In 2012, the big cities with the highest rates of inequality were Atlanta, San Francisco, Miami, and Boston. In each of these cities, a household at the 95th percentile of the income distribution earned at least fifteen times the income of a household at the 20th percentile. In Atlanta, for instance, the richest 5 percent of households earned more than $280,000, while the poorest 20 percent earned less than $15,000. In another six cities (New York, Oakland, Chicago, Los Angeles, Baltimore, and Washington, DC), a household at the 95th percentile of the income distribution earned at least twelve times the income of a household at the 20th percentile.[5] These are all cities with entrenched histories of concentrated punishment.[6]

Unlike actual peaks and valleys, the differences between advantaged and disadvantaged places are entirely manufactured. While Oak Park's strength is reinforced by a great education system and access to rewarding work, Austin's history has been marked by racially discriminatory policies, including racially restrictive covenants that prohibited nonwhite families from moving into communities, predatory lending that targeted low-income areas, and underfunded and shuttered schools.[7] Rather than seeking to level the playing field, Austin has been shaped by one regressive response after another, each one piling on new layers of social and economic exclusion.

Amid this history of regressive responses, the criminal justice system simultaneously fuels and conceals larger patterns of inequality. The "bad choices" of Austin residents are used to explain away huge gaps in wages, school quality, and investments in development. Meanwhile, the residents of advantaged areas like Oak Park are often immune to criminalization, a fact that allows them to make their own bad choices—from using drugs with near immunity to more serious, white-collar crimes—without ever facing life-altering consequences.[8] As a result, the driving forces behind Austin's and Oak Park's differences often remain invisible to the untrained eye, making the peaks and valleys of opportunity appear almost natural.[9]

This chapter seeks to lift that cloak. We connect the deep history of racial inequity in the US to the genesis of a high-incarceration area like Austin. Several scholars have already linked this history to the larger phenomenon of mass incarceration, notably Michelle Alexander and Loïc Wacquant, who trace it all the way to slavery, illustrating how blackness itself has long been associated with criminality in the minds of Americans.[10] In his *Atlantic* article "The Case for Reparations," Ta-Nehisi Coates connects structurally racist policies to the formation of neighborhoods on Chicago's West Side. He explicitly analyzes how "black people across the country were largely cut out of the legitimate home-mortgage market" and, during this same extended period, from the 1930s to 1960, "were herded into the sights of unscrupulous lenders who took them for money and for sport."[11] In this chapter, we draw upon lesser-known observers to show how these forces facilitated the rise of concentrated punishment and how Austin specifically was made and unmade through the persistence of structural racism, through a toxic mixture of segregation and extraordinary sanctions.

In so doing, we illustrate how valley and mountain neighborhoods have been formed over time, how economic pillars have been eroded, how racial segregation and generational poverty have been reproduced. We document the origins of the war on neighborhoods, from the segregation of the city to the changing composition of US police forces to the antiblack intentions that guided the genesis of the "war on drugs." And we begin to count the costs of this punitive direction in policymaking, pointing to the immense financial burden of suppressing entire communities. Finally, we show how local organizations have fought the uphill battle for progress and how they keep pushing ahead despite the odds and obstacles, carrying as much hope on their backs as they can.

HOLLOWING OUT THE VALLEY

The composition of Chicago's West Side changed dramatically in the twentieth century. Between 1950 and 1970, the number of African American residents grew from 77,360 to 196,482, while the number of whites dropped from 333,716 to 110,725.[12] It was impossible to predict at the time, but this massive shift laid the groundwork for what would become concentrated punishment.

This period of change, commonly known as "white flight," had many driving forces.[13] These were the closing decades of the Great Migration in which, between 1916 and 1970, more than six million African Americans left the South for the Northeast, the Midwest, and western parts of the US.[14] While Chicago's South Side was a primary destination during the early waves of migrants, the West Side became a major entry point in the later decades. Meanwhile, suburbanization had begun. Accelerated in the post-WWII years, the move to the suburbs provided white families a greater separation between work and family life, as well as between themselves and their African American former neighbors.[15]

In Chicago, the suburban exodus mapped onto the development of the Eisenhower Expressway, which officially opened in 1955. During the main construction period for the Eisenhower, from 1949 to 1961, an "estimated 13,000 people" were displaced from the neighborhoods surrounding Congress Avenue, upon which the expressway was built.[16] This dispersal forever changed the landscape of the West Side.[17] Though remnants persist today, large sections of Near West Side neighborhoods Greek Town and Little Italy were wiped out. The heavily integrated Near West Side community area, which was roughly 40 percent African American in 1950, was torn apart. East Garfield Park, West Garfield Park, and Austin, areas with large Jewish populations at the time, were also heavily impacted. According to historian Beryl Satter, the expressway's "construction was a physical manifestation of Jewish Chicagoans' political powerlessness."[18] Amid this displacement, white communities of the near and far west sides sought new lands. While many joined ethnic enclaves across the city's North Side, thousands moved to the suburbs. As with other expressway projects across the country, the Eisenhower brought an end to diverse and integrated communities across a key section of the city.[19]

There is no telling how the influx of African Americans on Chicago's West Side might have unfolded differently. In historian Robert Loerzel's words, the expressway "undercut any desire or any will to find solutions, to find ways to integrate the new arrivals. It was clear that the area was not going to stay all white. But that didn't mean there had to be this mass white flight that took place."[20] Even as this flight was unfolding, many small experiments in multiracial community building developed, including acts of solidarity in direct response to the racist housing policies of the time.[21]

However, prior to the construction of the Eisenhower, the dominant policy experiments reinforced racial tensions. In *The Condemnation of Blackness*, Khalil Gibran Muhammad shows how statistics were used in the late nineteenth and early twentieth centuries to associate African Americans with dangerousness. Crime statistics were used as justification for not investing in solutions to meet the social and economic needs of African Americans, who were already over-incarcerated at the time. While the crimes committed by Italian and Irish immigrants were said to be the fault of society, for not better supporting their successful integration, the same courtesies were not applied to groups with darker skin.[22]

This period, from the late nineteenth century through the first half of the twentieth century, is when "the greatest and most durable increases in racial disparity took place."[23] These disparities would prove foundational in what would become mass incarceration. In "Northward Migration and the Rise of Racial Disparity in American Incarceration, 1880–1950," Christopher Muller finds that "migrants left a region with a comparatively low, and entered a region with a comparatively high, nonwhite incarceration rate."[24] With the influx of African Americans, northern states became increasingly likely to put new arrivals behind bars—and they had already been more willing to do so than the states from which blacks were moving. Explaining this trend, Muller points to the tensions between African American migrants and white immigrants, whereby African Americans became the foil for many white immigrants in their efforts to assimilate. He documents how foreign whites like the Irish had successfully secured a growing share of patronage jobs, ultimately occupying a majority of police positions in northern states.[25]

These same white populations wielded the power of the law in the 1950s, as African Americans moved into the North Lawndale, East Garfield Park, and West Garfield Park areas following World War II.[26] And they held that same power in the 1960s, as demographics started to transition in Austin, the last of the major West Side neighborhoods to do so. This was a period rife with tension, as Amanda Seligman demonstrates in her book *Block by Block: Neighborhoods and Public Policy on*

Chicago's West Side. Rather than pack up their bags, many whites used a combination of intimidation, violence, and the law to try to keep their community from changing.[27] One white former Austin resident we interviewed recalls how heated confrontations between whites and blacks became common on outdoor basketball courts, until finally, white park operators chose to remove basketball rims rather than help to integrate the games. A hub for these actions was the Austin Town Hall Assembly, a sixty-member organization with prominent civic and political leadership.[28]

During the 1960s and 1970s, local civil rights leaders were pressing for progress at the neighborhood level. Organization for a Better Austin (OBA) was a 187-member organization formed to fight blockbusting and hold real estate firms accountable.[29] Meanwhile, both Austin Town Hall and the Austin YMCA were targeted for organizing by the National Association for the Advancement of Colored People (NAACP). Both had been whites-only spaces since their founding and the push was to get them to finally admit African Americans. According to one white former resident, "Whenever blacks walked in the gyms, they would just turn off the lights." And gym lights were not the only thing being turned off. These years saw the closure of a major elevated-train station, as well as several bedrock institutions, such as hospitals.[30] But none of these exclusionary shifts did much to slow the demographic change. Whereas the Austin area was 32 percent African American by 1970, that percentage grew to 73 percent in 1980 and continued to climb thereafter.[31] Austin's segregated future had been ensured.

DAWN OF WAR

When he launched the War on Poverty, in 1964, President Lyndon B. Johnson wanted to ensure that all Americans, no matter where they lived, had a pathway to prosperity. Spurred by the civil rights movement, his efforts to end poverty gained great momentum in their early years. Under the Johnson administration, and in the wake of John F. Kennedy's assassination, formal racial segregation was outlawed, school segregation was banned, college loan programs were launched, and programs for everything from early-childhood education to youth jobs were brought to life.[32] But along the way, something went terribly wrong. By 1996, nearly one of every three young black men in America was under some form of correctional supervision, whether in prison, on probation, or on parole.[33] Starting in the early 1970s, rather than double down on the War on Poverty, the United States had prioritized a parallel war in high-poverty communities like those on the West Side, a war that fundamentally changed the ways society understood disadvantaged urban areas, even as the racial composition of those areas continued to shift.

This was officially called the War on Drugs. The campaign, begun by Richard Nixon, had two fronts: an international focus on disrupting the production and shipment of drugs, and a domestic focus on punishing those who bought and sold drugs within US borders.[34] Domestically, rather than view poverty as the destructive force holding back many communities, the target was shifted to illegal narcotics, those who distribute them, and those who become addicted to them.[35]

From the outset, the domestic arm of this campaign was antiblack. John Ehrlichman, former advisor to President Nixon, has gone on record and declared that the true objective of the War on Drugs was to disrupt political threats to Nixon's presidential campaign and, later, administration. In Ehrlichman's words,

> The Nixon campaign in 1968, and the Nixon White House after that, had two enemies: the antiwar left and black people. You understand what I'm saying? We knew we couldn't make it illegal to be either against the war or blacks, but by getting the public to associate the hippies with marijuana and blacks with heroin, and then criminalizing both heavily, we could disrupt those communities. We could arrest their leaders, raid their homes, break up their meetings, and vilify them night after night on the evening news. Did we know we were lying about the drugs? Of course we did.[36]

Whereas tensions during the Great Migration contributed to racial disparities in northern cities, as reinforced by a greater share of foreign whites in law enforcement roles, Nixon's efforts ensured that these disparities would continue through the close of the twentieth century. Putting their plans in motion, the Nixon administration launched drug raids across the country, predominantly arresting African Americans.[37] But compared to shifts in policy and practice under the Reagan administration, the early days of the War on Drugs were mild.[38]

In 1981, not long after becoming president, Reagan declared, "We're taking down the surrender flag that has flown over so many drug efforts; we're running up a battle flag."[39] Delivering on Reagan's promise, his administration appropriated billions of new dollars to fund its war. It passed new property forfeiture laws for drug offenses and pushed a dramatic expansion of mandatory-minimum sentences, which included the launch of differential sentencing standards that punished cocaine offenses one hundred times more when the drug was found in its crystal ("crack") rather than powder form.[40] But none of these efforts stopped the spread of addiction across the country.

Turning fear and punishment into standard public policies, the Reagan administration delivered on the work the Nixon administration had begun. And the original antiblack emphasis only grew. By the close of the twentieth century, African Americans were far more likely to be arrested for drug offenses than any other group in the United States.[41] Once arrested, the likelihood of their imprisonment was also drastically higher. Research from 1998 showed that "African American drug users made up for 35% of drug arrests, 55% of convictions, and 74% of people sent to prison for drug possession crimes."[42] Consequently, African Americans were thirteen times more likely than any other group to be sent to a state prison for a drug crime, despite making up only a small percentage of routine drug users.[43] These disparities around drug crimes help to explain why 20 percent of African American men in the United States born between 1965 and 1969 have been imprisoned before reaching their early thirties.[44]

The war on neighborhoods has also misshaped how we understand and attempt to uproot violence, the larger driver of imprisonment. Concentrated punishment has created greater stress and tension among residents of impacted areas, without limiting their ability to illegally obtain guns.[45] It has also affected local institutions, the employers, schools, parks, libraries, afterschool programs, and faith communities that might strengthen and support relationships under stress. Meanwhile, the narrow focus on law enforcement has persisted, even through egregious cases of corruption and abuse of power, causing both the pain and the potential of entire neighborhoods to be ignored.

Today, students with learning disabilities continue to be suspended, struggling parents are removed from their homes, returning ex-offenders are systematically denied employment, and addicts go to jail instead of receiving treatment. This pushing away of problems began under Nixon, but it carried on not just through the Ford, Carter, and Reagan administrations but also through the presidencies of George Bush, Bill Clinton, George W. Bush, and Barack Obama. Though modest changes in federal drug laws were made under President Obama, the on-the-ground enforcement momentum begun by Nixon was far from reversed. Across these administrations, concentrated punishment steadily intensified, reshaping not just the handling of drugs, but the ways that society has understood and responded to social and economic disadvantage.[46]

END OF AN ERA

As the "war on drugs" raged on, fundamental shifts occurred in how policymakers saw poor people and understood the issue of work. Under the Clinton administration, with the support of advisor Rahm Emanuel, "welfare as we know it" was changed. In 1996, the Personal Responsibility and Work Opportunity Act was signed into law, giving states more power over the delivery of welfare and greatly reducing the role of the federal government. The entire piece of legislation was structured around the premise that people who wanted to work could do so. Knowing that work opportunities were still in limited supply, Clinton said upon signing that "the business community must provide greater private-sector jobs that people on welfare need to build good lives and strong families."[47] But little was done to actually expand the labor market opportunities of residents in areas like Austin.

There was not always a need for economic development on the West Side. Throughout the mid-twentieth century, workers lined the concrete floors of West Side factories with steel-toed boots. Those boots supported entire communities, helping residents stand tall through adversity and challenge. In 1968, near the peak of this manufacturing era, the unemployment rate for African Americans in Chicago was only 7.6 percent. West Side factories made candy, telephones, and plastic cups and other disposable products that were sold across the globe, as well as to other industrial cities such as Pittsburgh and Cleveland. Austin was the home of Brach's, one of the largest candy manufacturers on the planet. Nearby in Cicero, just south of Oak Park, was Western Electric's Hawthorne Works factory, where most of America's telephones were made.[48] In North Lawndale, a neighborhood just east of Austin, Sears Roebuck operated the largest mail-order distribution center in the world, what has been called "the Amazon of the 20th Century."[49] In addition to these nearby employers, Austin residents also traveled across the city to work in the steel mills and stockyards, two of the region's larger economic pillars.

But between 1972 and 2003, West Side factories went from a total workforce of almost sixty thousand to a workforce of just twelve thousand, and a similar gutting occurred across the city. By 2012, the official unemployment rate for African Americans in Chicago was 19.5 percent, nearly triple that of the midcentury figure.[50] In less than two generations, the steel-toed boots had vanished. And many struggled to keep standing tall.

Bert, both a police officer and a lifelong Austin resident, lived through these changes and remembers them well. Decades before joining law enforcement, he was a factory worker on the West Side. "You go down a lot of these side streets from Augusta and Chicago Avenue, there are a lot of old factories. Those factories had jobs. Now those jobs are gone. That's one of the main reasons the West Side is so devastated."

Judge J, both a long-term Austin resident and a long-term judge, remembers when times were good, before changes in the global market, shifts in corporate values, and breakthroughs in industrial technology. "I tell kids all the time, when I was in high school a kid could quit going to school. . . . You could walk up and down Lake Street, Cicero, Laramie, North Avenue. There were factories and they had the big signs outside talking about 'positions available' and 'go inside and get a job.' After you went inside and got you a job, you could find a furnished apartment, a one-room kitchenette that had the bed, and the tables, and the lamps and all that stuff. In some of the better ones there were even plates in the cabinets."

Factory work provided the young adults of Bert's and Judge J's generation immense freedom. It was a pathway to personal independence and a launching pad for economic stability. Judge J recalls, "All you had to do was bring your clothes and then you work for six to eight weeks, maybe three months, and you had your down payment for your little Ford or your Impala. You had a job, you had a place to live, and a way to get around." Today, no such pathways exist.

Austin's local economy is a shadow of its former self. Active industries include healthcare, schools, nonprofits, and commercial storefronts.[51] A small group of manufacturers still lingers on. Madison Avenue is the most active commercial corridor in the area, an exception to the vacancy that has come to rule much of the terrain.[52] It is lined with fast-food restaurants, sit-down restaurants, funeral homes, barbershops, convenience stores, small groceries, and a gas station. To the north, Chicago and Division Avenues both offer some similar wares, but Madison Avenue is the area's retail cornerstone.

Most Austin residents must look beyond the West Side in search of employment. Rather than finding a good-paying job down the street, residents search all over Chicagoland for a path to pay their bills. Those who find jobs downtown typically work in the low-wage service industry. These workers are part of a larger employment trend that holds true for many African Americans across Chicago and across the country. An estimated 46 percent of Chicago's low-wage jobs are held by African American workers—the percentage is even higher in New York City.[53] For readers who know Chicago only as tourists, Austin residents may have changed your hotel bedding, served your lunch, or helped you shop somewhere along the Magnificent Mile. They commonly have to work two or more service jobs to make ends meet, thereby facing a choice between feeding their children and providing them ample supervision. Jobs that pay higher wages can be much harder to reach. Commutes to suburban factories can last two to three hours each way, a voyage that requires multiple bus transfers for those without a car. Judge J says, "Sometimes that just breaks a person's spirit. You are leaving your house at five o'clock in the morning and you are making it back to your house at eight o'clock at night. And the amount of money you are making is still not enough for you to survive. So, people give up."

Tired of the search for honest work, many Austin workers turned to the street economy. As unemployment rates grew throughout the 1970s and 1980s, displaced workers often became the person on the corner facing arrest. Through major shifts in the classification and sentencing of criminal behavior, those arrests increasingly became felonies. And when displaced workers were felons, society no longer felt responsible for the astronomical unemployment rate. As Bert's and Judge J's stories show, many displaced workers also entered the criminal justice system as professionals, becoming police officers, jail guards, probation and parole officials, and judges. In his book *Locking Up Our Own: Crime and Punishment in Black America*, law professor James Forman illustrates the struggles that coincided with these radically diverging paths of employment.[54]

Rather than an economic concern, unemployment became an issue for the criminal justice system to manage, especially in African American neighborhoods.[55] Following deindustrialization, little public effort was made to step in and build a new economy. There were no public works programs, no creative financing for local entrepreneurs, no guarantee of basic income. Meanwhile, the number of residents with felony convictions skyrocketed. Over time, these felony records have obscured the ways that low-income African American neighborhoods are structurally excluded from living-wage jobs. The mark of a criminal record provides a perverse justification for exclusion that could otherwise only be attributable to race, thereby making the valley appear less man-made.[56]

A look at one of Austin's few employment agencies illustrates the point. When we interviewed Gerald at the Westside Health Authority's job placement office, the phone would not stop ringing. Calls were even crowding out the agency's main line. At the time of the visit, the Chicago Transit Authority (CTA), which oversees the city's buses and trains, had recently announced it would be hiring 260 positions. For the first time in history, the CTA was encouraging people with felony convictions to apply. And the Westside Health Authority was one of a handful of agencies in the city that would be asked to help with the hiring process.

Gerald explains how the CTA started "an apprenticeship program in which the unions allowed the formerly incarcerated to work." The program lasts for twenty-one months, and afterward the apprentice "has the right to actually apply to be hired as a regular employee." This rare public program is based on a logic in which need is met with actual, viable opportunity. In a city where those most desperate for work are often the first to be excluded, that simple logic makes the CTA program truly exceptional. People in Austin quickly took notice.

"We were averaging four hundred to five hundred calls per day. We literally could not take them. Every phone was jammed," says Gerald. At the time of our interview, he estimates they had a five-year waiting list. "It shows you two things. One, it shows you the number of individuals in this community who are formerly incarcerated. And two, it shows you the magnitude and the desperation of these individuals looking for work."

"MILLION DOLLAR BLOCKS"

Concentrated punishment is an expensive habit. In areas like Austin, incarceration has taken ever-greater shares of taxpayer dollars, more than housing, job creation, public transportation, youth development, or other essential systems. Since the 1970s, imprisonment has been the fastest growing of all public investments in Illinois, a trend that is maintained through the ways arrests are made, cases are processed, and sentences are assigned.[57] Unlike funding for youth or workforce development, approaches that seek to prepare individuals for successful, independent living in the world, dollars spent on imprisonment demand that society keeps pouring money into jails and prisons for the long haul, requiring constant reallocations.[58] With these shifts, government itself has become a dependent actor, constantly avoiding the real work of rebuilding opportunities for Austin residents.

Like Brownsville in New York and Highland Park in Detroit, Chicago's far West Side is full of "million dollar blocks," residential census blocks where state government commits to spending over a million dollars to incarcerate residents over the life of the prison sentences when considering the average cost of each prisoner.[59] This concept and the term "million dollar blocks" were coined by Laura Kurgan and Eric Cadora, who initially analyzed blocks in New York City; they have since analyzed the geography of incarceration in New Orleans and other US cities.[60] Applying their framework to Chicago (where data are available), we see that in the Austin neighborhood, each year, on average the state commits to spending over $100 million over the life of prison sentences of adults. This is a massive sum poured into management and monitoring, rather than addressing their underlying needs and providing meaningful supports to promote behavior change.[61] By comparison, the total dollar figure of all grants from the Illinois State Department of Human Services to the Austin Community was just over $6 million in 2016, and Chicago's signature youth violence prevention initiative, Get IN Chicago, committed to invest $40 million over multiple years to fund violence prevention programs for the entire city.[62]

Although it lacks viable economic pathways for its residents, Chicago's West Side is not experiencing a lack of investment. Rather, concentrated punishment represents a form of perverse misinvestment. Between 2005 and 2009, $550 million was committed to incarcerate residents of Austin, a massive sum that does not factor in the costs of patrol, arrest, detention, or prosecution. Commitments on individual census blocks often exceed $2 million.[63]

The dark areas on the map shown in figure 2 clearly stand out, denoting the millions spent on forced removal in small residential spaces. In one block alone, the committed public investment over a five-year period is up to $17 million. It is also important to note this same general area is home to those former industrial zones that were once the backbone of the Austin labor market. In essence, policymakers have been willing to pay to ensure absence and loss rather than economic revitalization.

In all of Chicago, there were 851 census blocks where more than $1 million was committed to incarceration costs during the five-year period from 2005 to 2009, and 121 of those blocks exceeded a million-dollar commitment just from nonviolent drug offenses.[64] Nearly all of these blocks were predominantly African American.

This perverse misinvestment is at the heart of the war on neighborhoods. But while high incarceration rates are at the center of the war machinery, punitive thinking has expanded well beyond courtrooms, jails, and prisons. The war has also fueled exclusionary school discipline practices, labor market behaviors that all but dismiss people from certain zip codes, and city budget decisions that consistently underfund mental health services.[65] Through this spread of punitive logics and policies, the war on neighborhoods has reshaped households, residents, businesses, and local organizations. It has further hollowed out the valleys while the surrounding mountain towns continue to thrive.

Since the dawn of mass incarceration, around 1980, the share of annual income going to the top 1 percent of households has more than doubled. And that lopsided share continues to increase.[66] Meanwhile, the punishment of disadvantage—the practice of making individuals responsible for major societal shortcomings—makes it seem as if mountains of opportunity and valleys of struggle are natural phenomena. It hides the deep and cumulative impact of policy decisions, so that the real work of solving

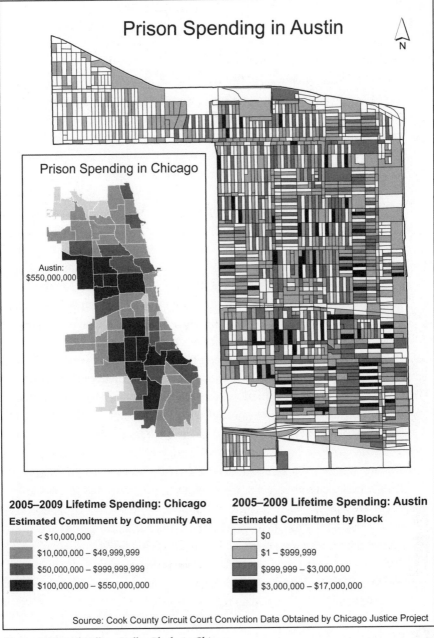

Figure 2: Map of Million-Dollar Blocks in Chicago

these problems never happens. High neighborhood-unemployment rates are never addressed. The foster care system is never repaired. Under-funded schools are closed en masse.[67] Affordable housing is uprooted while the foreclosure crisis leads to vacant blocks. The tax base is never expanded. And violence—both on the street and in households—is allowed to continue. At the same time, US cities grow increasingly strati-fied: home to luxury neighborhoods and communities full of foreclosed homes, magnet schools and empty school buildings, the global elite and those who must work multiple jobs to make ends meet.[68]

ELUSIVE MOUNTAINTOPS

In Chicago, as well as in Atlanta, Cleveland, Detroit, and many other US cities, there have been three constants across the last fifty years. First, the sale and use of illicit drugs has increased at alarming rates. Second, disadvantaged areas like Austin have experienced high incarceration rates that are unparalleled in world history.[69] Third, urban violence has persisted, fluctuating in ways that often appear independent of incarcer-ation practices.[70] Throughout this period, President Johnson's vision for social and economic inclusion has become a distant dream.

The institutions that were meant to help win the War on Poverty have been continually attacked and undercut. Meanwhile, policymak-ers have developed an addiction of their own, one that they still haven't shaken, regardless of the negative effects. This addiction—concentrated punishment—has reinforced long-standing practices of racism and led to a wide array of bad investment decisions in and for predominantly African American neighborhoods.[71] Under the war on neighborhoods, struggling parents are the first to be removed from their homes. Restless youth are the first to be kicked out of schools. The most traumatized are the most likely to be jailed. And those most in need of work are the least eligible for employment. Policymakers have not just avoided ad-dressing the problems of unemployment, struggling schools, addiction, and mental illness in African American communities; they have actively punished people suffering from these conditions.[72]

History did not have to play out this way. In 1966, Dr. Martin Luther King Jr. temporarily moved to the West Side of Chicago, uprooting his family to show that white supremacy was not merely a problem in Ala-bama, Mississippi, and Louisiana. On the corner of Sixteenth Street and

Hamlin Avenue, he, his wife, and his children took up a modest apartment for ninety dollars a month. This was his new base of operations for fair-housing marches, which sought to improve housing opportunities for African Americans.[73]

Chicago was King's first major campaign in the North.[74] His goal was to bring the city's underbelly of hate out into the open, and it did not take long for him to achieve it. At one march on the Southwest Side, where many white Chicagoans greeted him with Confederate flags and swastikas, King was struck in the head with a brick. Afterward, he declared, "I have seen many demonstrations in the South, but I have never seen anything so hostile and so hateful as I've seen here today."[75] As marches continued, Chicago's deep prejudice became undeniable. In exchange for an end to civil rights protests, the Chicago Real Estate Board agreed to support open-housing laws. It was, according to King, "a first step in a 1,000-mile journey."[76]

One of King's next steps was to focus on economic justice, to support organizers working for "Jobs or Income Now!" This was his issue of focus in March of 1968, when he was killed in Memphis, a short while after his Chicago victory. Following his assassination, riots erupted in more than one hundred US cities. Though those riots expressed the utter despair felt by African Americans across the nation, the gains of the civil rights movement were starting to become evident. For the first time in the nation's history, blacks enjoyed the same legal rights and protections as whites. Progress was also visible on the economic front, as poverty started to drop and wages for black workers began to rise.[77]

But those gains were short-lived. Despite the laws passed and discriminatory policies put on notice, racism continually found new ways to express itself. In his book *Stuck in Place*, sociologist Patrick Sharkey concludes that "the generation of African-American children raised during the civil rights era has made virtually no advancement out of the nation's poorest neighborhoods."[78] In 1960, African Americans in Chicago had a 69 percent chance of living in a predominantly African American neighborhood. They also had an average poverty rate of 29.7 percent and a median income of $4,800, compared with a 7.4 percent poverty rate and a $7,700 median income for whites. In 2011, African Americans in Chicago still had a 63 percent chance of living in a predominantly African American neighborhood, only now their poverty rate had increased to 34.1 percent, compared to 10.9 percent for whites. While the median income for African Americans had risen to $29,371, this was far outpaced by whites, whose median income was now $58,752. In Austin, according to the 2015 American Community Survey, the median income was $31,634.[79]

Decades of community organizing has fought to reverse this trend. In Austin, powerful organizers have emerged, many of whom were trained in Saul Alinsky's approach to creating change through public conflict. They've built dynamic organizations, led innumerable local actions, and brought together neighbors around shared, urgent messages. One Austin-based organizer, Gale Cincotta, went on to help pass the Home Mortgage Disclosure Act of 1975 and the Community Reinvestment Act of 1977, two federal laws that have sought to hold accountable the very banks involved in practices like redlining and mortgage discrimination by mandating the disclosure of racial demographics of loans originated and mandating lending in areas where banks receive deposits.[80]

Several community organizations founded in the 1960s, '70s, and '80s have tried to forge Austin's path out of the valley. These groups—all of which started as church efforts, informal networks, or secular organizing groups—have become providers of workforce development, early childhood education, senior housing, energy assistance, and supports for people returning from prison. From Bethel New Life to the Westside Health Authority to the South Austin Coalition Community Council, these agencies have never stopped working to make a new economy possible. In the face of persistent disadvantage, local leaders have consistently pushed for a brighter future. In addition to organizing, they've worked tirelessly to attract resources to the area, brokering relationships between insiders and outsiders, providing administrative capacity and professional expertise, and bringing other community stakeholders to the table. They have laid plans for creating a highly skilled workforce, connecting to advanced manufacturing and engineering opportunities. Seeds have been planted for world-class high schools that pave the way to future prosperity. Major Chicagoland companies and universities have been approached as possible anchors for these visions.

But Austin has continued to decline over time. If the visions of community-based leaders were embraced, nurtured, and brought to fruition, Austin residents might again be able to experience a world with abundant opportunities, though it would certainly be a much differ-ent world than what Judge J and Bert knew in the 1960s. What might the neighborhood look like if the state invested as much in innovation and small business development as it does in incarceration? Would vi-olence still persist if schools were better resourced, good jobs became more common, and the street economy was not the leading magnet for entrepreneurship?[81]

Rather than vacant lands and abandoned buildings, the infrastruc-ture of Austin might once again serve those who live nearby. More than any other site, the former Brach's candy factory has been the target for these aspirations. Gazing at its facade, local visionaries have imagined everything from a super school to a manufacturing innovation park. According to Manufacturing Renaissance, another Austin-based agency, with the right investments this site could become a hub for renewable energy for the city, or even the Silicon Valley of the West Side. It could be the production site for wind turbines and solar panels, a headquar-ters for the green economy in the Midwest, powered by well-trained and highly skilled local residents. Despite the best efforts of local champions, the investments needed for these projects have yet to arrive.

Without these investments, even the best-laid plans feel a lot like dreams. While tens of millions of dollars are poured into incarcerating residents on the blocks surrounding Brach's, the site itself receives only basic maintenance.

CHAPTER 2

ADDICTED TO PUNISHMENT

IN THE FINAL DECADES of the twentieth century, politicians and policymakers recognized the growing influence of illicit drugs on the lives of city dwellers across the country. They knew action must be taken. And they took it.

In Illinois, between 1984 and 2002, there were fourteen specific policy changes that substantially changed the ways drug offenders are charged and sentenced.[1] Half of these changes were geographically targeted, establishing "drug-free zones" around common locations that are essential to neighborhood life. Drug penalties were dramatically increased within one thousand feet of schools, parks, buses and bus stops, places of worship, nursing homes, public housing, and truck and rest stops. Of these locations, only truck and rest stops are not found in concentrated form in urban neighborhoods. Through these changes, Illinois became one of thirty-one states that established "drug-free zones" beyond just school areas.[2] Building on this momentum, there were thirteen enhanced drug laws enacted from 2000 through 2011, influencing approximately 5,761 sentences from Cook County alone.[3] One example is mandatory prison time for anyone selling more than five grams of heroin, a threshold that was later lowered to just three grams. Consequently, by 2011 almost half of all prison sentences originating in Cook County were for drug possession or dealing, and these sentences were, on average, seventy days longer than they were in 2000.[4]

It took less and less for Austin residents to be targeted for arrest, even as the consequences for drug-related convictions were expanded. Rather than address root causes, policymakers saw public safety through the lens of individual offenders. Issues of unemployment, addiction, and mental health were increasingly reduced to questions of personal decision making. In short, disorder was individualized.[5] The policy focus moved away from neighborhood-level needs and toward problematic people, rarely drawing the connection that the former provides the environment needed for the latter to emerge.[6]

Across the country and the hemisphere, across political parties and ideological lines, the US government has implemented a coordinated campaign to stop the sale and use of drugs, with local law enforcement playing a leading role. Though the so-called war on drugs included meaningful drug treatment and education programs, it primarily helped to fuel concentrated punishment, at great financial and human costs. All the while, it utterly failed to uproot the underlying drivers of illicit drugs in and around cities like Chicago. In fact, while drugs were always the presumed target of this chapter in US policy history, the actual use and sale of drugs is one of the few things its efforts failed to substantially impact.[7]

Recalling the days when drugs entered his community, a lifelong resident named Simon states that "drugs really became prevalent in Austin in the beginning of the '80s. I saw the effects firsthand. It hit family members. And it really hit South Austin hard, it hit South Austin first. Then it went to Central Austin. It made its way to North Austin—it took ten years, but it made its way to North Austin in the late '80s, early '90s. I had been living in North Austin since '81 and it was no different than being in Oak Park. In the early '80s, you couldn't tell the difference." Simon continues, "You could walk down the street, there were no problems, no crime like you see now. Purses weren't being stolen; nobody's trying to put you at gunpoint. There used to be a movie theater at Monitor and Division called the Rockney Theater with dollar shows. We used to go to the movies right there."

Dance clubs and other entertainment options also disappeared. As drugs spread throughout the 1990s, Austin lost the Factory, a youth dance club; the Rendezvous, a nightclub; Starville Recording Studio; and Music City, a banquet hall rental business. The loss of the Factory was particularly hard hitting, as it was well known as a safe haven for youth, where fighting was rare and young people enjoyed a much-needed respite from gang violence.[8] As drugs migrated, gangs became prevalent on each of Austin's major commercial corridors. From Madison Street to Chicago Avenue to Division Avenue, Simon recalls, these corridors morphed into "hot crime areas because of drug trafficking."

Simon's family was heavily impacted by these changes. Having grown up in South Austin during the early 1980s, he recalls that the younger generation of his family had enormous potential that was never realized. In place of upward momentum, many of these family members faltered and were drawn into the street economy. Meanwhile, as Austin was starting to decline, public officials in Chicago did little to tap into the latent potential of Simon's cousins, to draw them out of the streets, or to ensure that their younger siblings did not follow their path.

Austin's available routes for success became increasingly constricted and those, like Simon's cousins, who could not access those routes were met with punishment. Consequently, over the course of the 1980s and early 1990s, the whole of Austin was overtaken by the drug market, as was much of the broader West Side.[9] Violence escalated correspondingly, with West Side police districts regularly ranking as the most impacted.[10]

Though the intensified war on drugs led to regular arrests of local African American residents, several of the biggest drug busts in Austin involved white professionals who only worked in the area, including police officers. One of the largest drug convictions in Chicago's history happened on April 20, 1989, when Officer Rick Miller pleaded guilty to running a multimillion-dollar heroin and cocaine operation.[11] At the time, Miller was an active officer in Austin's Fifteenth District. A year later, Mario Lettieri, owner of a local butcher shop, was found guilty of operating his own multimillion-dollar drug ring from an apartment complex in the neighborhood.[12] Similar incidents continued throughout the 1990s, again involving local police officers. Five Austin-based officers were convicted in 2001 for robbing from local drug dealers throughout the mid-1990s.[13]

Though these incidents all made headlines, no prominent federal leaders questioned the effectiveness of attempting to uproot drug sales through aggressive law enforcement approaches. Nobody introduced broad new accountability paradigms for police officers. Meanwhile, the suppression-focused approach based in neighborhoods continued unabated and the convictions of residents piled up. As the following national and neighborhood histories reveal, a clear punishment paradigm emerged that shaped the trajectory of public policies. Instead of ending international trafficking or street corner distribution, this paradigm added new obstacles. In fact, there is evidence that some of the most aggressive policy responses actually drove neighborhood dealers to sell publicly on street corners—and to do so in increasingly chaotic ways.

NOW YOU'RE THE TARGET

Today, more than thirty years after Simon originally witnessed the visible spread of drugs in his neighborhood, Austin is at the center of the Chicago region's heroin market. The Chicago Police Department (CPD) has estimated that of all the heroin sold in the city, 60 percent was once sold along the Eisenhower Expressway, and drug sales along the expressway continue to be a central challenge.[14] As home to a major section of this highway, Austin's street corners are an extremely convenient stop for suburban heroin users, making the drug one of the neighborhood's largest exports.

In the words of Beth, a Fifteenth District police officer, "This is the major distribution point for heroin. You really don't get heroin so much on the South Side; you get crack on the South Side. If you want heroin you come to the West Side." In particular, many city-suburb commuters are attracted to powdered heroin that can be snorted rather than injected and thus used without the risk and inconvenience of needles. Describing this trend, Gil Kerlikowske, the former commissioner of US Customs and Border Protection, has said, "They think if they snort or smoke it, they won't end up injecting. Very quickly, they do."[15]

Michael, the white, suburban former addict with over one hundred court cases but no prison time, describes the Heroin Highway's customer base: "You just have these white people coming from everywhere." A lifelong suburbanite himself, Michael remembers regularly seeing working addicts from the suburbs come to Austin. He says, "I've seen a lot of white people in line on their own. One day I was sitting there waiting for my buddy and a car pulled up behind me and out got a nurse. She had her nurse's scrubs on and she went to the spot and bought dope."

Samuel, a Fifteenth District officer, affirms Michael's words, while also recognizing the customer base living within the neighborhood. "People working in the suburbs and living in the city detour a little bit, or the other way around, people working in the city but living out in the suburbs picking up their stuff." He continues, "You've also got the more twenty-four-hour-based addicts [functional addicts who are still able to hold down a job] that are already in the neighborhood." There are a lot of both, Samuel says, but "you see more from outside of the city, during, like, rush hour. There are many working addicts."

In recent decades, heroin use has grown rapidly in the suburbs surrounding Chicago. From 1998 to 2007, although heroin-related hospital discharges decreased 67 percent among Chicagoans aged twenty to twenty-four, they "increased more than 200 percent in the Collar Counties."[16] Compared to other major US cities, Chicago's metropolitan area "ranks highest in Emergency Department mentions in the nation for heroin and has the highest rates per 100,000 persons."[17] One study found that in 2010, more people were treated for heroin overdoses by hospitals in Chicago and surrounding suburbs than any other major city in the country.[18]

Nothing the City of Chicago has done has stopped the flow of drugs in and through Austin. From Harold Washington to Richard M. Daley, many major Chicago politicians played a role in the local implementation of the so-called war on drugs. For example, as part of a coordinated effort with the US Conference of Mayors, Washington declared November 18, 1986, to be "D-Day in Chicago," a day when he sought to focus the city's attention on "the elimination of this scourge from our society and the salvation of our people from its grip." Chicago was one of 349 US cities to coordinate activities that day. This nationwide effort came less than one month after Reagan signed his signature Anti-Drug Abuse Act of 1986 and on the same day that a US federal grand jury released the indictment of Pablo Escobar and other leaders of the Medellín cartel, which was named in the indictment as the world's largest cocaine-smuggling organization.[19]

Local government officials were focused on people much further down the food chain than Escobar. Patrol officers in Austin rarely encounter individuals who hold more than entry-level positions in drug distribution networks, making them largely blind to the inflow of drugs that they have been asked to control. Nonetheless, in a 1992 speech, then mayor Daley declared, "We are putting the gangbangers and drug dealers on notice. . . . For too long you have made the community a target. Now you're the target."[20] This was no empty threat. Under Daley's tenure,

Chicago became ground zero for locking up black men for drug offenses, with rates among the highest in the nation.[21] As Nancy Reagan starred in popular education efforts that called on the country to "Just Say No," the CPD was busy changing the ways it did business. In 1964, still seven years before Nixon first declared his War on Drugs, Chicago police officers made 2,232 drug arrests. By 2012, this number was at 35,088, a fifteen-fold increase, despite a decline in the city's total population during this same time period.[22] Although drug use also increased during this time period, that increase was in no way stalled by these efforts.

In his twenty-two years as mayor, Richard M. Daley displayed an amazing ability to double down on policies that benefited downtown at the expense of the West and South Sides. Like his father before him, Mayor Richard J. Daley, he deployed aggressive police measures that reinforced Nixon's antiblack agenda at the local level. Richard M. Daley's reign thereby deepened the war on neighborhoods, often in ways that intensified rather than prevented neighborhood violence.

MIGRATION TO THE CORNERS

As Austin's economy was collapsing, the new structure of the drug economy was taking root. This formation did not occur in a policy vacuum. The logic of punishment played a direct role in the emergence of the neighborhood's open-air drug market, a shift that led to a continued increase in Austin's incarceration rate.

Wilma, who was born and raised on the West Side, has seen the rise in the outdoor sale of drugs. She explains, "When I went off to college, I knew about drug sales and [that] people sold drugs in homes. If you wanted to get some drugs, you go into the home. It was that drug house or whatever; it was sort of isolated. But then when I came home in 1994, I would see kids on the corner shouting [about drugs for sale]. I was, like, twenty years old, twenty-one, and I had no idea what they were doing or what they were talking about."

Austin went from a place where Wilma knew everyone on the block to an area where "people weren't outside anymore because there were folks [selling] on the corners." Asked about the reasons for this turn to outdoor dealing, she says, "People were outside because [the police] were seizing the homes. If you were caught selling then that home could be taken away from you. People just moved out to the street corner, so that their mothers and their grandmothers and people they loved—they did love them—their houses wouldn't be taken away from them. So they migrated to the street corners."

The seizing of property in Austin was enabled by Comprehensive Crime Control Act of 1984 under the Reagan administration. Under this act, any real property—houses, cars, businesses, lands, and bank accounts—that could be said to facilitate illegal drug activity became subject to seizure, even when the owners themselves were not convicted of a crime. According to one estimate, over $12 billion worth of assets was seized by the US Department of Justice between 1989 and 2010. The seizures by the Justice Department grew "from $27 million in 1985 to $56 million in 1993 and $4.2 billion in 2012."[23] When the constitutionality of these seizures was brought before the US Supreme Court in 1996, the court ruled they were fair play, later amending the ruling to say that items seized had to be proportional to the seriousness of the offense.[24] Meanwhile, the number of federal statutes allowing for property seizure mushroomed, rising from two hundred in the early 1990s to more than four hundred at present.[25]

As forfeiture laws reached Austin, they had a direct effect on Wilma's own family. She recalls, "I had [an uncle] who was selling in my grandfather's basement. My grandfather was sixty at the time when [the police] kicked him out of his house. He had to come and live with my mother. They boarded up the building until the selling stopped. They had to see that my uncle was not even going to live there anymore . . . because he was selling drugs. The city boarded up all six units."

For families like Wilma's, the seizure of homes erased decades of intentional wealth building. She says, "All my parents' life, my grandfather owned property. He came from Mississippi and owned a six-unit property for the family. The entire family lived on one side of the six-unit and he rented out the other side." Wilma's uncle, who was "in and out of jail" for selling drugs, was forty years old when this building was seized from her grandfather.

With this seizing of private property, drug sales became a public affair. Young men flocked to the street corners, most of them adopting a standard uniform. The dealers were "out there with white T-shirts for their own safety," Wilma explains. "So if they ran they wouldn't be identifiable; it was white T-shirts and jeans."

As Wilma's story shows, the structure of Austin's drug market shifted in direct response to new law enforcement strategies. Drug dealers were driven to open-air selling, making them more susceptible to arrest and later incarceration. White T-shirts were an adaptation to that shift. As the work of dealing became more public, those doing the work now collectively shared the risk in ways that did not exist before. And with the migration to the corners, turf and territory became central issues.

Blocks and corners were now openly contested places of business. This shift required security measures that had been unnecessary when drugs were primarily sold in private homes. Describing the new reality, one Fifteenth District police officer puts it simply: "Guns and drugs go together. You need a gun to protect your drug spot." Similarly, explaining the role of violence in protecting and establishing drug turf, Harold describes the role that shooting plays: "Everybody wants to make money. If you move in on a certain area of the neighborhood where I'm making money, you [may be] two blocks away but you are drawing some of my customers down there. That means I'm going down there to shoot at you and try to get you off your corner so I can sell most of my product."

The logic behind this kind of drug-related violence is simple and is largely financial in nature. However, there are also real disincentives to using guns to establish or protect sales territory. The biggest disincentive is that competing dealers often carry guns as well. According to Harold, this is one of the dynamics that pushes people to work as a team. Turf security "all depends on how much manpower [the other] guy got. You can go down there and shoot at him but what difference is it going to make if he's got the same amount of guns as you? You all [are] just going to be shooting at each other all day until the police break it up." Another strong disincentive is that violence scares away customers, a fact that effectively reduces the street value of drugs. One study found that drug prices fell by as much as 30 percent during conflicts between gangs.[26]

Now, more than twenty years after Wilma's grandfather was forced from his home, there is some evidence that dealers are starting to move their work back indoors and away from contested corners. In addition to open-air markets, which she sees daily, West Side police officer Tamara says, "You'll have people selling out of their house, out of cars. That's one or two people [working a location]. It's from the protection of your house. We will see a lot on second or third floors where they will drop down a bucket, you put your money in; they pull it up and then drop the drugs down. There you only need one person because they don't really need security. I see it a lot with courtyard buildings." Each of these spots, Tamara says, typically moves the same kinds of drugs as the outdoor markets.

Michael has also observed a rise in people selling from their homes. When asked how drug sales in Austin today compare to the early 1990s, he says "the only difference is that a lot of guys get those cricket phones, a lot of dealers, and you call them and they meet you outside. . . . This is just recently, but for years it was on the street." Importantly, this move beyond the open-air market supports a more individual approach to sales that is less visible to outside scrutiny. It may also be traced back to a rise in home foreclosure and decrease in homeownership, whereby renting has become more of a norm, a consequences of the disproportionate percentage of subprime loans given to African American households.[27]

REALITIES OF ADDICTION

No matter where you call home, whether you are from Chicago's West Side, the surrounding suburbs, or elsewhere in the country, addiction is an incredibly destructive force. It steals lives, relationships, and dreams, with a legacy of pain that often spans generations. A mother dies too early, leaving her kids without a protector in the world. A father loses himself to his cravings, abandoning all that he had toiled to build and nurture. A young person who is suffering starts to self-medicate and ends up unable to remember years of his life.[28]

The death toll of addiction is massive. It kills over half a million people every year across the United States. Though their effects work more slowly, tobacco and alcohol are far more lethal than any other abused substance in this country. Of the more than half a million annual deaths from substance abuse each year, roughly 480,000 are related to tobacco. Alcohol is the second-leading killer, taking the lives of about 80,000 people a year.[29] Meanwhile, accidental drug overdoses have been quickly rising on the list, taking 59,000 lives in 2016.[30]

Though its numbers are much smaller than those of tobacco- or alcohol-related deaths, addiction to heroin in particular brings incredible agony. It is an equal-opportunity devastator, taking down anyone who gives it too much power, anyone who is unable to learn and adjust as the signs of decay creep into their lives. Even those who can successfully recover from their addiction must then work diligently to overcome the effects of their abuse. The last forty years of American drug policy have done little to help those fighting such agony, with treatment capacity actually shrinking in places that continue to fight the war on drugs.[31]

In her book *Unbroken Brain*, Maia Szalavitz argues that the idea that US drug laws are rational must be abandoned.[32] Szalavitz, a former heroin user herself, critiques the "idea that if we are just cruel enough and mean enough and tough enough to people with addiction, that they will suddenly wake up and stop."[33] This is simply not the case, as her work reveals, because harsh judgment does nothing to change human biochemistry. Rather than a force for real behavior change, drug laws were established to control groups of people, she argues.

If drug policies were actually designed to uproot substance abuse, Szalavitz argues, we would focus far less on punishment and much more on helping those struggling with addiction to learn from their mistakes and address their underlying pain. At the root, this pain is emotional, often stemming from people's exposure to trauma at a young age. Major studies by the Centers for Disease Control have confirmed this point, directly linking adverse childhood experiences to later-life substance abuse.[34] Gabor Maté, author of *In the Realm of Hungry Ghosts*, argues that addressing childhood suffering is the only real way to end addiction in the long term. Childhood is the period when trauma survivors' brains start to be reshaped, making them search out external coping mechanisms.[35] Though rarely touted by US legislators, this kind of approach is preferred by American voters, across the political spectrum.[36]

BREAKING THE HABIT

As decades have come and gone, policymakers' addiction to punishment has persisted. However, political attitudes around drug use and even sales appear to be shifting.[37] When you stop to talk to the people impacted by this addiction—whether former drug dealers, current police officers, longtime residents of areas like Austin, or recovering addicts—one thing becomes abundantly clear: *law enforcement will never be enough to uproot drug sales or usage.* When you look at who buys illegal drugs, where users come from, what life is like for frontline sellers, and ongoing changes to distribution and sales patterns, the point holds true. Law enforcement efforts can force drug markets to change, but those changes often have unpredictable and chaotic consequences. This is the price of treating root causes as afterthoughts.

As long as there is a demand for illicit drugs and unemployed people with access to those drugs, there will always be an active market. According to some economists, the biggest failure of the war on drugs has been its negligible impact on the price of drugs within that market. In theory, aggressive drug-focused policies are supposed to make drugs harder to access and, as a result, more expensive. In practice, they have done the opposite, effectively lowering drug prices over time and thus making them more readily available to users. In an article titled "The Most Embarrassing Graph in American Drug Policy," one author summarized this trend, writing that the price of street drugs "fell by roughly a factor of five between 1980 and 2008. Meanwhile, the number of drug offenders locked up in US jails and prisons went from fewer than 42,000 in 1980 to a peak of 562,000 in 2007.[38] Put simply, as the US locked up increasing numbers of people for drug offenses, drugs themselves actually became more affordable. In Austin, roughly 66 percent of convictions between 2005 and 2009 were drug related, with 40 percent of these for manufacture or delivery of drugs, meaning drug sales.[39]

The persistence of drugs is by no means limited to Austin. It affects the entire Chicago region. Despite the billions of dollars spent incarcerating neighborhood residents in the 1980s, 1990s, and early 2000s, Chicago is still a leading heroin market in the country, and drug-seizure data shows that the city's drug trade is stronger than ever. The region was ranked first in heroin shipments, second for cocaine and marijuana, and fifth for methamphetamine, making it the only US metropolitan area to rank in the top five for the four main categories of drugs. This inability to move the needle is not a Midwestern problem. It is nationwide, prompting even high-ranking law enforcement leaders to declare US drug law enforcement strategies a "wholesale failure."[40] In this failure, the war on drugs created a host of other problems for impacted individuals, families, and communities. As drug distribution continued, generational wealth built through homeownership was erased, marginalized youth were pushed into more violent confrontations, and high-incarceration neighborhoods across the country now face the added challenge of a revolving door of residents who must navigate life with a felony conviction.

How then can addiction be uprooted? In Samuel's words, "It has got to happen from a different influence from society. A lot of people think it is [police officers'] job to eliminate drugs. It is not our job. It is society's job." Whether the drug in question is heroin, crack cocaine, ecstasy, weed, or methamphetamine, law enforcement "can only minimize it or take care of it for a small snippet of time." As this officer highlights, the police cannot end addiction, they cannot provide work alternatives to street-level dealers, and they have little influence over the global supply chain of drugs into Chicago's West Side. Several officers we spoke with shared the sentiment that "society wants police to solve their problems," to respond to economic issues like unemployment and medical issues like addiction that are far outside their scope of influence.[41]

Addiction is not a technical problem. It does not have a simple answer. There are no handcuffs in the world that can make it go away. But when we treat law enforcement as the solution, that is precisely what we are pretending is possible. Progress must be seen as more than just another conviction. Addiction is an adaptive problem, one that can only be solved through compassionate and active attention to human development and the environments where that development unfolds.[42] And policymakers can certainly help lead the way. In Oakland, the city council has even started a reparations program to help people imprisoned under the drug war to now grow and sell marijuana legally.[43] Innovative programs like this are developing on the progressive fringes of the country, such as in California and Washington State, where meaningful drug policy reform has been implemented. There is no guarantee that such initiatives will be adopted elsewhere. But they certainly point to the possibilities, laying the groundwork for a new and desperately needed paradigm. Whether that paradigm takes root will affect generations to come. How we respond to addiction doesn't just influence recovery outcomes and illegal drug sales; it also shapes the conditions in which violence unfolds.

CHAPTER 3

A CYCLE UNBROKEN

EIGHT THOUSAND PEOPLE attended his funeral. All of Chicago's leading politicians were there. Mayor Harold Washington spoke. So did former state's attorney and later mayor Richard M. Daley and civil rights leader Jesse Jackson. This was November of 1984. They were all there to pay respects to Ben Wilson, the highest-ranked high school basketball player in the country, who had recently been shot to death by another student after a confrontation outside a favorite lunch spot, near Simeon, their South Side high school. ESPN even aired a special tribute about Wilson's life and his tragically lost potential. At that time in Chicago's history there was a profound outcry to end the violence that plagued young people and communities across the city. Today, over thirty years later, we are still hearing that cry.

Since Wilson's death, more than twenty-one thousand people have been murdered in Chicago. The news of young people being shot has become a tragic norm, an unacceptably routine reality. In recent years, many of these deaths have made national headlines: Blair Holt, who was shot and killed on a Chicago Transit Authority bus in 2007. Derrion Albert, who was beaten to death on his way home from Fenger High School after school in 2009. Hadiyah Pendleton, who was fatally shot in a park near her home in 2013. Tyshawn Lee, a nine-year-old who was shot and killed in November 2015. All of these murders were of young people who posed no threat to anyone. All of their deaths were covered by local and national media. But none of their stories led to lasting changes in how the City of Chicago understands violence or attempts to prevent it from happening.[1]

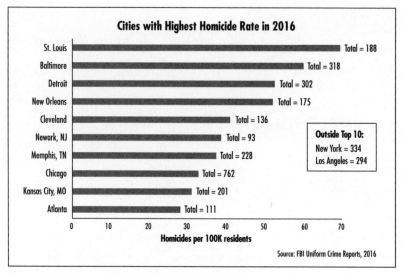

Figure 3: Murders and Violent Crime in Major Cities

The political will to address the root causes of violence has been missing in action. While there has been no shortage of powerful speeches, when it is time to set annual budgets, policymakers act as if deaths cannot be prevented. Every few years, old policing strategies receive new brands, buildings, and infusions of technology, but the fundamental strategy does not change. Just east of Austin, in Garfield Park, a $95 million police and fire training facility is being built, right next door to the shuttered factories that once brought economic stability to the area.[2] Meanwhile, community-based violence prevention programs struggle to keep their lights on. This is part of how the war on neighborhoods continues.[3]

In a now predictable pattern, signature prevention programs emerge and temporarily gain attention but the actual funds required to uproot violence are always missing. Task forces are occasionally organized, comprehensive plans are periodically developed, but these efforts have lacked the political willpower and financial resources to truly enact long-term solutions.[4] The majority of resources and staffing are poured into a narrow law enforcement focus, largely ignoring the potential role of community leaders and organizations in the work to make neighborhoods safer. Even as violence continues to plague Chicago streets in predictable ways, concentrated punishment has carried on, without interruption.

Today in Chicago, violence is back on the rise. Like many cities across the country, Chicago saw historic lows in violent crime near the start of the twenty-first century. From 2004 to 2014, Chicago had the lowest number of homicides it had seen since the early 1960s.[5] But in 2015 that trend started reversing sharply, and Chicago was one of a quarter of US cities that saw their murder rate increase. Although Chicago had the highest number of homicides in 2016, there were seven other US cities with higher homicide rates, when adjusting for population. All of them have disadvantaged neighborhoods similar to Chicago's Austin community, where the criminal justice system plays an outsized role. Tragically, Chicago's upward trend was no outlier. In 2016, there were 58 percent more homicides in the city than in 2015. In the decade prior, homicides had been trending down steadily. In 2017, the elevated rate continued.[6]

Violence in Chicago has become much more concentrated. Over the past fifteen years, the violence rate in Austin has been consistently around 50 percent higher than the average for Chicago as a whole, with the disparities much greater when compared to the North and Northwest Sides. During the early 1990s, the most dangerous third of Chicago neighborhoods had only six times more homicides than the safest third. Across Chicago neighborhoods today, the most dangerous third of the

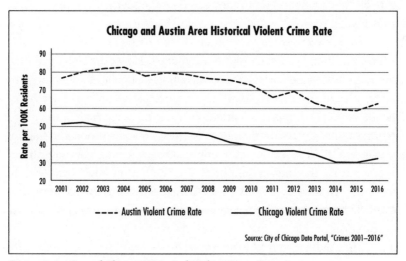

Figure 4: Austin and Chicago Historical Violent Crime Rates

city has somewhere between twelve and sixteen times more homicides than the safest third. This concentration has been called a "public-safety gap," "murder inequality," and "a tale of two cities"—descriptors that point to the ways residents' experiences of safety depend greatly on where they live. Areas like Austin are at the losing end of this gap.[7]

As the stories of Blair, Derrion, Hadiyah, and Tyshawn teach us, residents on the city's West and South Sides are incredibly vulnerable. To really understand these shootings, it is vital to take a more comprehensive look at violence, to see beyond the common stories found in news headlines and police reports. Well before Ben Wilson's shooting, in 1984, a powerful narrative existed that says violence results primarily from individual choices, that its effects are easily visible and thus containable.[8] Accordingly, removing those who commit violent acts has been the dominant response; condemning them as criminals and putting them away, for years or decades at a time, has been treated as a lasting solution.

But violence is not so simple. It cannot be explained away by individual choices, nor can it be fully understood by looking at environmental and external conditions. On the one hand, yes, most neighborhood violence involves one person harming another. On the other hand, it is clear that extended economic exclusion leads to desperation, and harmful acts are all but inseparable from the contexts in which they take place. This side of the equation is well represented by the saying "The best way to stop a bullet is a job."[9]

There are vast spaces in between these two poles, between individual responsibility and socioeconomic context. How do trauma and economic exclusion intersect? How do racially unjust policies—food deserts, under-resourced schools, toxic incinerators placed in poor neighborhoods of color—impact individual decision making? How is toxic and traumatic stress passed on from generation to generation? The field of public health offers some entry points into answering these questions. From tracing the impacts of childhood trauma on adult outcomes to mapping the ways that violent behavior spreads across social networks, this field has made powerful advances in helping us understand the drivers of violent behavior. But these drivers are rarely taken into consideration when public safety policies are set.[10]

Policymakers must learn to see the complexity of violent acts: A husband beating his wife in the name of control. A bully pushing a physically weaker student down the stairs. A struggling soul, unable to see the return of hope, taking her own life. These are all daily forms of harm. Often, they feed on one another. The exploited worker becomes the abuser. The child whose mother was beaten becomes the gang member who attacks another youth, picking up an easily available firearm. The young person shot becomes the bully in school, with teachers too overworked to trace when his behavior changed. The student pushed down the stairs becomes the struggling soul who takes her own life, a tragedy that forever lives in the minds of her younger siblings.[11]

This is how the cycle continues, with long-forgotten acts bearing influence in ways that can be hard to see, often blurring the lines between victim and offender.[12] Policies and individual actions are more connected than most like to admit. It is far easier to keep relying on suppression-oriented strategies that require no admission of societal guilt, no fundamentally new direction, no reallocation of resources. But only by facing the complexity can people, both policymakers and everyday leaders, begin to change the patterns.

MY SISTER'S KEEPER

Shootings are just one type of violence in Chicago. Sexual assault and domestic violence are also major problems across the city and concentrated punishment has utterly failed to uproot them. In turn, this failure has perpetuated other kinds of violence, driving many youth to prematurely leave their homes and many siblings, cousins, friends, and partners to harm someone in retaliation for hurting a loved one.

Several Austin residents spoke to us about these trends, about the ways people move to the streets because of abuse in their homes or turn to violence because there is no other solid recourse after someone they love is harmed. In the words of an Austin-based advocate for survivors of sexual violence, "A lot of these shootings that are happening have to do with domestic violence and abuse. They are not just these random attacks that they are made out to be. . . . Somebody's girlfriend or sister was attacked or abused, and they handle the retaliation. . . . Which again gets down to the issue of addressing the underlying issues with what is going on in homes, the domestic and sexual violence that could be taking place." Speaking to household violence as a driver for gang recruitment, a youth development professional in Austin explains, "When you really look at family dynamics, why youth are on the street, why they are turning to street mentors, you are going to find domestic and sexual violence within that." As he indicates, these young people may turn to gangs as an escape from difficult issues in their homes.

Though a major dimension in the cycle of violence, the harm women endure is often forgotten by outsiders. It is left out of both official tallies of violent crime and critiques of our criminal justice system. Scholar Beth Richie has addressed this issue at length, showing how the invisibility of violence against women in neighborhoods like Austin is linked to society's broader inability to understand the linked and cyclical nature of harm. She has created a violence matrix, which shows how physical assault, sexual assault, and social disenfranchisement intersect at the household, community, and broader societal levels. From the lack of employment opportunities to direct abuse by intimate partners, Richie argues that the many forms of violence are connected in ways that lock violence in place, keeping women of color especially exposed to systemic abuse.[13] As the war on neighborhoods perpetuates violence at all levels, these women are living on the front lines.

Emily, an Austin-based advocate for survivors of sexual violence, helps explain the deep vulnerability of women in high-incarceration neighborhoods. "Our clients aren't reporting. They don't want to deal with the police, they distrust the police." The ways law enforcement handles violence against women is not "the most survivor friendly," she says, and survivors may "have criminal backgrounds themselves and just don't want to mess with it." This underreporting perpetuates the invisibility of violence against women, keeping routine acts of abuse out of the spotlight. In turn, this invisibility leaves harmful social norms in place, where abuse goes undetected and unchallenged, which leads to continued underreporting.

Denial among police officers is a major part of the problem. They think, she says, "that a lot of cases are BS. That 95 percent of victims that come forward are these girls that have gotten drunk, or have gone on a date with someone, or cheated on their boyfriend or their husband and they just want to cover up their infidelity." Emily continues, "I've heard police officers say, 'Oh, they just wanted access to free STD medication or emergency contraception.'" Given the free health clinics scattered across the city, she points out, "Why would they go to a place that is mandated to call the police and go through the two- to three-hour evidence collection kit?'"

As Richie has argued, some of these limitations in protection stem from earlier shortcomings in the movement against violence against women, where advocates called for law enforcement to become the primary line of defense for vulnerable survivors. While expanded legal protections for survivors of domestic and sexual assault were vital gains for this movement, those gains had complex effects. In large part, they did not build up robust community resources and supports so that women in neighborhoods like Austin could live safer, more independent lives. Rather, the Violence Against Women Act of 1994 made many of the same mistakes as did other public safety legislation of the era: *it sought to create safety through criminalization and to end vulnerability through punishment.* Consequently, even with recent improvements in training and educational resources for law enforcement, the sector is incapable of directly tackling violence against women, especially without the help of shelters, counselors, and workforce programs, most of which often struggle to keep meeting their fundraising needs.[14]

On the ground, those who have endured physical and sexual assault in high-incarceration neighborhoods face no-win scenarios where they must risk taking matters into their own hands, asking or allowing someone else to do so, leaving matters unaddressed, or seeking support from law enforcement despite the dangers that doing so might pose to themselves or their loved ones. Such dilemmas, where every option involves some risk of violence, are not limited to Chicago. A recent national example was the murder of Korryn Gaines by Baltimore police in 2016. The officers who killed Korryn and shot her five-year-old son had originally come to her home to serve two arrest warrants: one for her failure to appear in court on a past traffic violation and the other for her boyfriend's past domestic abuses against her. Though not addressed in mainstream coverage of Korryn's killing, the fact that the officers thought it was appropriate to serve these warrants *simultaneously* must be called into question. They were literally trying to arrest her boyfriend for assaulting her and, at the same time, to arrest her for a totally unrelated issue that posed no immediate threat to anyone's well-being.

The law is frequently unable to protect or even support women. Another extreme example is child sexual abuse, a category of uniquely troublesome crimes that are often swept under the rug, both in high-incarceration neighborhoods and in areas of concentrated advantage. One Austin woman we interviewed shared she had been sexually assaulted twice by her brother when she was young. The harm she endured was never addressed, her brother was never held accountable for his actions, and the healing of her wounds was never supported. Explaining why survivors of family violence often don't report, Emily says, "A lot of victims are scared nobody is going to believe them. If it is somebody that is known to you, depending on that relationship, you could be fearful, you could not want your friends to find out, you could think you will be alienated from your social circle."

Survivors of rape and assault are often vulnerable in many ways before they first become victim to an aggressor. They may be facing eviction, homelessness, unemployment, and/or hunger, issues of basic survival that routinely put them in positions where they have reduced power over their lives. Illustrating the gravity of this, Emily says, "Our clients in Austin have so many issues going on. The sexual violence that occurs tends to be secondary to 'I don't have a job, I don't have a place to live, I can't feed my kid.' We end up dealing with a lot of those issues with our clients. It is like, 'Who has the time to worry about the rape I underwent when I have two kids I can't feed and I don't have a job?'"

Even when reporting does occur, Emily continues, "a lot of investigative strategies [for rape] tend to focus on the victim instead of the person that is being accused. In my experience, more times than not it is the victim that is really being the one that's kind of torn apart or interrogated about what happened." Citing one reason that police officers may take this attitude, she says, "I think law enforcement finds it very counterintuitive for a survivor not to run to the police department and report the crime right away. This crime is unique in that sense because it is so personal that delayed reporting is very, very common. I mean, we get survivors years later that finally get to a place where they want to report."

Society's solutions to violence against women must be as layered as the problems themselves, working across the domains of harm that endanger women. Real progress requires building much more holistic responses to assault, rape, incest, and other forms of abuse, with an emphasis on helping survivors to safely build independent lives for themselves and, when relevant, their children. This work can have enormous benefits, uprooting harm across generations, both in households and on the streets.

MISSING THE BOAT

The war on neighborhoods has been justified primarily in response to street violence. But as with violence in the home, the way harm happens outdoors has also been misunderstood. It has been treated as an almost corporate problem, where all the actors are organized around a central hierarchy that governs individual choices. In the minds of many law enforcement leaders, violence results from dangerous individuals who, in turn, manage and monitor other dangerous individuals. Accordingly, police solutions have focused on containing these influential figures, without ever giving real attention to the disadvantaged environments from which they emerge.

In an effort to break up the West Side drug market, many of the city's older gang leaders were successfully prosecuted on conspiracy charges throughout the 1990s and 2000s. Chiefs were stripped of their powers. Their lieutenants were taken off the streets. But these cases did not have the intended policy effect. Rather than ending or even slowing the distribution of drugs on the West Side, these high-profile incarcerations left power vacuums, laying the groundwork for a wider group of new leaders to enter the market and compete for their share. Yes, these prosecutions disrupted channels of influence and traditional lines of authority. But their biggest impact was shifting the ways gangs operate. Large centralized units have all but disappeared, and new, smaller factions have taken their place.[15] Meanwhile, gang identity has become more porous, so that becoming a member is less a question of choice and more a matter of location. It is "the water everybody swims in."[16]

Describing these shifts from the police perspective, West Side police officer Tamara says, "When I started is when a lot of the higher-ups in the gangs were catching conspiracy cases and going away for longer amounts of time. Now you don't have your big chiefs on the street anymore, running things." As a result, Tamara says, "I think the breakdown of the higher-ups is where the problem is with a lot of these street gangs. They're all in jail, or they've got their other things going on now, they're not so much worried about leadership. You've got the main guys that run the spots, but it's just different. . . . There's definitely more gangs, every corner has their own faction of a gang now. So there's a lot more chaos in the gangs, there's not a mom and a dad to tell you how it is. It's just a bunch of kids playing gangs." As Tamara describes, the loss of gang chiefs is akin to a loss of authority figures, something many Austin youth have also experienced in their home lives, with parents taken away by incarceration, violence, and/or addiction.

Elaborating on these shifts, Harold says, "It is more of a renegade thing out here now." While a few of the long-standing West Side gangs still have a hierarchical structure, many do not. The "Travelers, New Breeds, and the Black Disciples, all the classics," still exist, but now there are many nonhierarchical groups "out there doing their own thing. . . . That's what you call renegades." According to Harold, the rise of renegades is tied to a resistance to authority figures, even within gang life. Reinforcing Tamara's insights, he says, "The young guys, they don't want to listen to nobody. They feel like can't nobody tell them nothing. That's how they are in their households. So if they are doing it in their households they ain't going to come to the street and listen to you. 'I ain't even listen to my own momma, what makes you think I'm going to listen to you?' That's how they look at it."

Members of these less organized groups have little concern for the hierarchies of old. A looser, more freelance culture has emerged, operating in parallel to many elements of the formal economy. But, according to Harold, because of their lack of leadership, these young groups also lack the experience that a cross-generational alliance can bring. "It is easy for renegades to collapse," he says. "They never stand strong for long because they never had that leadership quality." Even if business is thriving, renegades may still be likely to go out and shoot at competitors. Harold compares the renegades to the gang structure he worked in, where if what you are doing is working, "you keep doing what you are doing and try to do it better. If they can hire more people over here to sell their drugs then it makes no sense to go over there into someone's territory. Because they are structured a little bit better, they are going to stay right here."

Another major change is easier access to large quantities of drugs for distribution. Harold explains, "You had to be a major player back in the day to get a large amount of drugs. You had to be somebody." Now the barriers to entry are lower. Young people "get in the game with a corner strip and talk about how they have weight. There's too many people in the way." As a result, "there's no instruction in the gangs. A lot of outlaws. They don't think they have to ask anybody permission."

These changes can lead to an increase in shootings. Describing gang factions on the east side of Austin, Tamara says, "Right now, the intra-gang conflicts are what the problem are. A lot of the higher-up guys are incarcerated and they haven't trained these young guys to stay in line. One young guy wants to run the corner that the other young guy is running, so instead of doing it how they used to do it—ask permission, work up through the chain of command—they just go and kill them. So it's different than what it used to be."

Though the dynamics of street gangs have changed dramatically, police strategies have seen only minor reinventions. Efforts like the Violence Reduction Strategy (VRS) were designed to bring a new approach to the table by introducing both a carrot and a stick—potential connections with community resources or a law enforcement response. But, at least in Chicago, the VRS effectively continues policies implemented in the 1980s and '90s, when law enforcement agencies aggressively arrested tens of thousands of residents in low-income African American areas. The strategy invites community leaders to meetings so they can promise social service supports, but it fails to actually build out the kinds of community capacity needed to do more than just put black men in handcuffs by the dozens. Mentors are not recruited. Peacemakers are not trained. Youth programs and job training efforts go underfunded. And all the while, violence is said to be a product of individual actions and personal choices.

For cities outside Chicago, places that are still deciding what their violence prevention efforts will look like, it is essential to do more than just target "gang leaders" and warn them of zero tolerance. Such approaches work from a false understanding of the world. They fail to account for the limits of concentrated punishment, for the ways that removing people by the thousands—be they drug dealers and/or parents—creates vacuums for the next generation to navigate. To be effective, government leaders across the country must account for the environments in which individual choices are made and for the shaping force of policy on these environments. They must do more than simply punish disadvantage.

A TRUE INDIVIDUAL

Influential gang leaders have not been the only ones targeted in the war on neighborhoods. When seeking to explain neighborhood disorder in areas like Austin, the mainstream narrative has focused on the failings—or perceived failings—of residents in general, often criminalizing the most vulnerable. Disconnected youth have routinely been called thugs, gangbangers, predators, and worse. Meanwhile, parents are frequently blamed for the struggles of these youth, deemed bad, irresponsible, and absent.[17]

All of these labels make people's underlying humanity harder to recognize and their substantial disadvantages easier to ignore. For decades now, this labeling has been used by media, politicians, voters, and law enforcement executives to explain away complex social issues, reinforcing the distance between themselves and the struggles of everyday residents in places like Austin. Taken together, these terms have functioned as obstacles to empathy.[18] They have shaped a landscape that regularly divides the social world into good and bad people, rather than, say, good and bad environments. In turn, policies rooted in this binary frame separate people into law aiders and disorderly threats, into those worthy of support and those who can and should be discarded.

This kind of binary thinking is not routinely applied across all communities. Few observers go into wealthy white neighborhoods and start dividing the populace into good and bad. No, this lens is primarily applied in low-income neighborhoods of color, with the most severe depictions often reserved for predominantly African American areas like Austin. While low-income white communities struggle for adequate opportunities all across the country, they have not faced the same levels of outside demonization. The areas most impacted by this labeling are places where the poverty, crime, and incarceration rates are all high and there are long histories of racially discriminatory policies, from redlining to predatory lending to underfunded schools.

In other words, your humanity is most likely to be called into question when you are struggling economically, marginalized racially, and living in a place that is historically disadvantaged. Your value is up for grabs only if you are navigating daily challenges that most others cannot easily fathom. Responding to this framing, juvenile justice reformers commonly use the refrain "No child is born bad." The phrase asserts that the differences between most people and those behind bars are differences of context, not of innate capacity or character. Criminal behavior is never natural; environments and experiences, not genetics or inherent traits, are what ultimately drive some people toward harm and wrongdoing. This truth is often lost in media portrayals of Chicago's violence, where punitive responses to tragedy and pain are rarely called into question.

Most dehumanization of youth and residents comes from total outsiders, people who are comfortable seeing communities through labels like "thugs" and "bad parents," looking down on them from the confines of their suburbs, well-off neighborhoods, or distant towns.[19] This tendency has had massive effects on the general electorate, both rewarding and being fed by "tough on crime" politics. While the worldviews of the general electorate are well-charted territory among researchers, the perceptions of police officers are less well known. For officers, the psychic life of dehumanization often goes much deeper. They are working in contexts where they must stay vigilant for their own safety, where they receive little incentive for building caring relationships with those they serve, and where their only available tools are designed to sever rather than repair relationships. They accept these pressures every time they report to work, every time they choose to put on the uniform for another day or night. As their shifts pile up, whatever empathy they first brought to the work often gets depleted.

Samuel is a police officer in the Fifteenth District who works the overnight shift, which runs from 5:30 p.m. to 2:30 a.m. Working these hours, Samuel responds to many shootings. When asked how he processes those shootings, he says, "I don't. It is just a disconnected psyche. It is a mechanism, a mechanism to keep your sanity. To me, it is not that much different than going to a traffic accident. It is a disconnect." Elaborating on this disconnect, Samuel says, "A lot of it has to do with the lifestyle of the victim. If you see a true individual, a regular working guy that was victimized, it may be different, but even then there is a disconnect. I mean, there are a few times you feel bad for seeing something, people dying, but most of the time there is a complete disconnect." While Samuel occasionally experiences an emotional connection with those he serves, most of the people he encounters are not considered "a true individual." Though this clearly serves as a psychological coping strategy for Samuel, it is a strategy that introduces its own dangers, taking emotional separation to such an extreme that "true individuals" even disappear from view.[20]

Police officers aren't trained to see many elements of human contexts and conditions, even though these contexts and conditions have enormous influence over human behaviors.[21] These blinding effects may be especially bad for officers working the night shift, but we also talked to daytime patrol officers who described sections of Austin as "Afghanistan," implying a war zone mentality. If we lived in a world where law enforcement coexisted with abundant youth workers, mental health responders, family crisis specialists, addiction counselors, and workforce recruiters, such worldviews might not matter. Law enforcement officials could then put on their blinders and do what they must. But we do not live in such a world. Besides paramedics and firefighters, police officers are the only emergency response force that exists in most disadvantaged communities.

When police officers do not recognize the reasons why a young person sells drugs, or a child carries a knife to school, or a father struggles to break his addiction, or a mother cannot find legal employment to pay her bills, these needs have no outside witnesses. Police officers have neither the departmental resources to adequately respond to these challenges nor the partnerships with other types of emergency responders that would allow them to do so. This is how we lose sight of the human potential within entire neighborhoods. Left unaddressed, the needs and promise of residents in these areas—and the intricate dynamics of violence—become all but invisible to policymakers.

HEALING IS PREVENTION

Violence creates many complex emotions. For the survivor of a violent crime, any harmful act can lead to a sense of powerlessness and a reduced agency that is difficult to accept. So how does that person regain power?

In the criminal justice system, crime survivors rely upon the state to take action. They call the police and notify authorities of the wrongdoing.

If an arrest is made, the victim then relies upon the state's attorney to prosecute whoever is apprehended. The state's attorney becomes the victim's sole advocate for justice and punishment is the domain of government. If the state uses its power in a way that leads to a conviction, then that transfer of power is meant to result in some level of relief for the victim.[22]

In so-called "street" justice, the quest for relief is much more direct. Survivors take matters into their own hands or they call upon allies from their social network. In this equation, police officers are not trusted intermediaries.[23] Instead, the offended parties seek out the offender directly and exact whatever vengeance is deemed appropriate, often within a very short period of time. Power is reclaimed quickly and with little outside support. In the context of gangs, primary agents in street justice, the battle for justice is also enveloped in a complex web of economics, family, identity, and trauma, any of which can serve as a trigger for action. In place of the government, the social group becomes the advocate for justice, either supporting an individual's quest or taking action on that person's behalf. Though more direct, street justice is also much more brutal, as attacks replace state action.

Both methods of justice have deep flaws. Whereas the criminal justice system relies on forced removal, removing people from their homes for extended periods of time, the street justice system depends on violence and, all too often, on the ultimate act of murder. To varying degrees, both systems remove key actors from family and community life, and as a result, both perpetuate cycles of trauma within communities. Though damaging to individuals and families, the removal created by jail and prison is typically temporary and does not preclude any further contact between the prisoner and their loved ones. In stark contrast, the removal created through homicide is final and irreversible, ending all possibility of contact and all hope for reconciliation among the parties involved in previous acts of wrongdoing. These two approaches feed each other: whereas street violence drives up prison admissions, the failing of the formal justice system all but ensures that street justice will continue.

There is a third alternative path. Restorative justice offers a healing and transformative approach to repairing harms and addressing the underlying reasons for any offense. It places decisions in the hands of those who have been most affected by a wrongdoing and is concerned for the well-being of not just the victim but also the offender—and the surrounding community. Rather than a focus on the rules that have been broken, restorative justice pays attention to the harms that have been done. Participants in a restorative justice process, be it a peacemaking circle or a victim-offender panel, agree to work together to reach consensual outcomes. These processes involve listening to one another and respecting one another's ability to work through difficult emotions.[24]

Though it does not repair the economic damage done to areas like Austin in recent decades, restorative justice is a serious tool for rebuilding community relationships. On an interpersonal level it is an approach that invites people to deal with the existing tensions in their lives. When communities sit down in a circle and talk through difficult issues, some real truths are going to be raised: the ways we fear our youth, the ways we sweep issues of childhood trauma under the rug, the ways removing fathers en masse from their homes impacts future generations.[25] Restorative justice says "We have to wake up and face these realities." And it gives a practical, nonclinical starting place for doing so, helping practitioners to create safe spaces for very difficult conversations. From supporting restorative justice hubs for youth to consulting for a Restorative Justice Community Court in North Lawndale, we have actively worked to help build Chicago's restorative justice infrastructure.[26] We have seen how powerful leaders and policymakers in the Chicago area, including Judge Colleen Sheehan, County Commissioner Jesus "Chuy" Garcia, and State Representative Juliana Stratton, help to advance a restorative agenda. And we have seen incredible facilitators train literally thousands of everyday Chicago heroes in this approach.[27] Figure 5 illustrates the latent community peacekeeping capacity that exists across the city. There are myriad leaders trained in restorative practices who could, with the right supports, help mitigate conflict in areas that are over-reliant on the criminal justice system.

One reason restorative practices are effective is that they make space for the multitude of pains that both victims and offenders bring to any exchange. They are no replacement for therapy or clinical supports, but they can offer an entry point to trauma recovery. Built on the recognition that "hurt people hurt people," restorative philosophy asserts that healing is prevention, that cycles of violence are only interrupted when past experiences can be safely processed. Drawing from First Nations

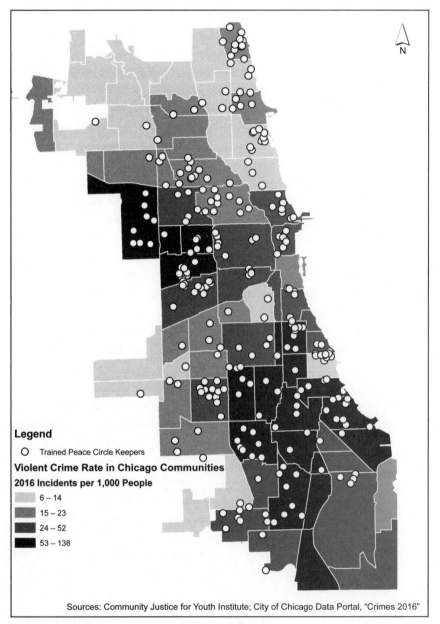

Legend

○ Trained Peace Circle Keepers

Violent Crime Rate in Chicago Communities

2016 Incidents per 1,000 People

6 – 14

15 – 23

24 – 52

53 – 138

Sources: Community Justice for Youth Institute; City of Chicago Data Portal, "Crimes 2016"

Figure 5: Map of Restorative Justice Circle Keepers Trained

traditions of conflict resolution, the accompanying practices help all people involved to share power in difficult conversations so that deep social harms can be repaired.[28] In so doing, these stakeholders tap into the reality that our brains are built to work in and through relationships.[29]

When the underlying traumas of people who commit violence are shut out from the process of justice, there is no reason to expect their behavior will change.[30] The symptoms of their pain—which can include low academic achievement, sleep deprivation, depression, anger problems, nightmares, and substance abuse—will persist, no matter what punishments are issued. But while "million dollar blocks" of misinvestment have been created, very little capacity for healing has been developed within high-incarceration neighborhoods. Meanwhile, many young people in areas like Austin experience a constantly high state of alert, triggered by a consistent stream of perceived threats. It causes young people with high levels of exposure to violence to move through life in a state of alarm, making it harder for them to access their deeper reasoning skills.[31] Without greater resources invested in services to address underlying traumas and their related affects, violence is likely to continue unabated.

Building community capacity for healing is essential for violence prevention. Community capacity should include strengthening the social fabric among households and neighbors, developing local restorative justice leaders, providing excellent clinical allies and supporters, and training trauma-informed professionals such as teachers, preachers, youth development workers, and police officers. Each of these layers of support should be robustly developed, prioritized in budgets, laws, and other strategic decisions. There should be no half-hearted measures. If professionals in areas like Austin become more trauma informed, but the other layers of capacity are not enacted, then little will change. For example, if all the best therapists in the world descended upon high-incarceration neighborhoods, but families and community members were not empowered as experts in their own right, then even well-resourced efforts would come up short.

New patterns will take root only when other models of violence prevention are fully funded, and when law enforcement is no longer looked to as the sole solution. From community leaders trained in restorative justice, to visionary employers committed to social responsibility, to social healers and organizers of all stripes, new allies must be empowered in the fight against violence and despair. These strategies must be more than campaign promises and political facades; they must be primary investments of government.

Such an approach is a major departure from the current public safety paradigm. Rather than help people process their pain, concentrated punishment freezes pain in place. It cements society's image of people as "ex-offenders," causing them to be forever viewed by their past actions. These "ex-offenders" are continually marked as a threat, in part because society never actually dealt with the emotions surrounding that person's wrongdoing. Similarly, for those directly impacted by harm, there is little opportunity to process the loss they've experienced. And for those who are indirectly impacted, there are few chances to support those who've been wounded or to help hold accountable those who opened the wounds. Though only a beginning, restorative practices seek to reverse this pattern, giving everyone affected by violence—from the victims to the perpetrators—the opportunity to safely move forward with their lives.

To date, the punishment paradigm has kept policymakers from fully exploring the possibilities of restorative justice. The punitive paradigm oversimplifies violence. It says that racism, trauma, and emotions have little to do with the perpetuation of harm.[32] When policymakers cling to this narrative, little change is required to the ways we seek safety. Criminal justice officials can continue hammering away at problems that actually demand much more sophisticated solutions than arrest and incarceration. They can keep imprisoning the children of those who were locked up a generation prior, without ever thinking about the deeper patterns at play. But doing so represents a costly misuse of the powers of the law, one that may help to explain why violence in Chicago is back on the rise.

The examples of violence shared in this chapter show the complexity that must be addressed by anyone wishing to create a lasting peace. The diversity of these examples was inspired by Richie's violence matrix, which shows how multiple forms of violence—sexual assaults, shootings, negative media images—play out across multiple contexts.[33] When we look comprehensively at these dimensions, it becomes possible to see how violence is fueled over time, how antisocial behaviors are often the result of antisocial conditions that were not created by those enduring them. But far too often, we falsely assume that behavior of residents in neighborhoods like Austin is irrational and counterproductive and, on the flip side, that the behavior of authority figures is rational and well justified.

More than thirty years after Ben Wilson's death, courtrooms and holding cells are still at the center of our public safety universe. The mass incarceration era has not eliminated violence. Bloody Fourth of July weekends are still a tragic Chicago tradition and, in far too many neighborhoods, roadside memorials that mark where someone was killed are still a regular sight.[34] But most violence is invisible to the broader world. Sexual assaults seldom make headlines. Shootings may be mentioned briefly but the victim's name is rarely even given. Even homicides do not hold our attention for long. And when instances of violence do receive public attention, it is almost always as short segments on the evening or nightly news.

Deeper attention is rarely paid. The concentration of violence has only aggravated this problem, making it easier for outsiders to ignore both violence and the flawed war being waged against it. In effect, the war on neighborhoods represents a devastating case of work avoidance, where consideration of how to change the fate of communities like Austin is minimal. Many public officials simply accept as second nature that violence is common in some places. Meanwhile, residents in areas like Austin must squint to see public investments in the capacity of their communities to heal, grow, and thrive.

CHAPTER 4

THE SPACE BETWEEN

SIMON IS AMONG the roughly 40 percent of his Austin peers who have never been convicted of a felony. Despite his clean record, he has had his own harrowing interactions with the law. He grew up witnessing the involvement of local police officers in the drug market, memories that will always be with him, no matter how sweeping the reforms have been since. More directly, he had a series of personal encounters with officers that changed his life forever.

"I was attending a local college, just going to class. I was leaving home; it was in the daytime. It was probably around ten, ten thirty. I was driving my car. I had a test that day. This Chicago police officer, he comes behind me. I had a cracked taillight. I didn't have money to get the car fixed. It still rolled, so I'm driving it; the lights and stuff still worked. Anyway, he pulls me over; he says it's because of the taillight. Mind you, I'm trying to get to school. I say, 'Okay, are you going to give me a ticket? I'm not speeding or anything, but I'm in a hurry.' I was very polite. I know the drill."

At this point, recalls Simon, the officer walks back to his car and sits in it "for literally twenty minutes. . . . I'm waiting there; I'm very disgusted, trying to figure out why this is taking so long. But I'm patient. He comes back to the car; he comes up to the vehicle, and he asks me to step out. When I get out of the car, he immediately grabs me, to put me on the car. . . . He didn't say anything; he just grabbed me. My first instinct is to pull away. I'm confused now."

Simon recounts what he said to the officer: "I've been waiting twenty minutes, gave you everything that I needed to give you; the next step should either be a ticket or an explanation. Not 'I'm going to grab you and put the handcuffs on you.'" He recalls the officer began "ranting and raving, like 'Get on the ground.' So I get on the ground; I'm surrendering. He put his cuffs on me, put me on the curb. Then he starts calling me all types of names: 'You nigger' and this and that. It was very demoralizing. How did I go from going to class to this scenario? He took my car keys, threw them in the grass. He's just going on and on. His partners get there, and I swear to God, if there weren't thirty cops out there. Thirty police officers for me, one guy. Paddy wagon, detectives, all these cars. We are in front of this church, and the neighbors, they are starting to come out. I just can't wrap my mind around it, I can't believe this, [I'm thinking,] 'I don't even jaywalk, this is crazy.'"

Explaining what happened when the additional officers arrive, Simon says, "These guys get there and they're even worse, 'You black guys, you nigger.' . . . I'm just like sitting there corralled, not showing any emotions or anything. I'm like, 'Hey, whatever y'all are going to do to me, you're going to do, I don't know. But I'm not going to give you any reason.' They put me in the wagon and took me over to the station."

Simon describes the scenario at the station: "I'm in this holding cell, and a white shirt [ranking officer] comes in there as soon as I arrive—the white shirt, he comes in there in the holding cell and starts to engage in a conversation. Now, this is where I wish I had been wiser. I shouldn't have said anything. I shouldn't have tried to plead my case; I shouldn't have talked to this guy at all. But I'm still thinking, 'Maybe I can just walk out of here, this is a misunderstanding and it will be looked over, I can explain it to him and he'll see that this is an error and say [I'm] free to go.'"

At this point in the story, says Simon, the police district had realized the depth of the initial officer's error: unlawfully arresting a man with no prior offenses. It was also at this point that, according to Simon, the truth of the encounter started to be buried. Explaining his precarious situation, he says, "The arrest was never explained, but it doesn't matter; I had no witnesses. It's just me. Nobody's in the car with me. Long story short, they end up sending me to the county [jail]. I'm thinking I will end up in court; they will say I have a fraudulent insurance card; I'm going to prove that it was a real insurance card." When Simon gets to court, he recalls, "I'm thinking, 'Okay, cool, I can probably bond myself out.' I think I had a couple hundred bucks on me. Come to find out, they didn't send any of my stuff with me when I got transported. They told the officers that they couldn't find it. I had no ID, no nothing. That was the first thing I noticed: I was being set up to fail. Second thing is, when I go before this judge, the state's attorney steps up and she's like, 'He was pulled over in a traffic stop; he had a fraudulent insurance card, Judge, but he violently resisted arrest and assaulted the officer. And he tried to take the officer's gun.' I was floored.

"Sure enough, when she said I tried to take that officer's gun, I saw the look on the court officer's face go to like, 'You? I thought you were a good guy.' I am looking like I saw a ghost; I couldn't believe she just said that. After all of that, she said, 'Oh, and by the way, he has no priors.' But she said it like it doesn't matter. So the judge is like, 'Give him an $80,000 bond.' They charged me with three felonies. Now, I have to fight a case for three, four years of my life. They were literally trying to give me eight years behind this. . . . I had to fight for my freedom."

Simon ended up taking a plea bargain to win that freedom, but only after spending weeks in Cook County Jail. The false admission of guilt that came with that plea meant he could never file a suit for the behavior of the officer who pulled him over. In his words, "They made sure I could not walk away from this case totally vindicated, because I could have sued them immediately." This experience is what led Simon to agree to be interviewed for this book. "That's one of my stories that propelled me to even talk to you. I know how many other guys have been in situations. They may not have been just like mine, but [they were] still wrong, because they are on the other side of this police officer and they are literally at the mercy of what these guys want to do with their authority."

Simon's experience is extreme but not out of the ordinary. It is indicative of the larger chasm between residents of areas like Austin and the police officers who patrol them. For many in Austin, officers are not seen as allies. Children are taught to keep their distance, to navigate interactions with extreme caution. Youth pressure one another to withhold information. The law is seen not as a supportive power but as a force to be avoided at all costs, even when a person has no objective reason to steer clear. Not all residents feel this way. But the feeling is strong and increasingly embedded into the hearts of new generations, a fact that was made clear both by officers and by residents throughout our fieldwork.

As city police departments have relied on forced removal to address crime and disadvantage, overall community health in places like Austin has decreased, as measured by standard mental health indicators.[1] Meanwhile, the core operating strategies of police departments go unchanged. On Chicago's West Side, at the very site where Sears Roebuck once operated the world's largest mail-order distribution center, the Chicago Police Department has been operating a highly controversial interrogation complex that was, until recently, off the grid and invisible to public scrutiny.[2] This site came to public attention in the same period that the City of Chicago was finally coming to grips with the CPD's history of torture in unmonitored locations during the 1980s.[3]

The space between police officers and disadvantaged African American communities is wide and cannot be easily bridged. Many activists do not believe that such a bridge is worth building. Police departments have missed the mark by too much, for too long. Their strategies have continued to punish poor people who live in disadvantaged environments, to occupy their neighborhoods in order to surveil residents of color. For many activists, reform efforts are to be treated warily, like signing a peace treaty without the cosigning aggressor actually ending the war. Such efforts may expose their communities to even greater danger, allowing antiblack strategies to keep disrupting their lives under new names and titles. Even for those seeking to reform police departments from the inside, the space between officers and residents can feel unbridgeable, a fact that has long been true for change agents in and beyond Austin.[4]

QUESTIONS OF IMPACT

The fundamental purpose of policing is to increase public safety, but the strategies and tactics that guide contemporary policing often miss that vital mark. In the process, these limited approaches frequently obscure the need for the creation of parallel safety efforts and infrastructure.

In 1992, under the leadership of then mayor Richard M. Daley, the Chicago City Council passed an anti-gang loitering ordinance that allowed police to arrest any young people who "remain in any one place with no apparent purpose" and were determined to have at least one gang member among them. By the start of 1996, implementation of the ordinance had led to eighty-nine thousand orders to disperse and forty-two thousand arrests. These arrests were not for drug offenses, illegal weapons possession, or even soliciting. They were for loitering, for standing outside in the open air. And they primarily targeted young men of color on the city's West and South Sides, a fact that points back to the tensions between ethnic white officers and African American citizens that had intensified during the Great Migration.

Throughout the implementation of the ordinance, city leaders made no systemic effort to positively engage those young people "with no apparent purpose." They did not ask Chicago police officers to round up youth and take them to open gyms, GED programs, or job-training sites. Instead, they created a world where a young person's mere presence was deemed dangerous. Laws like this helped the war on neighborhoods take root, arbitrarily dividing the world into lawbreakers and law abiders, into those who warrant the extended reach of the punitive state and those who may walk the earth freely.[5]

Though this ordinance was struck down by the US Supreme Court in 1999 as unconstitutional, lawyers for the city immediately went to work on a revised ordinance, which was implemented, although critics remained concerned that it asked "the beat cop to serve as a constitutional scholar."[6] Under the revised ordinance, the police department could only issue orders to disperse within predesignated "hot spots," which were areas where crime was said to be particularly intense. The public defender at the time, Camille Kozlowski, critiqued the law for criminalizing people's intent instead of their actual behaviors. As with the original ordinance, people were still being punished for being perceived as gang members rather than for committing criminal acts.[7] Ordinances like these are an example of "order-maintenance" policing, which was popularized through the broken windows theory. In the broken windows theory, regulating even the smallest displays of disorder—vandalism, loitering, public drinking—is seen as important for establishing norms of order and preventing the spread of further lawlessness.[8] According to scholar Bernard Harcourt, order-maintenance policing labels some people as orderly and others as disorderly, based largely on imaginary grounds. By falsely grouping people into these two camps, order-maintenance policies reinforce the idea that certain people belong in public urban spaces while others do not.[9]

A related trend has been the idea of "hot-spot policing," which still shapes much of contemporary police practice. Built on the notion that crime is concentrated in certain places, hot-spot strategies flood those places with law enforcement resources.[10] A recent example of this approach in Chicago is the "impact zone," introduced in 2012 after a historically violent March. Within these police-designated zones, communities are flooded with police officers. Squad cars occupy blocks. Officers patrol residents by car, by bike, and on foot. And street interrogations are a normal part of the operation.

In these areas, residents can experience temporary declines in crime, but the benefits are short-lived once officers leave. Meanwhile, those arrested and/or incarcerated by these operations are not less likely to commit future offenses.[11] These zones are based on a faulty model that assumes all we need to end gun violence is more police officers on the streets, whether or not illegal-gun users have access to meaningful life opportunities, supports, or positive investments. In theory, this strategy targets places where serious violent crimes occur on a regular basis, and the police are there to protect resident survivors of that violence. In practice, the strategy consists of nothing more than temporary interventions with no long-term commitments to building resources in the targeted areas. According to some officers we spoke with, there are also many times when an area is named an "impact zone" for political, training, or loose operational purposes, with minimal underlying violence to justify the incredible police presence. Importantly, this is only a new iteration of failed hot-spot strategies that had been tried before in Chicago.[12]

Another recent intervention is the Violence Reduction Strategy (VRS), which in Chicago has often operated alongside impact zones. In this strategy, police reach out to gang leaders and threaten "zero tolerance" if any of their members shoot someone. And, as a carrot for good behavior, they offer social services to anyone in need. In concert with chosen community leaders, high-ranking law enforcement officials personally warn gang leaders of severe repercussions for any violence occurring in their neighborhood.[13] Together they give gang leaders a unified message: "We will help you if you will let us, but we will stop you if you make us."[14]

After one such meeting in Austin in 2012, a community leader recalled how then superintendent Garry McCarthy told a group of high-ranking Insane Vice Lords and other gang factions that any shootings would be met with the full force of the CPD. The night after that meeting, there was a fatal shooting nearby. The police responded with 147 arrests. Meanwhile, as the summer progressed, the Fifteenth District went on to have one of the most violent summers in the city, at twice the rate of the Chicago average at the time.[15]

Why didn't all those arrests lead to a decrease in violence? Because, like so many other recent public safety initiatives, the VRS misunderstands the problem of violence, failing to see the root causes of traumatic stress, economic isolation, and violence against women. It also overestimates the existing capacity of local agencies to respond to those drivers. From ordinances and designated zones to personalized warnings, the CPD's idea of impact has had everything to do with forced removal and little to do with local capacity building. They are only short-term solutions that are aimed at immediately decreasing violence, and they come at the expense of longer-term investments that, while likely slower to show impacts, have greater potential for lasting positive change.

Even when community policing strategies were officially rolled out in the Fifteenth District in the early 1990s, rank-and-file officers were largely uncooperative, refusing to walk beats with block captains, act on the information citizens provided them, or respond to the priorities the citizens set.[16] Though cooperation improved as years passed, the underlying strategies never changed. Similar to the police executives in power, the mayors and city council leaders responsible for overseeing the police have had massive blind spots.[17] They have viewed safety as a direct by-product of suppression, something to be managed and patrolled, not a function of community relationships and resources, something to be created and nurtured.

SOLDIERS IN THE WAR

In Chicago's Fifteenth Police District, one of two districts within Austin, an officer's professional advancement can be implicitly linked to the number of arrests they make. It is an often unspoken management metric, a dynamic that is also true for those policing low-income communities of color well beyond Chicago.[18] Arrests—independent of actual public safety goals—are the defining feature of the occupation.

A Fifteenth District officer named Tom says, "District commanders are telling the beat officer and the tactical officer to make arrests. Well, the easy arrests are your bullshit possession—one rock, two rocks. . . . We are being told to make that arrest and if I don't make that arrest I am not going to get my management spot." Tom, a veteran of the department, describes a clear incentive structure for making arrests, even when officers don't believe doing so is in the best interest of public safety. According to him, such practices distract from many larger safety issues: "Why am I going to take time out of my day and be unavailable for a domestic call, or a criminal sexual assault, or some in-progress call to arrest you? So you can go to court and it's tossed out? Let's not waste the state's attorney's time." This pressure to arrest contributes to "a big circle of inefficiency" within the broader criminal justice system. It bogs down the court system administratively in ways that increase prosecutors' reliance on plea bargains, effectively randomizing who will be punished for what offenses.[19]

When asked if other officers also dislike arresting users and small dealers, Tom says, "Yeah, but at the same time it's a necessary evil if you are in management. If you are on a tactical team, you just have to do it. Or if you don't have the seniority to work on day shifts, you will make arrests that you don't always agree with or feel like is benefiting anybody." In other words, officers routinely opt in to an unjust system, reshaping the lives of those they put in handcuffs even though they know such actions won't positively influence human behaviors. "If you have one crack rock on you, you are a user. Me arresting you isn't going to make you not use. It's not going to stop you from burglarizing someone's house for scrap metal to get that crack rock."

This same dynamic appears in many police departments across the US, extending well beyond the Fifteenth District and the CPD. From Los Angeles to New York City, long-standing incentive systems have come to light in recent years, typically through courageous critiques by officers themselves.[20]

As illustrated through anti-loitering ordinances, impact zones, and other hot-spot strategies, these pressures are not applied equally across all Chicago police districts. They are often unique to low-income neighborhoods of color, a fact that contributes greatly to the unequal enforcement of criminal law. These disparities in arrest practices are clearly revealed by the ways that African Americans are arrested for marijuana possession. In 2010, Cook County had more arrests for marijuana possession than anywhere else in the country, with 33,068 such arrests in all. Meanwhile, as of 2011, African Americans in Chicago were arrested for marijuana 15 times more than whites, even though whites use marijuana at equal or greater levels.[21] This disparity only intensifies when analyzed at the neighborhood level. Even after a city ordinance was passed to decriminalize marijuana, arrest rates in predominantly African American and Latino West Side neighborhoods were 7 times higher than the city average and 150 times that of the lowest-arrest neighborhoods.[22]

The vast arrest differentials between Chicago neighborhoods are undeniable evidence of systemic racism. Defenders of these differentials might say that West Side marijuana arrests are a result of broken windows policing, where punishment of low-level disorderly conduct offenses is said to deter more serious crime. But the evidence of that deterrence is nowhere to be found.[23] Making matters worse, whereas patrol officers are pressured to make arrests, those arrested often receive undue pressure to make confessions. This pressure was made clear in an interview with a lawyer who works at an organization dedicated to providing free legal counsel to people arrested in Chicago neighborhoods like Austin. In her eyes, guaranteed counsel for every arrested person is an essential step toward a more accountable system.[24]

Quoting a *60 Minutes* episode that aired shortly before our interview, she says, "Chicago is the false-confession capital of the nation, and that means this police department has more innocent people actually saying they did it in that first forty-eight hours than any other police department in the country. And not only are we in first place, if we want to call it that—I guess last place—but [there are] twice as many false concessions out of Chicago than even the next runner-up." Without legal defense, people frequently just waive their right to counsel, thinking they don't have a real choice. As seen in Simon's story, this can have devastating consequences.

This lawyer's vision for change is that the police "would have to call us as soon as someone is taken into custody. They would have to let us know where they are at, what their name is, what their birthday is, and when they got picked up. Then we could actually protect everybody's rights when they are in custody. Right now we need a phone call; we need somebody to call us because we can't just go in and be like, 'Let me see my client!' We have to say, 'Here's the name of the person.' Every single person who is charged with a felony has a state's attorney that shows up at the station and says, 'Yes, police, we have enough evidence to charge them with a felony.' But there's no such thing for public defenders."[25]

Without this line of defense, high numbers of arrests have flooded court systems, where judges, state's attorneys, and public defenders are overwhelmed by the sheer number of cases they encounter—a fact that often makes effective representation difficult.[26] Without time, energy, or resources for due process, plea bargains have become a practical solution to a huge administrative burden. Across the United States today, more than 90 percent of all felony convictions are decided without ever going to trial. Of the roughly twenty-eight thousand felony cases that are adjudicated at the Cook County courthouse each year, 85 percent end in a plea bargain.[27] Describing how the plea process works from the perspective of the defendant, Simon explains that prosecutors "use the leverage of time and their abundant resources. It's like, 'I've got too much to lose.'"

DEADLY INSTINCTS

Eric Garner was selling loose cigarettes at a convenience store. Sandra Bland was pulled over for a minor traffic violation. Alton Sterling was selling CDs and DVDs outside a gas station. These were all minor infractions by individuals who did not pose a public safety threat. But Eric and Alton were murdered by police officers anyway, and Sandra was unjustly detained until her body was found mysteriously hanging in her jail cell. Because of the ceaseless work of activists and movement leaders, these deaths, which occurred between 2014 and 2016, were made visible to the nation rather than swept under the rug, was the pattern for decades.

Chicago is no stranger to such murders. In December 2015, an unarmed nineteen-year-old college student named Quintonio LeGrier was killed in his family home on the West Side. Concerned about his behavior, which was driven by an apparent mental illness, Quintonio's parents had called 911 thinking the police would take their son to the hospital. But the young student ended up being fatally shot by an officer. In the process, an elderly neighbor named Bettie Jones was also shot and killed by the officer.[28] Despite the two deaths, no charges were filed against the offending officer. Quintonio and Bettie died as part of a larger pattern of police killing citizens in the midst of an emotional or a mental health crisis.[29]

Story lines of police murders are far too familiar, as is the lack of accountability for the officers involved. In 2014, seventeen-year-old Laquan McDonald was shot sixteen times without cause by CPD officer Jason Van Dyke. Video of Laquan's murder was captured by a police cruiser's dashboard camera, but was suppressed for over a year. As so often happens, the protective instinct of police officers was profoundly misapplied, used to defend peers and professionals from facing justice at the expense of truth and credibility. Upon the eventual release of the videos, major protests were organized by groups like Black Youth Project 100. These demonstrations led to the high-profile ousting of both Chicago police superintendent Garry McCarthy and, through a hard-fought election triumph, state's attorney Anita Alvarez.

But what was not seen in most headlines was the difficult life that Laquan had endured prior to his murder. Laquan had experienced different degrees of homelessness throughout much of his young life, moving in and out of foster homes, the homes of extended family members, and the Cook County Juvenile Detention Center, never receiving the robust supports he needed to escape the difficult conditions of his childhood and youth.[30] Only in his death did Laquan get public attention.

In 2013, twenty-two-year-old Rekia Boyd was killed by CPD detective Dante Servin while he was off duty. Her alleged crime? Talking too loudly. Servin shot her in the back of the head from the comfort of his car, without ever even identifying himself as a police officer.[31] Rekia was one of hundreds of unarmed women and girls who have been killed by police officers in the United States in recent years, including Aiyana Jones, a seven-year-old sleeping on her couch, and Natasha McKenna, who was already shackled and in jail when she was tasered to death.[32] Of all unarmed people killed by officers since 1999, an estimated 20 percent have been black women and girls, despite the fact that they account for just 7 percent of the country's total population.[33] Despite overwhelming evidence, Rekia's killer was found not guilty. As seen in Laquan's case, law enforcement frequently circles the wagons when police violence becomes too publicly visible.[34]

In stark contrast to a police culture where the minor infractions of residents can somehow justify lethal action, police officers themselves rarely face meaningful accountability. Between March 2011 and September 2015, 28,567 misconduct allegations were filed against CPD officers.

Of those misconduct allegations, 1,732 were filed against officers in the Austin neighborhood, and 202 of those were for use-of-force violations. Though frequent, these allegations rarely led to any accountability for the officers involved. Citywide, less than 2 percent of the charges resulted in any level of discipline. In Austin, only 20 of the 1,732 complaints resulted in any disciplinary action, and half of those actions were only "reprimands," meaning a written or verbal warning. Of the remaining 10 cases resulting in discipline, only 2 led to a suspension of more than nine days.[35]

What underlying beliefs allow officers to become judge, jury, and executioner? And to do so with relative impunity? The deaths of Rekia, Laquan, Bettie, Quintonio, Sandra, Eric, Alton, and countless others do not indict just individual police officers but also the broader policies and strategies in which they are embedded. For decades now, police officers have been taught that low-level offenses lead to larger crimes, that financially struggling black people are criminals and are thus subject to lethal force, and that any attempt to hold police accountable is itself a threat to public safety. These are not the beliefs of every officer in America. But they are dominant positions within almost every police department.

The police executions we've named are the result of the pressure to arrest, of officers' blindness to "true individuals," of notions of safety that punish those who are already struggling the most. They are symptoms of a criminal justice system that is decidedly antiblack, where the full humanity of residents in areas like Austin is rarely recognized. In this vacuum, protective instincts turn deadly. They are warped to defend broken strategies, to double down on past failings, to extend the paradigm of concentrated punishment even further. Even as police departments across the country have come under the microscope, larger questions around the role of law enforcement in the work of creating safety are often missing from the conversation. In cities across the United States, police departments continue to be seen as the only legitimate institutions in creating public safety, rather than one of many resources that are needed.

BEYOND HAMMERS AND NAILS

Wielding only hammers, law enforcement executives typically treat the world as if it were made of nails. Within the CPD, this limited worldview has led to fatal flaws in departmental strategy and culture, flaws that are frequently mirrored at the federal level.[36]

At their best, police officers are the ultimate protectors. They intervene at the most dangerous moments in community life, showing up when the bullets are blazing, when the intruder is in the home, and when nobody else feels safe enough to respond. But as the Movement for Black Lives has made clear, police officers are often far from their best. And their shortcomings must be recognized. Not only is that recognition essential for helping communities grow safer, but it is also a vital step in protecting police officers from the greatest threats they face—suicide and alcoholism, two forces that are uniquely high in law enforcement communities. The suicide rate among Chicago officers is somewhere between 22.7 and 29.4 per 100,000 department members. Even the low end of that range is significantly higher than the national average.[37] In the words of one former Justice Department official, "Suicide is killing officers, alcohol is killing officers, at a far greater rate than ambushes, but there is not the same sense of urgency around this issue."[38] As this correlation suggests, there may be deep links between officer well-being and officer performance, between the health of those charged with protecting communities and their actual ability to do so.

Officer wellness is a prerequisite for changing the role of policing in areas like Austin, so that officers might become locally respected allies in the work to create safety.[39] This is one of many issues covered in a 164-page report on the CPD by the US Department of Justice (DOJ) released in January of 2017. The report drew from meetings with "over 340 Chicago Police Department members and 23 members of the Independent Police Review Authority."[40] It covers a litany of civil rights violations by the CPD, with a primary focus on the department's "pattern or practice of unconstitutional use of force." Arguing for strategies such as robust mental health supports for officers and deeper accountability efforts, the report calls on those who govern the department to ensure that "officers police fairly and compassionately in all neighborhoods, including in those with high rates of violent crime and in minority communities."

But it is not enough to simply help police departments get better. If departments are reformed but larger enforcement strategies are not shifted, then hammers will continue chasing nails for decades to come. Police officers will continue relying on a set of tools that is insufficient to create lasting peace in areas of high disadvantage.

In his outgoing letter as the US attorney for the Northern District of Illinois, written in March 2017, Zachary Fardon identifies many of the broken logics that stand in the way.[41] His policy vision covers a lot of ground. Though he gives a general nod to youth centers, his agenda is primarily based on the idea that more resources toward a punishment agenda will create peace and, somehow, help to restore the law's legitimacy in South and West Side areas like Austin. For example, he wrote, "You can't have a top-flight police department on the cheap. For decades, CPD has been run on the cheap. Officers don't have the training, the supervision, the equipment, or culture they need and deserve." He leaves this point especially open-ended, so that some readers can see it as a call for officers to have access to higher-grade assault weapons, while others can see it as a plea for officers to have better counseling to process the intensity of their jobs.

Throughout the letter, Fardon references the Laquan McDonald case multiple times. It is a rare through line for his arguments: "By January 2016, the city was on fire. We had no police superintendent. Cops were under scrutiny. . . . And many of them just no longer wanted to wear [sic] the risk of stopping suspects. . . . So cops stopped making stops. And kids started shooting more—because they could, and because the rule of law, law enforcement, had been delegitimized. And that created an atmosphere of chaos." Although Fardon was a coauthor of the DOJ study of abuses of power within the CPD, he explicitly blames the nongovernmental efforts at police accountability that followed Laquan's murder for many of the ills Chicago faces. Spikes in street violence, distrust of law enforcement, cultural changes in gangs' online behavior—he traces them all back to the efforts of activists to make police officers answerable for their crimes.

Fardon makes a dangerous argument. It reads like a twisted version of the self-protective instinct, where accountability is treated as the real threat. On their own, many of Fardon's basic observations are insightful: Street violence has been on the rise. Trust in the rule of law has continued to plummet. Social media perpetuates cycles of violence in ways that are historically unprecedented. But all of these trends were unfolding well before Chicago police officers were under national scrutiny.[42] The conclusions that Fardon draws from these observations miss the mark by miles.

In particular, Fardon's claim that police accountability is responsible for increases in violence must be unpacked. By his reasoning, the video of Van Dyke killing Laquan forced a contract between the CPD and the American Civil Liberties Union (ACLU), which had previously sued the department over stop-and-frisk practices. Fardon views that contract as the precipitating force for declines in police officer performance, under the assumption it tells officers that before talking with "kids on the corner," they must now "take 40 minutes to fill out a form" and then give them a receipt with their badge number on it.

This argument has several deep flaws. First, the paperwork Fardon mentions is meant to ensure and document that their searches are based on probable cause, a basic right of every US citizen. Second, street violence was already on the rise in Chicago in 2015, well before the ACLU agreement.[43] Third, Chicago's spikes in violence are part of a broader national trend impacting cities from San Antonio to Louisville.[44] But even if Fardon was right, even if declines in police morale led to declines in suppression and, in turn, less aggressive policing allowed for more violence, then another problem would have to be addressed. Why is Chicago still so dependent on strategies that threaten First Amendment rights and lead to massive spending on punishment? More than thirty years into the city's, county's, and state's broad investments in mass incarceration, why has there not been a turn to a much wider peacemaking portfolio?

BEYOND WINDOW DRESSING

Chicago's police department has a vast and complex history of racial injustice. Recalling one of the major police corruption scandals in Austin, Simon says, "The drug scene was real tough in Austin during the late '80s, early '90s. It really boomed. You had a lot of police officers making big money. Even before that big sting where they took down all those detectives in the Fifteenth District, part of that federal investigation. I knew some of the detectives that got caught up in that, I knew they deserved to be caught up in that. They were literally serving the dope spots, keeping these guys working and coming to collect money. I was not surprised when they got arrested and everything came down on them. That type of behavior was totally corrupt, it was purely financial. It literally helped escalate the drug scene in North Austin."

Simon is referring to one of the most notorious cases of police corruption in Chicago's history. It went public during the very same years that the anti-loitering ordinance was being launched. In this case, "seven Austin District tactical police officers, plainclothes cops assigned to root out gangs and drugs on the West Side, were convicted in a series of robberies, home invasions and extortions of narcotics dealers in 1995 and 1996."[45] According to one of the lead prosecutors, US assistant attorney Brian Netols, "Two of the convicted officers admitted that it was routine for officers in the Austin District at the time to take money from people who were arrested."[46]

Witnessing cases like this had a deep impact on residents like Simon, especially when considered in concert with his experience of being wrongfully detained and falsely accused of a crime. His worldview has been changed, perhaps forever. "We've had a lot of police that were corrupt. They're literally facilitating and encouraging the system because it keeps them able to manipulate things to serve their own means. Let's face it, crime for cops gives them a smoke screen to do what they want, to bend the rules and have things the way they would need them to be [able] to facilitate their own means." Simon is not the only Austin resident to hold these views. And, counter to Fardon's claims that the rule of law was delegitimized in the wake of Laquan McDonald's case, his words reveal a long-standing tension in how police officers are perceived.

Although he knows high-integrity police officers, Simon's views persist. "I like to think that there are some good cops, I know that there are some good cops. I know some police officers personally, in my family and things like that. But even though I know there are some good officers out there, I can't honestly say they haven't had a situation where they didn't take advantage of their authority in some form or fashion. Even just taking advantage of it in that little instance adds to the problem, because it affects the people who you serve."

When viewed alongside district dynamics like the pressure to arrest and to extract confessions, it should be no surprise that many residents are doubtful that law enforcement officials can ever truly make neighborhoods safe. Many police officers are also doubtful. As Tom shared, they are routinely asked to arrest people for minor infractions, even when they know those arrests will have no safety benefits. And, because of residents' growing distrust of the profession, patrol officers, detectives, and special units must all work extra hard to gain the kinds of information they need from residents to solve cases, a fact that has huge implications for how success in law enforcement is defined.

Taken together, these trends have weakened the authority of the law in community life, advancing a broken model of accountability that frequently violates individuals' rights. Other ways of working must be cultivated. As long as policymakers attempt to solve complex social problems primarily with law enforcement tools, their efforts will fall tragically short. To date, law enforcement has been the force that steps in when street corners are allowed to falter, when jobs have not been created, when human worth has not been validated, when community structures are not repaired, and when community development prospects remain just prospects.

But, as seen in Fardon's letter, many prominent voices are still suggesting that the real key to safety, in one way or another, lies with law enforcement. Whether it is better training, better policing methods, or better oversight, these suggestions fail to enact any structural reform. These positions reflect their misunderstanding of the underlying problems at hand, within both disadvantaged neighborhoods and the police districts they oversee. Without the right opportunities, supports, and positive investments in place, there will never be enough police officers to make communities safe. And even the most enlightened, community-focused officers will fail if they don't have a robust portfolio of community-based service partners for making referrals. These realities make it hard to believe in a more hopeful horizon, where forced removal is treated as a last course of action rather than one of the few areas where government is willing to make dramatic investments in neighborhoods.

From the outside looking in, it can be difficult to see how structural racism undergirds so much of daily policing activities in high-incarceration areas, how old ideas like hot-spot policing are reinvigorated through new brands, without ever really changing local conditions. Though these strategies fail to consider crime generationally, they have been a mainstay of police training for decades, keeping society in a state of hyperdependence on law enforcement. Meanwhile, new generations of officers—Darren Wilson, Jason Van Dyke, Daniel Pantaleo, and so many others—have killed unarmed African American residents as if doing so were routine, without facing repercussions.

While in some neighborhoods the law protects, in places like Austin it often blinds us to the actual needs of people and the contexts of their actions. It blocks our ability to see how trauma, loss, poverty, and racism have accumulated in people's lives. When we respond to higher levels of poverty and trauma with more punitive sanctions on behavior, we are not creating public safety. We are ensuring perpetual disorder. To reverse course, we must look deeper at both the root causes of danger and the many potential solutions.

CHAPTER 5

MISSING PARENTS

IT IS A WIDELY HELD BELIEF that having two active parents is critical to a young person's development and life trajectory. When then president Barack Obama visited his own South Side Chicago neighborhood of Hyde Park in 2013 to give a speech on violence, he stated that "there's no more important ingredient for success, nothing that would be more important for us reducing violence than strong, stable families, which means we should do more to promote marriage and encourage fatherhood."[1] Obama's speech amplified a common public refrain in discussions about youth violence: the notion that the epidemic is really a crisis of parenting.

Parental responsibility, or a lack thereof, features prominently in explanations of just about any youth outcome, especially violence. But one question is rarely asked: What are the larger forces that have weakened two-parent households in high-violence areas?

The juvenile court judge for Austin says the "majority of kids that come through my courtroom are angry and hurt over the fact that fathers have not been involved in their lives." Explaining the underlying forces at play, she continues, "I was always taught that vacuums don't exist in nature. Something is going to rush in and fill up the space. You take a father out of the home away from the children, something is going to rush in and fill up the space. Gangs have rushed in and filled up the space. Drugs have rushed in and filled up the space. Despair. A belief that 'there is nothing else for me out there.'" Speaking to the anger she sees in her courtroom, Judge J says, "Mothers will come in and they have their fourteen-year-old, fifteen-year-old, sixteen-year-old sons and they share, 'He's just got this nasty attitude! He's just angry all the time!'" However, she adds, the "kid doesn't understand why he is angry all the time. He doesn't know why he is fighting at the drop of a hat all the time. And when he is not doing that, he is smoking marijuana, and when you ask him about his father, he says, 'I don't care about him. I don't think about it.' That's what is coming out of his mouth, but it is all over him, the hurt from [his father] not being involved in his life."

In 2016, Chicago mayor Rahm Emanuel delivered a nationally covered speech to address what was turning out to be the city's most violent year in nearly two decades. In a preview to stakeholders at city hall—a dry run to workshop his major themes—he leaned hard on the explanation of absentee fathers. He mentioned that in all of his visits to funeral homes and hospitals, after a shooting or death of a young person, he had seen only one father.[2] After receiving pushback from community groups, he softened his tone; instead, in his public speech Emanuel mentioned the need for mentoring and role models, setting off public debate about how much responsibility fathers bear for youth violence, in a year when homicides hit 762, a number not seen since the 1990s.[3]

Mayor Emanuel ultimately listened to the community voices that roundly rejected blaming fathers for neighborhood violence. But most public figures do not. One need not search very far to hear some variation of this theme in national conversations about urban violence. Cable television news personality Bill O'Reilly, in discussing Chicago violence in 2012, noted that out-of-wedlock births had been much lower in the black community before civil rights legislation and are much higher in the current era. Musing that "it's all black crime going on in Chicago," O'Reilly connected the violence with poor parental responsibility. He also went a step further to conclude that "things have gotten worse as society has gotten more progressive," implying that government intervention to help achieve greater equity has somehow only made people more irresponsible.[4] The viewpoint that attempting to correct historical injustices engenders violence is particularly disjointed, but parallel arguments about personal responsibility are common on both the political right and left. President Obama castigated black fathers more than once. In a 2008 Father's Day campaign speech, he said, "They have abandoned their responsibilities, acting like boys instead of men."[5]

So, had Emanuel erred by not mentioning fathers in his speech? After all, there are many people on both sides of the political spectrum who identify the home environment as a major element of youth struggles, including Judge J, who sees young people in her courtroom every day. Why might community groups challenge the notion that absent fathers are the root cause of an epidemic of violence? It is because it ignores the fact that generations of caretakers have been forcibly removed due to mass incarceration.

Punitive policies are a major driver of parental absence from the home in areas like Austin and of the subsequently large racial disparities in rates of both marriage and divorce.[6] The *New York Times* documented the issue of parental absence in urban areas in an infographic piece titled "1.5 Million Missing Black Men."[7] For every one hundred black women in the United States, there are only eighty-three black men available for partnership, family, and parenting (assuming a heteronormative parenting relationship). The other seventeen men are typically either in prison or have suffered an early death because of myriad health disparities that are disproportionately experienced by black men. This equates to roughly one out of every six black men between the ages of twenty-five and fifty-four missing from the general population. There is no similar gender-absence gap among the white population—there are ninety-nine white men for every one hundred white women in the United States. The majority of the US black population lives in an area where there is a profound absence of black men. This is a major element of the war on neighborhoods like Austin. In Chicago, men make up 43 percent of the black adult population, meaning that roughly forty-five thousand men whom we would expect to be a part of family and neighborhood life are absent.[8]

Although mass incarceration is often discussed as a male phenomenon, black women are also incarcerated at twice the rate of white women.[9] And the number of women in local jails has been growing faster in recent years than the male population.[10] For the generation of children born in 1990, about 5 percent of the black population—those now entering young adulthood—have experienced a mother's incarceration, compared to only 1 percent of whites.[11] Thus, concentrated punishment does not just affect black fathers but black parents writ large. In turn, forcibly removing parents from the home has a lasting ripple effect on youth and, ultimately, on neighborhoods that spans generations. But these consequences are rarely discussed in relation to urban violence and seldom, if ever, taken into account by lawmakers. More commonly, and perhaps because of "irresponsible parent" narratives, we personalize the problem of absence and assume it is one of moral failure, born of a lack of skills or the motivation to do right by children.

These common narratives about parental absence miss the forest for the trees. Progressive civil rights legislation did not cause a sudden explosion of poor parental responsibility, resulting in the need for a tenfold increase in the national prison population. In reality, we witnessed a shift in punitive justice system policies that locked up generations of black caregivers. National public figures continually fail to mention this point, opting instead for the simple explanation of culture and behavior.

Moreover, it turns out that the irresponsible black father is mostly a mythical figure. Black fathers work as hard as most parents, and sometimes harder, to play a role in the lives of their children.[12] Black resident fathers—those who are either married or cohabitating with a partner— have been shown to spend just as much time with their children as white fathers. In addition, black nonresident fathers spend even more time with their children than nonresident white fathers.[13] Though removed from their families and children at astonishing rates, black men appear to be putting in extra effort to stay connected as parents.

Meanwhile, much of society remains blind to the systematic removal of parents from homes and the fact that black parents work extremely hard to care for their children. More commonly, we blame those parents for not being present to provide a stabilizing force for their youth who are involved in violence. Consequently, most of the solutions that policymakers identify to support low-income black households are limited. They involve minimally funding programs aimed at teaching parenting skills to fathers—like how to reconnect with children after being absent—rather than doing everything possible to keep families together in the first place. This error has long-term consequences for families and, by extension, entire neighborhoods, perpetuating violence over generations.

Another Chicago research report, titled *Two Sides of Justice*, helps document this trend. The researchers share the story of Warren, a West Side resident whose family is experiencing third-generation incarceration: "When I got arrested, my son was going to be one year old. When he got arrested, his son was, like, two years old, so the cycle that people talk about, it really happens. It really does happen, as much as you hate to admit it. . . . My son was arrested for carjacking. He was twenty years old when that happened. He was a troubled youth. . . . He was sentenced to twenty-two years, so he copped out the minimum and got half the time. I was in prison when he caught the case, on a twenty-two-year sentence myself. When I found out he was going to do time, I was hoping he would get a continuance long enough for me to come home and see him but it didn't work out, . . . therefore I missed out seeing him in Cook County [Jail]. He's from the same neighborhood I'm from so he grew up in the same lifestyle, so to speak, [but a] different generation. My son has a son. . . . He's running around doing wild things too. . . . We're going through something. . . . My son's girl, they're not letting me see the grandson because she's with some other guy. So, we're both going through it in the sense of not seeing him."[14]

Warren's story illustrates the negative cascading effect that forced removal has on families, spanning generations. Once a parent has been removed from the family, it creates very real barriers to meaningful participation in a child's life. As a direct result, inequalities have widened for black families. And these inequalities will not automatically disappear even if the imprisonment rate returns to what it was before its explosive growth in the late 1970s.[15] It will take substantial and sustained policy attention to uproot them.

As of the year 2012, 11 percent of all black children were estimated to have a parent in prison, a prevalence that has increased in recent years while that of whites has remained low.[16] For a black child born in 1990—those currently in early adulthood—there is an approximately 25 percent chance of having had a parent incarcerated before they turned fourteen. It is only 3 percent for a white child. And the 25 percent chance for black children is roughly the same likelihood of having a parent who has completed a college degree.[17]

These statistics are more than merely academic. They have real life consequences for children. An incarcerated father is less likely to obtain a college degree, will accumulate less in lifetime earnings, and be less likely to own a home. This is important because homeownership stabilizes neighborhoods, lowers crime rates, and is a source of wealth that can be passed on to the next generation.[18] But such benefits are less likely to be transferred to the children of the incarcerated. Instead, vulnerable children are made even more vulnerable. This is how disadvantage accumulates over generations.[19]

We made our own estimations about missing parents in the nearly all-black community of Austin during the years of 2005 to 2009.[20] According to the 2010 American Community Survey, between 2005 and 2009, the community area had seventy-eight adult black men for every one hundred black women.[21] During the same period, 5,983 men and 1,123 women from Austin, whom we can assume are almost entirely black based on neighborhood demographics, were sentenced to prison. If these men and women were not sent to prison, the gender gap would disappear. Further, national surveys tell us that approximately 52 percent of prisoners have at least one child.[22] If this statistic holds true for Austin, we may assume that nearly 3,700 children in the community experienced the removal of a parent due to incarceration, just during that five-year period between 2005 and 2009.

PARENTAL ABSENCE, FAMILY STRESS, AND DISCONNECTED YOUTH

In our research, the story of West Side resident Harold captures the parenting challenges that emerge when one has been removed to spend time in prison. Since his last release, Harold has been working to rebuild a relationship with his oldest son. Having been imprisoned for much of this son's young life, Harold has a limited influence on his child. Harold's years of addiction and absence all happened during his oldest son's formative years—a pattern that is repeating itself as his grandchildren now watch the struggles of their father. Twenty-six years old at the time of our interview, Harold's oldest son has already been to prison and back, and still he "is really out there, selling drugs."

Both Harold's and Warren's stories demonstrate the legacies of incarceration. We have entered the second and even third generation of the mass-incarceration era, where the next wave of parents, brothers, sisters, and cousins are being removed from their families and from their communities. Explaining how missing parents can affect an entire neighborhood, one Austin resident said, "You know, the children of the people incarcerated in the '80s and '90s are now on the street, trying to figure out who they are, without a lot of guidance." While there has been powerful scholarship about the negative impacts of this widespread removal, many of the long-term consequences will not be fully understood for years to come.

Families and neighborhoods both provide opportunity structures for young people that are responsible for healthy child and youth development.[23] But parental absence ultimately breaks down these structures. Worse yet, it creates stress that negatively impacts development in numerous ways, some of which are tied to the violence we are currently witnessing in many neighborhoods. When looking at family structure, the forced removal of incarceration is directly related to the racial disparities in marriage rates that are constantly identified by politicians and media figures as the problem. Consequently, fatherhood looks very different for black men because of incarceration. Although being locked up doesn't limit fatherhood prospects—men who have served time still have children at similar rates than those who haven't—it does alter family prospects, as Warren and his son found out. Only 11 percent of incarcerated young black men are married, compared to 25 percent who have not been to prison.[24] Incarceration clearly decreases the likelihood of participating in a marriage.

The proliferation of black households led by single females follows the growth of the prison rate very closely. During the initial phase of the prison boom, from 1980 to 1990, the number of single-female-headed black households grew by 19 percent.[25] It is not simply that absence reduces the opportunity for marriage, though of course that is true. The differential in the marriage rate is also related to the stigma of incarceration, in terms of both economic earning potential and social status. Those with criminal records face significant barriers to employment and to providing for a family economically. Would-be partners may be hesitant to marry someone because of this, because of a fear the person could be reincarcerated or because of the perceived social stigma of partnering with someone who has been in prison.[26]

As Warren and his son experienced, romantic partners may be hesitant to allow a father back into the life of a child once he has spent time in prison. For those who have been incarcerated and do marry, there is a greater risk of divorce. And such marriages typically end sooner than those in which a partner hasn't been in prison. Beyond marriage, the 46 percent likelihood of black families separating after the birth of a child is much higher than for any other racial category.[27] These data tell a story of generations of men in high-incarceration neighborhoods who are re-moved from their children and then face barriers to playing a strong par-enting role in their lives. Our nation's prison boom ushered in the era of the missing parent, but rather than naming the culprit, popular accounts instead often place the blame on irresponsible men and "welfare queens."

Black men are more likely to be removed from the home and incar-cerated, and black women are more likely to bear the brunt of the added responsibilities, challenges, and vulnerabilities. Matthew Desmond, in his book *Evicted*, writes, "If incarceration had come to define the lives of men from impoverished black neighborhoods, eviction was shaping the lives of women. Poor black men were locked up. Poor black women were locked out."[28] In Milwaukee, a city divided and segregated much like Chicago, one in five black female renters had been evicted in the years immediately following the Great Recession, triple the rate of white women. In segregated black neighborhoods, females are twice as likely as males to face eviction.[29] This is just one of the additional strains that incarceration adds to families.

THE CYCLE OF TRAUMA

Without question, the removal of active parents has a profound impact on children. The literature on trauma has grown extensively in recent years and has pointed to significant, sustained impacts on stress levels.[30] Having a parent who is incarcerated is considered an adverse childhood experience (ACE), as are other destabilizing events such as physical, sex-ual, and emotional abuse. Taken together, ACEs are predictive of a range of outcomes later in life, from low educational attainment to poor health outcomes and early death.[31] These stressors are traumatic and they are thought to be responsible for stunting normal brain development in young people. Moreover, when the underlying stressors in the lives of trauma survivors are never alleviated, there is little opportunity for heal-ing and recovery. As the ACE research indicates, if persistent unresolved pain reaches a certain threshold in a person's life, unhealthy outlets for that pain emerge.[32]

Not everyone who survives trauma becomes an aggressor; in fact, the majority do not. But among those who experience ACEs, violent be-havior is one established response.[33] Low-income and minority youth are many times more likely to have experienced parental absence as a result of incarceration. They have also probably witnessed violence in the home or community, making it more likely that these children may be prone to develop post-traumatic stress disorder (PTSD) or experience similar symptoms.[34] Whereas poverty has been shown to create high levels of stress—impairing such important stages as early linguistic development—trauma also creates dramatically increased stress levels and has been conclusively linked to disruptions in both neuro-emotional and social-emotional development.[35] Recognizing that cognition is a finite resource, the daily challenges associated with surviving both trauma and poverty consume high levels of people's available cognitive capacity, leaving minimal space for succeeding at activities associated with upward mobility, such as learning and education.

The *Chicago Reporter* chronicled the case of a sixth-grade Austin student identified as "James," a star student who inexplicably displayed a reversal in behavior:

> [Sanya] Gool, James' social worker, says it took a couple of years for her to learn that James' behavior problems were tied to [both parents'] imprisonment [for drug charges]. She can only wonder how many other children at Howe [Elementary] are dealing with similar issues. "There are probably a lot more than we know about, but there's no way to identify those students," Gool says. "It's not like we can send out a survey."[36]

The impact of parental incarceration on James's educational performance was clear and, in his case, made even more complicated by the residential mobility he experienced as he moved around with different caretakers. With only one paid social worker, the underfunded public school he attended didn't have the resources to identify the source of his struggles in school right away. Like many students in West Side schools, the family roots of James's educational challenges trace back to parental incarceration; in his case, at least they were identified.

When these underlying traumas are not addressed, symptoms can become visible in the form of low academic achievement, sleep deprivation, depression, anger problems, nightmares, and maladaptive coping behaviors such as substance abuse.[37] Affected youth, however, may not seek mental health services and may avoid seeking treatment for fear of being perceived as weak.[38] Even if they do seek treatment, options are often limited in high-incarceration neighborhoods due to rollbacks of government provision and funding for services—Chicago closed half of its mental health clinics in 2011, almost all of which were located in South and West Side neighborhoods. In the absence of necessary supports, young people are left to deal with high levels of exposure to personal trauma and community violence on their own.

Another adverse childhood experience is exposure to domestic violence, which is harmful to children in many ways. Incarceration has a complicated and troubling relationship with domestic violence. Incarceration will at times serve as a protection for family members who are enduring domestic violence by removing an abuser from the home. However, people who have been incarcerated are also more likely to assault their partner, a fact that illustrates the toxic nature of prison environments. The rate of men who assault their partner before a pregnancy is nearly three times higher among men who have been incarcerated for any type of offense. The rate is five times higher for those who assault their partner after a child has been born into the family.[39] Rather than having a rehabilitating effect, incarceration adds stressors to households without ever addressing the underlying reasons for why men batter, or why women often stay in abusive relationships. It may actually leave women and families more vulnerable. As decarceration policies are expanded across the United States, this is an area that needs special attention. Only then can the multiple drivers of childhood and adolescent trauma begin to be uprooted, and the cycles of violence actually addressed.

BEYOND THE HOME: PARENTAL ABSENCE SPILLS INTO THE NEIGHBORHOOD

The parents missing from places like Austin are also absent from participating in the civic life of their community. Although involvement in neighborhood life may seem at first blush to be a leisure activity, the bonds that form between neighbors who know and look out for one another have actually been shown to regulate crime and disorder. Across Chicago, neighborhoods that have strong norms of trust and cohesion between residents have less violent crime.[40] These norms might not be as strong in Austin as in other neighborhoods because parents are constantly being removed or cycling back into the community after being released from prison. This has major destabilizing effects, which criminologist Todd Clear has demonstrated through decades of research that point to incarceration as a primary driver of disorder and crime.[41]

Neighbors only get to know one another when there are opportunities for interaction and expectations of sticking around for a while. But concentrated incarceration disrupts social networks and bonds among neighbors. Residents may not feel any motivation to form a strong connection with others if they believe that either they or others will only be there temporarily. These connections, between people and also between individuals and institutions in a neighborhood, are referred to as "social capital." This kind of capital affords residents access to resources that might otherwise be out of reach, giving them a psychological and social bond that allows for greater opportunity and stability.[42]

Meanwhile, concentrated incarceration keeps urban black neighborhoods segregated and disadvantaged, thereby making the uphill battle for success even steeper. Racist institutional practices like redlining gave way to predatory lending, which resulted in black neighborhoods disproportionately experiencing high foreclosures during the Great Recession.[43] Many market forces are already creating disorder and instability in urban black neighborhoods. And, as mentioned previously, women are even more vulnerable to negative housing trends. Concentrated incarceration is only adding more neighborhood disorder, creating a cumulative punishment effect that extends well beyond the justice system. This amounts to a one-two punch of neighborhood instability, with multiple forms of forced community removal that are ultimately responsible for more crime and disorder.[44]

As the cycle-of-stress model highlights, many black neighborhoods are trapped in a downward spiral of absent parents, stressed and traumatized youth, and highly mobile, unstable households that decrease opportunities for strong bonds between residents. These are the ripple effects of concentrated punishment. Youth, families, households, and whole neighborhoods are trapped in this spiral of disadvantage, which is passed on to the next generations. Trauma, broken households, a lack of social capital, and violence only widen the inequalities in outcomes such as educational attainment, employment, and wealth accumulation. This is precisely why our cities are divided into two different places: one of thriving white and ethnically mixed neighborhoods and one of disadvantaged neighborhoods of color.

Figure 6: The Cycle of Stress and Forced Removal

But instead of investing in solutions to these complex problems, we continue to employ a one-dimensional approach—trying in vain to incarcerate our way to public safety. In doing so, we've made neighborhoods worse. This has been demonstrated through careful research across numerous cities. In neighborhoods where prison cycling is high—including a steady rotation of parental absence and return—the crime rate is actually often higher as a result.[45] Conversely, if fewer people had been forcibly removed from places like Austin, we might see more families who live in one place for a longer period of time and who spend more time in the workforce, allowing them to save money for things like homeownership and enabling the expanded sense of investment that comes with it.[46] In turn, greater trust and interaction among residents who aren't forcibly removed may lead to greater social capital and opportunities for young people. This is what a virtuous cycle looks like, as opposed to the current vicious cycle in place.

BREAKING THE CYCLE OF STRESS AND FORCED REMOVAL

It is true that black fathers are more likely to be missing from the general population and thus from the lives of their children when they are incarcerated. And this is especially true in areas like Chicago's West Side. But a narrow focus on this point is lazy at best, and dishonest and stigmatizing at worst. It points out an effect without identifying its cause. Parents in Austin are not absent because of inherent cultural values, irresponsibility, or progressive social policies—far from it, in fact. The absence is due to an intentional policy shift in how we've decided to punish disadvantaged neighborhoods of color, by meting out harsh sentences and locking up their residents instead of investing in human and community development. This policy shift to concentrated punishment was anything but progressive.

Despite the fact that our justice system is often a barrier to a two-parent household, black fathers nonetheless make extra efforts to remain involved, and black mothers persevere through the additional challenges and vulnerabilities of raising children, often alone. This is a reality that many residents of Austin live with and know very well. And it is why community groups would prefer to hear a mayor, president, or national commentator talk of ending mass incarceration in order to make neighborhoods safer rather than lazily blame fathers or individual behaviors.

Such acknowledgments would be an important first step for enhancing public safety in disadvantaged places like Austin. In the long term, however, we must stop the parental vacuum created by prison sentences and deal with the lasting effects of the current vacuum.

We have created complex neighborhood challenges and, unfortunately, merely cutting back on prison sentences won't solve them. There are now additional problems to reckon with. Decades of overreliance on incarceration has created disastrous ripple effects for families and neighborhoods that call for much more comprehensive solutions. When you run up a large balance on a credit card, you eventually have to deal with the compounding effect of interest. This is the current state of high-incarceration neighborhoods. We have run up a huge balance that won't go away even if we stop making charges on the card. We have to reckon with disconnected youth who have experienced multiple traumas and with disconnected neighbors who may feel alienated from their community.

The good news is that research on neighborhood social ties points to a clear way forward. The structure of leadership connections in a community—meaning organizational leaders or stakeholders who are identified as being able to get positive things done—makes a difference in terms of positive neighborhood outcomes. In neighborhoods where civic leaders are strongly connected and aligned with one another, rather than fragmented and uncoordinated, there is less crime and better health outcomes.[47] Further, when these civic leaders are connected to other leaders outside the neighborhood, it means better outcomes for residents. This suggests that cohesion and bonding between key leaders within a community is important for everyone accessing resources both inside and outside the community. A strong network of civic leaders from diverse sectors, connected to resources beyond the immediate neighborhood, can help pull residents together and establish norms of social control and, ultimately, greater safety.[48]

So, an important aspect of breaking the vicious cycle, aside from immediately ceasing the forced removal of parents from the home, is building a strong neighborhood civic infrastructure, where organizations and stakeholders share a common vision, goals, and understanding about the root cause of problems and the most effective solutions. Such an approach, widely known as "collective impact," has the potential to align organizations and leaders in building a cohesive community and ensuring that all youth are connected to positive adult role models and mentors.[49] Indeed, many such positive efforts are happening in high-incarceration communities, but they are often fragmented, underfunded, and operating separately from other efforts.

The year 2016 was the deadliest the city of Chicago has witnessed since the late 1990s, with 762 homicides—more than those in New York City and Los Angeles combined.[50] There is indeed a crisis, and parenting figures into the equation but not in the way popular narratives often portray it. Youth violence is the product of the complex ripple effects of parental absence, family and youth stress, and a lack of social capital and strong civic leadership infrastructure.

Meanwhile, a truly connected community is a major part of the antidote to gangs and violence. Douglas, a youth outreach worker in Austin, asserts that gang involvement can provide rhythm and relationships that help young people build a basic identity in the absence of community structures. These youth desperately need new opportunities for meaningful belonging, or else violent peer groups like gangs will continue to be a dominant option.

Many of the incidents that result in a shooting start out as minor and escalate from there. Given that so many of these trends and outcomes co-occur with parental absence, a mandatory starting point for reform should include halting the flow of parents from high-incarceration neighborhoods to prison, investing in leadership development efforts that build individual and community capacity to lead positive change processes, and ensuring that all youth are connected to positive adult supports, whether it be a parent, guardian, or mentor. To date, the federal government has invested some funds in fatherhood programs for low-income and formerly incarcerated fathers, some of which have been shown to be effective at improving relationships between parents and children.[51] These programs are very welcome; however, if the investments are only in a handful of interventions without considering proper scale and context, there is a real risk of treating symptoms while not addressing root causes. Investment must go beyond just individual-level solutions.

As discussed earlier, the social environment—the trust and bonds among neighbors and civic leaders and their connections to resources outside the community—is crucial for producing better public safety outcomes. Aside from individual programs, intentional coordination between leaders and community efforts is a critical factor in building a strong community that has the capacity to work with youth who have been repeatedly exposed to trauma, parental absence, and other adverse childhood experiences. Such efforts exist but are fewer in places like Austin, and they are underfunded and perhaps misaligned with the goals of government and foundations, which encourage competition among community institutions for individually focused programs with modest outcome goals.

Austin Coming Together (ACT), a collective impact network rooted on the West Side, has sought to align the goals of key leaders and institutions in order to create the density of infrastructure that has been shown to produce safe and cohesive communities. ACT takes a holistic approach by trying to understand and intervene at multiple entry points within Austin's complex ecology of challenges and assets. Aware of the research on how incarceration produces parental absence and more challenges for youth, ACT's goal is to identify areas with the greatest disadvantages—such as Austin's million-dollar blocks—and work collaboratively with young people and families in an effort to break the cycle of violence and disadvantage. This model represents a good start in terms of intervening at a community level. However, much outside support is needed to scale up their work within the Austin community, let alone across Chicago's other high-incarceration neighborhoods.

There is no simple parenting solution that will solve challenges such as violence. Because we have removed so many parents from places like Austin, the effects have compounded across generations and made neighborhoods worse off. We have racked up too much debt in the form of generational youth trauma and fragmented neighbors. The challenges are complex and deeply rooted. Stopping the forced removal of parents from their homes is a mandatory first step in solving the problem of concentrated disadvantage, as is building the parenting capacity of the formerly incarcerated. But there is now an even greater need to invest in building strong networks, institutions, and systems that can fill the vacuum and provide positive supports and opportunities for young people.

CHAPTER 6

MISSING SYSTEMS

WHEN RAHM EMANUEL first ran for mayor of Chicago, before he identified missing fathers as the problem, he frequently talked about getting
"gangbangers off the streets." In multiple speeches and advertisements,
he advanced a notion of safety based on the removal of dangerous young
people. This was an old refrain, one that portrays Chicago's disorder as
a problem caused by youth roaming the streets.[1] But over the course of
his first mayoral term, Emanuel's biggest policy decision might have
driven young people *to* the streets. In 2013, the Chicago Board of Education closed forty-nine public elementary schools, most of which were
in neighborhoods heavily impacted by violence. The closings were a
historic divestment in both public education and neighborhoods themselves. None of the projected savings created by the closings were committed to build other types of infrastructure for children and youth in
the most impacted neighborhoods.[2]

Four of the schools closed were in the Austin neighborhood. Shortly
before these closings took place, one Austin mother said, "That mayor,
whatever his name is, he is trying to close these schools. But he should
be trying to pull everybody together. If you take that education from the
kids, that's going to make them want to pick the guns up. They are going
to be mad. Now they can't go to school, because some of the people in
the neighborhood don't have cars to go all the way out to other schools."
In recent years, violence in Austin has indeed increased, though scholars
still debate the precise cause.[3]

The schools that remain are overstressed and underfunded. In the
words of one formerly incarcerated resident, there's "a lot of stuff going

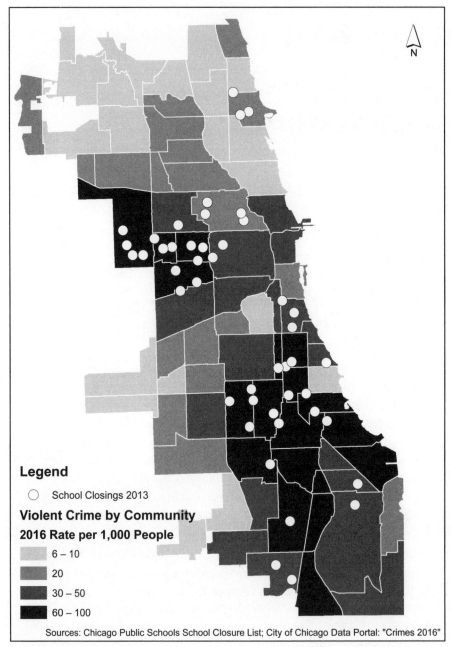

Legend

◯ School Closings 2013

Violent Crime by Community
2016 Rate per 1,000 People

☐ 6 – 10
☐ 20
☐ 30 – 50
☐ 60 – 100

Sources: Chicago Public Schools School Closure List; City of Chicago Data Portal: "Crimes 2016"

Figure 7: School Closure Map

on with these kids that better schools could help with. Classes are over-crowded, teachers underpaid, textbooks outdated. . . . That's not a nur-turing learning environment. How can somebody be productive in these circumstances? I think that education with tax dollars should be a level playing field, it actually should be distributed equally no matter where you are from; that way we would not be the haves and the have-nots."

Given the challenge of parental absence in high-incarceration neighborhoods, schools often play an especially important role in the lives of young people. They are supposed to provide a safe space where youth can escape the turbulent streets and find positive guidance from adults. But in terms of spending, schools are lower on the priority list than prisons. In just the census tracts of the forty-nine schools closed by Emanuel, one analysis found that more than $2.7 billion was com-mitted by the state to be spent on prison sentences handed out over a twelve-year period. Meanwhile, the school closings are estimated to save the entire Chicago public school system $43 million a year, or $430 million over a decade.[4]

Nationally, from 1980 to 2013, the growth in prison spending far outpaced the growth in preschool-through-high-school education. Whereas expenditures on preschool through high school increased only 107 percent during this period, prison expenditures rose at triple that rate, or 324 percent. In Illinois, this differential was actually less stark than in the large majority of states.[5] Given the incredible concentration of people being imprisoned from certain community areas, it is likely that the differential for Austin is dramatically higher. We are so caught up in investing in prisons that schools are often an afterthought.[6]

Young people become an afterthought as well. Disadvantaged stu-dents are frequently pushed out of their classrooms. They are dispro-portionately suspended and expelled, often ending up in the justice system. This is what scholars refer to as the school-to-prison pipeline.[7] Susan, the juvenile probation supervisor for Austin, says, "We have had kids that are out of regular school attendance for over a year. You know, even in the elementary level." Until probation gets involved, there is of-ten little effort to draw those children back into the school system. This same neglect can also be seen toward students with learning disabilities, whose individual educational plans frequently go unfulfilled. At times, juvenile probation is more of an advocacy force for these students than the schools themselves.

Meanwhile, the people involved in West Side gun shootings are getting younger. In the 1980s and 1990s, West Side resident Charles recalls, "the people who were dying were actually heavy in the life. The thing that has changed the most is there are no rules of engagement. When I was coming up when I was younger in the gang, you wouldn't [attack someone] if there were kids or any people out there." That code of restraint has vanished. Too many parents have disappeared. And we've failed to provide positive supports elsewhere in their absence. As a result, guns seem to have lost their safety catch.

A probation supervisor for Austin sees the trend toward younger offenders as well. Cases that she saw happening with fifteen- or sixteen-year-olds in years past now involve twelve- and thirteen-year-olds. Douglas, the West Side outreach worker who supports gang-affiliated youth in Austin, has also seen this downward shift in age. He attributes it to all the death young people see in Austin. There are too many streetside memorials, where teddy bears and bottles mark the remains of a future that will never come. Like youth outreach workers across Chicago's South and West Sides, his waiting lists are too long and he has been to too many funerals. For young people across Chicago, their place of residence has an incredible bearing on how safe they are. Of the 530 youth killed in the city between 2008 and 2011, approximately 80 percent were from low-income areas on the West and South Sides that account for just one-third of the city's overall population.[8] Thus, the majority of youth homicides are almost exclusively found in high-incarceration areas. These are the places where, since the advent of mass incarceration, homicide has become increasingly concentrated, where the public safety gains of downtown Chicago or huge swaths of the North Side are still distant dreams.

But even within areas like Austin, risk is not equally distributed. There is growing evidence that the likelihood of a young person being a victim of a shooting can be predicted based on a combination of their social networks and expulsion from school, two factors that heavily overlap with geography, poverty, and race.[9] Young black men within high-vulnerability social networks are nine hundred times more likely to be shot than the general population.[10] Not surprisingly, the youth in these high-vulnerability networks have routinely been excluded from key community institutions.

When eight-year-olds are lined up in handcuffs on the sides of their school buildings, a deadly predictive pattern begins. Many of the youth Douglas serves never complete grammar school, let alone high school. They "have never had a job or been part of team sports," he says. "These kids have never been a part of anything organized." And so, street activity becomes their path to achievement, their pretense at organized activity. "That gives these guys a sense of working together, recognizing each other as individuals, as humans." In his efforts to draw these youth away from violence, Douglas focuses heavily on providing positive reinforcement.

As Douglas's work demonstrates, schools are not the only places with the power to keep young people out of trouble. Many residents in Austin talk about the need to get back to an "it takes a village to raise a child" approach in the neighborhood. Doing so would require more safe havens, more places that can help keep youth off the streets and provide a positive influence. Talking about the dearth of such options in the neighborhood, a lifelong resident named Bobby recalls, "When I went to school, we had social centers after school. You go home and do your homework for an hour, come back to school, and you had a social center. And if you needed extra help with something the teachers would be there to help. But now there is nowhere for these kids to go." Describing how the neighborhood landscape is different than what he had growing up, Bobby says, "It is more fragmented. Fewer resources. Fewer places for the kids to go."

At the Peace Corner Youth Center, an Austin safe haven for youth, only twelve- to fifteen-years-olds are let in through the building's glass doors. But as street dynamics have shifted, the Peace Corner has had to change its rules as well. The director, Gavin, now makes exceptions to allow younger children into its programs. He recalls letting a third grader join the program because the boy was out pumping gas for money and the people at the center knew he needed a meal. "He was pumping gas for the same reason many kids try to sell drugs—they see their family struggling," says Gavin.

Having grown up in the Chicago suburbs, Gavin recalls all his fellow students having a hopeful vision for their futures. "It gets very disheartening when you ask a fourth grader their dream and their dream is to make it to fifth grade. That's if they even have a dream." Homelessness is high among the youth the Peace Corner serves. Many of the youth participants just roam the streets when they leave the center, a fact that clearly motivates the staff to be as inclusive as possible. "If I have a ten-year-old [who] comes in here under the influence of marijuana, we tell them they have to come back the next day. We don't want them to feel like they can't come back, because then we may lose them forever."

In stark contrast, rather than figure out what is troubling these young people, many police officers, news anchors, and elected officials dismiss them as "gang involved." With that label, they attempt to deny responsibility for their trauma, their hunger, and their sense of hopelessness. When these young people are murdered, their deaths somehow become warranted or excusable. The circumstances that preceded their actions are unexplored, and the impact that their death has on their younger family members is almost never taken into account. All because of the tattoos on their arms, the friends on their Facebook page, and the city blocks where they hung out.

The story is different for those who build real relationships with disconnected youth. Like Douglas and the Peace Corner director, caring neighbors, teachers, and youth workers see a much more nuanced reality. They see how gang affiliation can be almost automatic, resulting more from circumstance than from personal choice. It is a composite consequence, a product of the house you were born into, the opportunities available to your parents and siblings, and the resources within reach. Where parents are absent, so are other supports that might provide desperately needed opportunities for growth. When present, these opportunities can mean the difference between potential realized and another life lost.

Thanks to Chicago City of Learning (CCOL), a youth development network that the Emanuel administration has modestly supported, it is now possible to track which youth are accessing learning opportunities outside school and which ones are not. CCOL measures the participation of Austin's young people across available programs, within the area, beyond the area, and online. With the right investments in their community-level partners, it would be possible to ensure that all Austin youth are connected to meaningful out-of-school-time learning opportunities that connect with their interests and meet their deeper social and emotional needs in powerful ways.

Raised in a two-income household in North Austin in the 1980s, Simon benefited from many advantages that his cousins in South Austin lacked. He was surrounded by less drug activity than his cousins. His parents sent him to top schools. During that time, the park district still operated intensive athletic programs throughout the summer. This combination of a peaceful environment and investments in his development helped Simon get on a path to college and, eventually, to a successful career.

Much of Simon's family has not had the same success. By the 1980s, South Austin was already heavily affected by the drug market, and imprisonment was already a common outcome for those caught dealing. While Simon was attending college, many of his cousins were in prison. Simon still lives in Austin and sees this same pattern playing out. "There is nothing for individuals to do in Austin, outside of whatever they can get into in the street. There are no activity centers or programs for youth that are really promoted."

When Simon was growing up, his "days and nights were taken up by school activities and extracurricular activities that were related to school." Attending an elite school gave him these opportunities. Among the other young people in North Austin at the time, those kinds of around-the-clock programs were rare. "Only maybe two guys on my block went to this school." Of peers from his school, Simon estimates that 90 percent are living safe, productive lives and have never been to jail. In contrast, of the young men who went to schools that are continually underfunded, the large majority were caught up in the gangs and drug markets that migrated to North Austin. "That either led to their death or caused them to be locked up for a ridiculously extended amount of time, which is almost like death."

Positive supports are no less important for young people who have become deeply affiliated with a gang or clique. When a young person's identity becomes tightly fused with a gang, when his whole sense of self runs through the prism of a star or a crown or a set of colors, then healthy developmental relationships and opportunities are even more crucial.[11]

For gang-involved youth, one's identity and network serve as an emotional and economic survival strategy. The gang provides an immediate sense of backup within an antisocial environment. But as a consequence, the young person faces even more peril than before.

Mashawn grew up in South Austin. He remembers sneaking into an abandoned school around the age of thirteen. "We just broke into it to smoke weed and run around the school and have a little fun. We went in there and tore up the school, sprayed the fire hydrant all throughout the school, busted windows. Somebody called the police. We all ran out, and my brother and I made it safely home. But a few got caught and told on us, so they came to our crib and arrested us. That was my first case, for burglary." In Mashawn's case, adolescent misadventure led to the first of what would be many interactions with the criminal justice system. When his dad died from a medical condition, the risks Mashawn took grew more and more serious. He became what Judge J calls a "frequent flyer" in the system, a young person who keeps coming back. With each flight, he went deeper into a life of violence and further into the criminal justice system. By the time he realized that a new direction was desperately needed, there was almost nowhere for him to turn.

DETAINING FUTURES

Susan's office is deep within the Cook County Juvenile Temporary Detention Center (CCJTDC), a vast red brick building on the inner edge of Chicago's Southwest Side. Her desk is on the third floor. Not far from her station is a glass wall overlooking a first-floor courtyard. All the balconies on the higher levels have been locked up, and rumored to be locked to ensure that no employees use the space to take their own lives. Susan's team of probation officers maintains a caseload of about 150 youth at a time. As Austin schools struggle to fund supports for students with even low levels of mental health challenges, students with deeper needs frequently end up on Susan's caseload. She estimates that more than half of the youth her team supports have serious mental health issues. Though they display clear signs of bipolar disorder and schizophrenia, she says they have been "undiagnosed, unserviced, or uncared for." Estimates place the percentage of justice-involved youth with at least one mental health diagnosis between 70 and 95 percent.[12]

Working outside of the juvenile justice system, Douglas sees the same dynamics among the youth he supports through his outreach work. Post-traumatic stress is common and largely undiagnosed. A best friend shot in front of you, holding someone as he dies in your arms—"That's something these kids know." Last year alone, four of Susan's probationers were killed. So many of the youth on her caseload have lost close relatives that she has added a bereavement program to her unit, in addition to the individual counseling and fatherhood programs that already existed.

For both Susan and Douglas, success means keeping youth alive, out of the juvenile detention center, and as engaged as possible with school. The less contact young people have with the juvenile justice system, the more likely they are to reach all three of those goals. There is now a mountain of evidence that the younger a person is when he is first held in detention, the more likely he is to reoffend later.[13] When comparing detained youth with youth from a similar background who've committed comparable crimes, one study found that the decision to detain a juvenile in Chicago makes him "13 percent less likely to graduate from high school and 22 percent more likely" to be incarcerated as an adult.[14]

The juvenile detention rate in the United States is many times higher than anywhere in the world.[15] Every young person who is detained and incarcerated faces a major disadvantage, over and above the challenges faced preceding imprisonment. Within detention, young people are forced to rely on basic survival skills, a situation that often reinforces the very worst of what they have learned in their lives outside. For youth who have survived family or community violence—which is the majority of young people entering detention—healing from past experiences can become significantly harder, as they are now isolated from friends and immersed in often hostile surroundings.[16]

Spending time in detention does not rehabilitate young people. It actually does the opposite: it increases their likelihood of further contact with the criminal justice system compared to other available treatment options.[17] In Cook County, almost two out of every three young people who are detained will return to cells after their release. In 2011, the CCJTDC had 249 admissions from Austin alone, at an approximate cost of $2,833,310. These youth are often arrested many times each year, with few nonpunitive, community-based supports.[18]

Wilma, both a long-term West Side resident and an Austin community leader, is deeply concerned about how many youth are being brought into the juvenile justice system and kept there. "One thing I am interested in changing is some type of way that all crime is not so full of penalties. Like, really? Do they really have to be locked up for that? It is like once they are in the system then that is it." Through her work for a local youth development agency, Wilma sees the very worst of the juvenile justice system. "We have one young man who at age seventeen has been locked up twenty-seven times. I don't see how it's possible that a seventeen-year-old can be locked up twenty-seven times. . . . I'm sure there could have been twenty-six other interventions that could have been done other than locking him up."

Judge J sees many young people in Austin getting "arrested every six to eight weeks," often for minor offenses. Despite the low threat these youth pose to public safety, she often has nowhere to send them that will break the pattern of arrest. Probation officers will come into her courtroom to talk about how youth are "not going to school, not living in the home of their parents, testing positive for drugs," or otherwise violating their probation, she says. But she has few community-based resources with which to respond to these violations. There are few places where these youth can go to return to a stable place. The kinds of programs Douglas runs are an exception and the expanded referral services that his clients need are nowhere to be found.

This is concentrated punishment. The young people most in need of learning are the most likely to be expelled, just as those most in need of healing are frequently detained. Changing course means reimagining what happens to young people when they act out or commit offenses. From the principal's office to the police officer's handcuffs, we must recognize that intervention points for troubled youth are the moments when their futures are written.

RESTORING INDIVIDUALS, SUPPORTING EVERYONE

What if every young person's arrest led them to more supportive systems—surrounding them with tutors, mentors, and support for their families? A pilot of this approach is currently being tested in select Chicago police districts through a program called RISE, which stands for

Restoring Individuals Supporting Everyone. RISE works with youth on their second to fifth arrest and diverts them to a community-based leadership development program. Though RISE is only one step, it is a powerful example of the kinds of no-entry interventions that can be advanced moving forward. It is also a rare example of the Emanuel administration embracing a vision for public safety that invests in communities' ability to support their most vulnerable youth at the point of arrest, taking their criminal justice contact as an indicator of need rather than innate criminality. But even as RISE offers a promising model, its funding and scope pale in comparison to the public investment in youth detention, and still dozens of other intervention points are being ignored.

Judge J sees alternative schools as another golden opportunity to keep youth out of the system. They are a gathering place for students who were expelled or pushed out of their first assigned schools, a common referral point for probation-involved youth and also one of the few welcoming points of return for youth leaving the juvenile detention center. In other words, these schools are where all the youth with the greatest needs meet. But despite being such an ideal potential intervention point, alternative schools operate with even fewer resources than regular public schools and often have the highest rates of youth who are shot.[19]

Speaking about this missed opportunity, Judge J says, "[It's] like they got the worst of the worst in there, and it is not like they have the best of the best in terms of personnel and services. That's a recipe for disaster. I had a kid [in court] once, he left school every day right before lunch. They would ask him why and he says, 'The lunch they serve us is this big chunk of bologna and a piece of bread.' I said, 'Every day?' He said, 'Every day.' I turned and looked at the person who was there from the school and said, 'Is that what lunch is?' They replied, 'Yeah, pretty much.'"

Institutional neglect has a cost. From the bench, Judge J often sees no solid options for the young people that come through her courtroom. There is great awareness about the adverse effects of juvenile detention, but that awareness has failed to translate into action. "Increasingly, we are being asked not to send kids to the Department of Juvenile Justice. They are trying to come up with all of these other ways to address the problems, but they are not putting money into those [options]. So it becomes a Band-Aid."

Judge J's insights point to the limits of reform strategies that fail to build up community-based supports. Keeping youth out of the justice system should always be the top priority, but the needs of these youth for healing and support cannot be ignored. Douglas feels strongly that with more investment in the youth he serves, they would be able to get away from a life rooted in drugs and guns. "Whatever it is these kids have a passion for, whatever they have interests in, you can nourish that with an afterschool program."

The few programs that exist for these youth are constantly struggling for funding. Douglas has had to open and close his program's doors on multiple occasions, and this instability makes his efforts to build trust with vulnerable youth even more challenging. The Peace Corner also scrambles to maintain its operations. Like all the nonprofit programs in the area, it is competing for dollars from a pool that cannot meet the demand. Many of the best ideas for strengthening Austin never even get off the ground. Community leaders have done extensive planning to create a new high school, to launch an innovative manufacturing district, and to build a unified improvement strategy for all Austin schools. These initiatives could have had a transformative impact on youth in the area and also helped to build a stronger, more connected neighborhood. None of them saw the light of day.[20]

Meanwhile, who will be a victim of gun violence is now more predictable than ever. By analyzing social networks and histories of social exclusion, public officials can estimate young people's likelihood of facing death. This is a major breakthrough in predictive research. How it gets applied is literally a matter of life and death. If local leaders like Douglas are empowered with the information and given the resources to grow their outreach efforts, then high rates of youth violence could become a historical artifact, a tragedy that is remembered but not constantly relived. If linked to interventions like RISE, then peace might reign again.

There is no guarantee. Although Chicago has a reputation for violence, public officials have done far too little to alter the city's destiny. To date, only police officers have been equipped with this predictive data and the budgets needed to act on it. But they are trained to arrest rather than heal. For officers, uprooting problems means arresting people, not solving the generational reproduction of disadvantage. That may be where their focus should stay. But a broader strategy for public safety is crying out to be born, and many of the community leaders who can give this strategy life are already in place.

CHANGING DESTINY

On a corner in Northwest Austin is Ruth Channing's childcare center. A red awning wraps the north and east sides of the building. The center perfectly bridges the intersection where a commercial corridor and residential block meet, a uniform junction along Division Avenue. In the back, a large outdoor playground was built so that children had an outlet for their energy in the summer months. Walk down Waller Avenue, on the east side of the building, and you will see parked cars, trees, and fences in front of one- and two-story homes featuring brick, wood, or aluminum siding. Two lots on the block are empty, with futures still unfolding. As the seasons pass, these lots become home to fallen leaves, snow piles, blades of grass, and, eventually, wildflowers.

Ruth is a well-known leader in the Austin community. In addition to running her own early-learning center, she actively supports other early learning providers. As founder of the Austin Childcare Providers' Network, Ruth works to connect parents to high-quality, licensed providers in the area. She also helps connect those providers to ongoing professional development opportunities.

Ruth knows that birth is not neutral. Without the right supports for children, geography may be the closest thing there is to destiny. Where people grow up influences almost everything about their path—the schools that are available, the food that is accessible, the level of safety outside their home, and the challenges and opportunities that shape their parents' or caregivers' lives. People's place of birth often shapes how much adversity they will have to face and what resources they can call upon to face it. Opportunities and stress are both handed down within particular places, with major implications for life expectancy.[21]

Efforts like Ruth's should never have to struggle for the investments needed to scale up to make a broader impact in a community like Austin. But to date, criminal justice reformers have made little room for building infrastructure for children and youth. Instead, reform efforts have been dominated by a reentry focus, which accepts the initial institutional channeling of millions of Americans into prisons. Successful reentry is essential, but it is limited by an inability to prevent the future generations of people from entering prison. To do so requires investing in and strengthening the institutions that can improve the quality of life of children and youth, as well as the resources that their family members need to thrive.

Much of the foundation for this strategy already exists. Over time, the social service sector has become one of the largest employers in places like Austin. As deindustrialization intensified on the West Side, several long-standing community organizations, founded in the 1970s and 1980s, have become integral parts of the neighborhood landscape, taking on greater importance and influence. Today, these groups—which often started as church efforts, informal networks, and secular organizing groups—are the primary providers of everything from senior housing to workforce development to energy assistance to reentry supports. Key organizations of influence include the Westside Health Authority, Bethel New Life, and the South Austin Community Coalition. These larger, established organizations often serve as resource magnets for adjacent neighborhoods and have the capacity to convene other community partners. In addition to attracting resources, these groups broker relationships between insiders and outsiders, provide administrative capacity and professional expertise, and bring other community stakeholders to the table.

This is not to say that only paid professionals are leading meaningful social change efforts. Block clubs are common in Austin and often work independently of nonprofit channels, leading everything from community gardening to old-fashioned relationship building. These clubs are a way for neighbors to band together for block improvement and social cohesion, to share information and resources, and for efforts such as recycling. Yet block clubs also work in partnership with larger agencies, which typically recognize the importance of a block-by-block framework in their own initiatives. In particular, the Westside Health Authority, whose organizational mantra is "It takes a village," places a great deal of emphasis on its partnerships with block-club leaders. Other vital examples of grassroots leadership include the Austin Green Team, which leads local gardening efforts, and the Westside Historical Society, which seeks to expand residents' awareness of their local and cultural heritage. Generally speaking, the Austin neighborhood is a welcoming home to many different types of leadership, as well as to both established and emerging organizational efforts.

REBUILDING OPPORTUNITY

Even the strongest leaders struggle to move mountains, and few mountains are bigger than Austin's employment challenge. Among local nonprofit agencies such as the Westside Health Authority, two main employment approaches have emerged for helping the formerly incarcerated to regain stability: one is to help these residents connect with existing market opportunities, serving as the advocate, trainer, and coach they require to get through the door; the other is to actually create jobs. Several nonprofit organizations have sought to become the employers that these residents so desperately need by enabling residents with felony convictions to become property managers, run urban farms, and join catering companies, to name just a few examples. These groups help residents rebuild independence and, where family is involved, contribute once again to the financial stability of their household.

Neither of these strategies is able to keep up with demand. The sheer number of job seekers far outweighs the opportunities that can be created or identified. Chicago's black unemployment rate of 25 percent is in the top five of the highest rates in the nation, so even the most inspiring attempts fall exceedingly short.[22]

In the face of such demands, other local agencies have started creating their own jobs. One effort, run by the Friendship Community Development Corporation of Austin, employs the formerly incarcerated to maintain vacant, bank-owned properties in the area. Because of the size of the properties and the amount of work required, the agency has determined that maintaining thirty properties is enough to keep four individuals working thirty-five to forty hours a week, every week from April 1 to November 1. Despite a strong track record, the agency has had a hard time persuading banks to support the effort and has struggled to employ more than four people at a time. In the beginning, there were talks of Chase Bank turning over 150 of its substantial portfolio of troubled properties, but that never came to pass.

At Austin Polytechnic High School, educators work to prepare students for high-tech manufacturing jobs. While this approach has little to offer those returning from prison, it does show promise for their children. The school's flagship program has brought advanced manufacturing equipment into the classroom. A lead partner agency called Manufacturing Renaissance works with the school, raising funds, providing expertise, and brokering partnerships with regional employers looking for these advanced skill sets.

These are all laudable efforts. They are well-conceived and often well-executed interventions aimed at supporting those most in need of work. But on their own, neither social service agencies nor committed neighbors can change the jagged terrain of opportunity. Without equally bold investors, without governments, corporations, or wealthy universities sharing responsibility for job creation and placement, the mountaintop will remain out of reach and many of those seeking honest work will be caught in a perpetual search.

While government officials have been laser-focused on punishing disadvantage, other resource brokers—such as major corporations—have been missing in action. The few large corporations that have rooted in Austin, most notably the Walmart store along North Avenue, have not helped residents secure living wages. Whereas some local politicians and residents cite the entrance of Walmart as a boon to the area, others complain about the lack of quality products sold in the store and the lack of respect they receive when shopping there. Residents who used to work at this Walmart have also issued similar complaints. Meanwhile, most of Austin's established community-based organizations prefer economic development solutions that do not give undue control over neighborhood quality of life to outside actors like a multinational corporation. Though they certainly see such outsiders as possible partners, these stakeholders tend to promote ventures that might position Austin residents for a more substantive economic revival.

In the wake of forty years of struggle, Austin's grassroots organizations have taken a number of approaches to uplifting their community. Like most Chicago neighborhoods, Austin has a diverse range of stakeholders that includes churches, nonprofits, block clubs, government agencies, health providers, and small business owners. Leaders across these groups often work together to meet pressing challenges, building and maintaining vital organizational infrastructure along the way. But the large-scale investments this ecosystem needs are missing, and they are not likely to come from the philanthropic sector. If private foundations pooled all their funds, they would still not be able to match the potential of government sources. As noted elsewhere, one of the biggest areas of potential funding—where we see some consensus that funds are being wasted—is in corrections.[23] Money can and should be repurposed from the prison system into education and other neighborhood institutions and systems. However, in practice, entrenched interests make such a paradigm shift a challenge.

CHAPTER 7

FROM URBAN TO RURAL AND BACK

FROM INDIVIDUALS TO families and neighborhoods, the ripple effect of punitive policies further divides cities like Chicago. This is abundantly clear to residents and stakeholders in high-incarceration communities like Austin. So why have we not implemented any strategies to undo the damage that years of punitive policies have done to neighborhoods? Or, at the very least, why aren't we investing in better systems to support youth and families in places like Austin?

An answer to this question can be seen in competing demonstrations that took place in the Illinois capital of Springfield in 2008. One of Chicago's largest community development corporations (CDCs), Bethel New Life, was located in Austin at the time. Its work included developing affordable housing and providing employment training for formerly incarcerated individuals, among many other things. Like many CDCs, it was heavily dependent on state-government grants and contracts to carry out its services.

In early 2008, in the midst of what would later become known as the Great Recession, the West Side was awash in foreclosed homes, and the finances of the state of Illinois were in dire shape. Most state contracts require monthly billing after services have been delivered, and the state was behind on its obligations to the tune of approximately $9 billion. This translated into a seemingly random and unpredictable schedule of payments to service provider organizations. These providers often had to wait upwards of six months to be reimbursed for services already delivered as the state sifted through its backlog of bills. For nonprofit organizations without large reserves or endowments, such a delay was a real threat to keeping the doors open.

Being steeped in a tradition of community organizing, Bethel New Life chose not to sit back and hope that reimbursements would be forthcoming. Instead, it organized several buses full of West Side residents, some formerly incarcerated, to travel to Springfield and demand a meeting with the governor and the comptroller. The group was perhaps one hundred strong and staged a demonstration inside the capitol building aimed at raising awareness about the dire consequences of the state's shortcomings for West Side Chicago residents who depend on human and social services. During the action, their chants echoed throughout the rotunda of the capitol building and outside the governor's office: "*Pay your bills!* You owe the West Side of Chicago! *Pay your bills!*"

Such advocacy efforts don't typically result in an audience with the governor. For these protestors, the goal was to meet with key staffers who would listen to the demands and assist in any way they could, or to get senators and members of Congress to acknowledge the seriousness of the state's delay in paying its obligations—the resulting threats to housing and services for youth, families, and seniors. But on this day, the biggest benefit may have been that it helped empower the Bethel staff and residents who took part in the action. There was no immediate positive resolution, but West Side leaders gained experience advocating their cause to legislators. It's not every day that you gather with one hundred other people to publicly speak truth to power.

However, this particular demonstration was dwarfed by another that was much larger, much louder, and much more organized. On the front lawn of the capitol building, decked out in matching shirts and carrying banners and signs, was what could have appeared to a public official as the entire rural town of Pontiac, Illinois. The mass of people were holding a demonstration to protest the governor's proposed closure of the Pontiac Correctional Center. The governor had proposed closing the facility to reduce costs and also because many state prison facilities were no longer full. Both crime and incarceration rates had been ticking down slowly but steadily for years. But even with prison admissions falling, the forced removal of residents from high-incarceration areas like Austin was still the lifeblood of corrections-related jobs for some Pontiac residents. Where one West

Side Chicago organization had shakily found its sea legs in a public action aimed at the state, the union representing corrections employees appeared to be in full command of a navy. And its members were likely just as certain in the righteousness of their position that the state had an obligation to the people of Pontiac, an obligation to keep prisons open and full of prisoners in order to provide jobs in a town otherwise void of major employers.

The thousand demonstrators on the lawn were ultimately successful. The Pontiac Correctional Center remained open, and still does to this day. On the other hand, after barely weathering the recession years, Bethel New Life—one of the key civic institutions in Austin that helped fill the void of parental absence—ended up shifting its strategy away from providing services reliant on government funding. Its budget and scope of services are now much smaller, and it no longer has the same capacity to serve families, parents returning from prison, and youth. It is no longer in the business of developing affordable housing or providing many of the other services it had in the past. It is very tough to provide services in a neighborhood decimated by market forces and government policy and where there is little political will to invest in its improvement. The business of urban community development in a high-incarceration neighborhood quite literally doesn't pay. Or, at the very least, it is locked in a zero-sum competition with prison towns for scarce and ever-decreasing levels of state investment.

These two demonstrations represent a critical battle line drawn around perhaps the most important racial justice issue of the twenty-first century: what to do about the problem of mass incarceration. Why is there scant political will to invest state dollars into human and community development? And why are there ample resources to maintain a costly system of incarceration that both major political parties agree is not working? When viewed from thirty thousand feet, the justice system is more akin to a living ecosystem than a single organism. Much like that day at the state capitol, activists, scholars, and reformers are currently up against the same long odds for true justice reform—a reform that would repurpose public dollars spent on incarceration into rebuilding the damage caused to communities like Austin. Uncovering the barriers to deep justice system reform requires a comprehensive orientation—like an ecologist examining the entire ecosystem.

The examination must begin with place. Mass incarceration is rooted in specific places, most notably in a highly visible war on disadvantaged, urban black neighborhoods. Yet, the carceral state in the United States is part of a much larger, complex web of policies, systems, interests, and ideologies that play a role in its growth and maintenance. Peeling back the layers of the larger political economy of incarceration illustrates why there are many barriers to ending the war on black urban neighborhoods, let alone investing to improve them.

FROM CHICAGO TO PONTIAC

If you drive on I-290—the Heroin Highway—far enough away from Chicago, out to the vast western suburbs, the expressway stops, curving north before it merges with others. Along the way you can transfer to a number of other highways, roads that will take you almost anywhere in Illinois. These roads link a loose network of rural towns with their own struggling economies and complex histories. In many of these places, as in Austin, high unemployment reigns. In these towns, as manufacturing jobs were lost and family farming was displaced by a new model of agriculture, their leaders bet on prisons as a strategy for revitalization. Each prison was a dart thrown in the dark, propelled by desperate and fear-driven promises.

Today more than thirty correctional facilities dot the flat and lonely landscape of Illinois. They house nearly fifty thousand inmates, many of whom are from Austin and areas like it. The prison buildings stand near cornfields and windmills. Old barns, rarely used, can occasionally be found nearby, remnants of a time that predated the expressways.

For every high-incarceration neighborhood where people are removed en masse by the justice system, there is a counterpart, a largely rural, white community like Pontiac, similarly impacted by deindustrialization and unemployment, where prisoners are sent to serve their time. For prison towns, the high-incarceration neighborhood, and its prisoners, represents a desperate promise of employment where few other obvious options exist. Across the United States, prison construction in rural places has served as an economic development strategy, with prisoners as the commodity that provides corrections jobs as well as some related service jobs, such as hotels for visiting families and health and legal services.

As it turns out, this is largely a false promise of economic development.[1] The actual boost to employment is minimal, though in some places that minimal boost may be the only existing economic stimulus. Nonetheless, the fates of poor urban neighborhoods of color and rural towns are perversely linked in the political economy of mass incarceration. Residents of rural towns have a vested interest in seeing the status quo maintained or, worse yet, even more punitive policies put in place to ensure that prisons are kept full and operational. But it is not simply a matter of rural residents wishing incarceration upon a poor urban black population. These two types of communities have been pitted against each other because of larger political and economic forces that invariably include privatization and profit motives, shifts in the role of government in contributing to job growth, and rising concentrations of wealth inequality across the US. The parasitic relationship between high-incarceration neighborhoods and prison towns provides a strong starting point for understanding the complex, entrenched nature of the US justice system.

The population of Pontiac is just shy of twelve thousand residents, more than 85 percent of whom are white and approximately 10 percent of whom are black. The majority of the prison population, however, is black—nearly 60 percent of the 2,018 inmates, which accounts for most of the town's black population. Meanwhile, the maximum-security Pontiac Correctional Center, in operation since 1891, employs approximately 750 people.[2] For the mostly white corrections employees, inmates from places such as Austin are a guarantee that the facility provides stable employment in an area whose economy is largely stagnant. Like Austin, Pontiac has lost population since the Great Recession.

Both places have been left behind by the market and both are in need of greater government investments. But the current misinvestment in Austin—as indicated by the "million dollar blocks"—is in removing residents, under the faulty pretense of rural economic development. This has been the status quo for decades, since the prison boom began in the late 1970s. Many now take it as a given that the government must continue doing this. Breaking the status quo and reforming our justice system would mean fewer prisoners and by extension fewer corrections jobs. Chicago, already a divided city, is also part of the divided state of Illinois, where there is often "downstate" resentment of Chicago for its outsized influence on the rest of the state's politics. In a small town of mostly white residents, it is likely that many of the people of color who visit are from larger cities like Chicago and are there either to be locked up or to visit someone who is locked up. Perceptions of racial division, and urban-rural division, are necessarily tied up in this parasitic relationship.

Why would a Pontiac resident want to see increased investment in human and community development in black communities like Austin, and fewer prison sentences? Likewise, why would Austin residents want to see Pontiac Correctional Center employees maintain their jobs housing inmates?

West Side resident Alvin spent time in Pontiac. He says, "My first experience with the system was 1974. I got convicted to a three-to-nine, did seven-and-a-half years in Pontiac, . . . and that's when I really found out about racism. I learned that you're not going to win with the system. The justice system is not for the Austin area, the West Garfield area, the Englewood area, anywhere that there's poor neighborhoods. It's supposed to be rehabilitation. It's not. They stop people from getting educational degrees. They don't want people to come home with degrees. Because now they say you're too smart. We don't need them type of people, we need you to keep coming back [to prison]. You know, we're going to keep putting narcotics in your neighborhood. You can catch every little kid out here with these little plastic bags or whatever they got. But you can't catch the people that's bringing it in? Come on, there's something wrong with this picture."[3]

Alvin's story illustrates just how deep the perception is that the system is set up to make people fail. After all, his failure means jobs for another town's starving workforce. It is understandable why he might feel that prisoners like him are viewed as an employment commodity rather than a person to be invested in. And this undoubtedly complicates racial dynamics between the two struggling places of Austin and Pontiac. We have set up a zero-sum competition where jobs and livelihoods are on the line. It is true that the case for keeping prisons open and running has little to do with crime trends or with questioning the logic and efficacy of harsh punishment. It typically has everything to do with jobs and, specifically, with the government doing great harm to places like Pontiac by not continuing to provide prison jobs. In an era in which government spending is contested in just about every area, prisons are often exempt from tough scrutiny and the budget ax.

And yet prison-dependent communities like Pontiac continue to struggle. In 2008, at the time of the competing protests, the 5.8 percent unemployment rate in Livingston County, where the Pontiac correctional facility is located, was at its highest in the previous two decades. For the first time in as many years it was nearly on par with that of Chicago's Cook County. Both places were already feeling the effects of the Great Recession.

For a small town feeling the pressure of an economic downturn, the loss of a large employer can be a major blow to the economy. The demonstration on the steps of the Illinois capitol building in 2008 was not the only organizing effort undertaken by residents of Pontiac and corrections employees. Later in the summer of that same year, the town organized a "Save Pontiac Prison" parade, attended by the mayor, local lawmakers, corrections employees, and residents. The estimated four hundred residents, nearly all white, listened to speeches and posed for photographs on the Pontiac courthouse steps.[4] They marched past homes where residents waved and showed their support with signs and banners. A website called Save Pontiac Prison was created to advocate for keeping the prison open.

Later, when the state's Commission on Government Forecasting and Accountability made the advisory recommendation to reject the

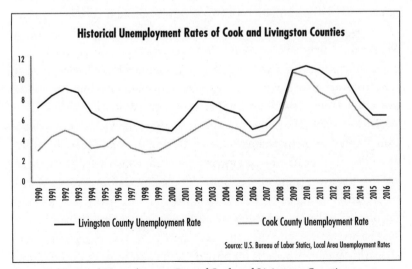

Figure 8: Historical Unemployment Rate of Cook and Livingston Counties

proposed prison closure, the town homed in on the report's quantifying of the projected economic impact—between $7 million and $17 million in economic output would be lost annually to save an estimated $3.6 million.[5] Local lawmakers made this their central argument for keeping the prison open. Since the prison infrastructure was already in place, it made economic sense to keep it running. For people whose jobs are on the line, it was simply common sense: why should we ever close prisons down? Missing from this argument was anything about crime and sentencing trends, whether prisons are effective, and whether there are even more cost-effective ways of handling public safety challenges. Ultimately, the economic argument carried the day. The governor and other public officials were unwilling to face the blowback that would result from cutting so many jobs, no matter how unjust their foundations or how obsolete their future.

Bethel New Life and Austin residents were also making a case for government investment in employment: human- and community-development jobs with the potential to keep people out of prison or to help them successfully reenter their communities after serving prison sentences. Both groups are impacted by how the state decides to allocate its resources to support local economies that have been left behind. Why is it that Pontiac has been successful in its narrative about government investment and not Austin, especially given prisons' dubious track record of successfully rehabilitating prisoners? This question cuts to the heart of the biggest division in our politics today: the role of public spending. Many rural towns have been left behind and, much like coal companies in an era of cheap natural gas and emerging alternative energy technology, look to government support to keep unemployment rates low. Prisons are portrayed as a necessary government economic stimulus.

This was not always the case. Prior to 1980, the majority of prisons were located in metropolitan regions. During the subsequent incarceration boom, over half of all new prisons were constructed in rural areas.[6] In order to secure new prisons, rural communities competed with neighboring localities by providing economic incentives such as land, tax breaks, and other subsidies, all at the expense of local taxpayers.

The promised economic benefits of these rural prisons have been elusive. Although new prisons do provide some new jobs, studies find that the larger economic benefits are often negligible for the counties that sell the farm to build the prison. For instance, there appear to be no discernible differences in the employment rate of counties that host prisons versus those that do not. And prisons do not spur any new economic growth in their surrounding communities, making these communities totally dependent on this one industry.[7] There is some evidence that new prisons have a positive impact on the per capita income of very poor rural communities, but the quandary is that these gains are contingent upon the prisons being full.[8] For towns betting everything on prisons as their economic growth engine, reductions in crime and subsequent prison sentences in urban neighborhoods like Austin present a threat to any economic gains that rural communities have witnessed. Again, this leaves these communities totally dependent on what is beginning to be accepted by people across ideologies as a misguided approach: incarceration.

THE ENTRENCHED PRISON SYSTEM AND THE BROADER US POLITICAL ECONOMY

The justice system has grown so large over the last forty years that it now affects innumerable aspects of politics, the economy, and the everyday lives of a broad spectrum of people. If we are ever going to embrace bold policy solutions to dismantling the prison system, especially ones that undo its years of damage, we must understand how deep its roots reach within the broader political economy. Rural communities and the public-sector unions that represent local corrections employees have an economic incentive to keep their prisons full. Since those prisoners disproportionately come from low-income African American urban communities like Chicago's Austin area—black people account for 58 percent of the total prison population but just 15 percent of the Illinois state population—deep justice-system reform means having to answer to these vested interests that stand to lose from it.[9]

Ultimately, public-sector unions representing corrections employees are just one force to contend with. Other deeply entrenched stakeholders also have an interest in preventing any truly deep justice system reform. Outside Illinois, many states have privately run prisons without unionized labor forces. The ecosystem of political and economic forces that sustain the carceral state and prevent it from being dismantled have not remained constant over the entire period of prison population growth. Rather, they are varied, ever shifting, and adaptive.

The explosive growth and reach of the justice system began with a political impetus and evolved to include economic and corporate interests as well. One thing that has constantly remained central, as pointed out elsewhere, is the punishment of disadvantage, whether the driving factor was political jockeying or public demand. The rise of the high-incarceration neighborhood coincided with a shift in urban policy away from fighting poverty and instead toward punishing disadvantage associated with segregation and the loss of industrial jobs. Whereas urban policy at the beginning of the 1970s saw crime and disorder as the result of disadvantage and poverty (for example, President Johnson's War on Poverty), this view began to reverse later in the decade and then to harden into an entrenched ideology in the 1980s.

Urban policy started to reflect the premise that crime and disorder were the drivers of disadvantage rather than the other way around. This marked a shift toward law enforcement solutions and away from social programs aimed at alleviating poverty.[10] What has followed are decades of policies rolling back the welfare state at the expense of people of color in disadvantaged urban neighborhoods and the slimming down of government services with the exception of law enforcement and justice systems, again at the expense of disadvantaged neighborhoods. Illinois expenditures on prison and social welfare were equal as recently as 1997, but by 2008, the state was pouring nine dollars into prisons for every dollar invested in social welfare.[11] The rollback of public and affordable housing, income supports, and job training, among others, has disproportionately impacted places like Austin. This has created a negative feedback loop in which disadvantaged neighborhoods continue to decline due to a lack of private investment and public support and then become further disadvantaged by punitive justice policy approaches.

The 1980s saw the fastest growth in the US prison population of any single decade.[12] It is common to associate the rise of mass incarceration with Reagan-era neoliberal policies that sought to shrink the role of government in providing services, with the exception of law enforcement and corrections, whose budgets were greatly expanded by the war on drugs.[13] But an important precursor to this was the aforementioned shift toward policing and punishing urban disadvantage, which was ultimately how the roots of the entrenched prison system took hold. For example, in the 1970s, the Nixon and then Carter administrations concentrated surveillance and law enforcement efforts in urban areas. Neighborhoods with large concentrations of public housing were a major surveillance target under the Carter administration.[14] Public housing is almost exclusively located in segregated, disadvantaged places, much like the high-incarceration neighborhoods in West and South Side Chicago.[15] It was no coincidence that in the 1970s the prison population began to grow in tandem with this shift in approach.[16]

The war on drugs in the 1980s took the targeting of urban areas to a new level, as has been noted by Michelle Alexander and others.[17] However, the war on drugs wasn't simply a shift in our approach to punishment; it was a shift in the ways Americans think about disadvantaged places. The shift in how presidential administrations in the 1970s viewed urban crime and disorder—that is, beginning to see it as the driver of disadvantage in urban neighborhoods—was a significant first step in deeply embedding a narrative of fear of urban black neighborhoods. This opened the door to more punitive approaches to addressing disadvantage.[18] Alexander notes that at the outset of Reagan's ramping up of the war on drugs, only a very small percentage of the American public viewed drugs as an important issue facing the country. By 1989, after years of the administration promoting the dangers of urban crime and drug dealers—accompanied by increasing federal funding for law enforcement agencies while cutting others such as the National Institutes of Health—nearly two-thirds of the country saw drugs as the most significant issue.[19] In other words, the policies themselves were likely key in shaping public perceptions about drugs and urban neighborhoods of color, rather than the trends on the ground. And now, the notion that urban neighborhoods are dangerous and need to be heavily policed is deeply ingrained in the public consciousness.

Geographer Ruthie Gilmore notes that in California, a state that witnessed one of the most rapid increases in prison construction, crime rates were actually declining when this prison growth took off in the 1980s.[20] Increased investment in law enforcement and prison construction when crime was not on the rise and the public was not concerned about drugs points to other potential motivations. Prisons served as a perverse distraction from the economic havoc that deeply affected urban neighborhoods of color during this era.[21]

The high unemployment rates that came along with jobs moving overseas in the 1970s and 1980s also impacted rural towns. This translated to a hunger for any economic development strategy and less resistance to prison construction than might be typical of urban areas.[22] The same scenario played out in rural areas across the United States without generating the promised economic development benefits beyond the prisons themselves. Instead, it has made this segment of public-sector employees odd bedfellows with private companies (which are decidedly unfriendly to organized labor) that run prisons or contract with prisons to deliver services. Both of these groups wield power—in the form of organized employees or organized money—to lobby against any reforms that would meaningfully reduce prison populations. Without this organized power, the town of Pontiac would not have been successful in getting its message across and halting the closure of its prison.

The economic imperative that helps maintain the justice system status quo has evolved over time in ways that have made the carceral state highly resistant to deep reform. At the same time that unions representing corrections employees push back against efforts to shut down prisons, private corrections companies lobby to buy state-run facilities from cash-strapped governments with the guarantee that they will be kept full of prisoners, forcing states to maintain strict sentencing laws even when the crime rate decreases, as it largely continues to do across the US overall.[23] More and more, private companies are also getting into the business of providing reentry services for prisoners who are released back into the community, something once largely the domain of nonprofit service organizations.[24]

Many interconnected policies and stakeholders have led to the entrenched punitive approaches to public safety. It is vital to recognize that law enforcement solutions were not always widely seen as the sole path for addressing crime and disorder. This narrative did not evolve from a spontaneous sea change in US cultural values; it resulted from the concerted efforts of myriad invested stakeholders. And it is these same stakeholders that present the biggest barriers to dismantling the justice system and investing in human and community development approaches to rebuilding high-incarceration neighborhoods. These groups, with strong economic interests, have the power to influence public discourse and political actors to continue punishing disadvantage and maintaining the pipeline of Austin residents to prisons such as the Pontiac Correctional Center.

ILLINOIS: GROUND ZERO IN THE BATTLE TO INVEST IN HUMAN AND COMMUNITY DEVELOPMENT

Disinvestment in urban neighborhoods of color, along with justice policies that punish the resulting forms of disadvantage, have left high-incarceration neighborhoods stuck in a downward spiral—a spiral that many justice system stakeholders depend on. In 2008, as the Great Recession began unfolding, social service agencies struggled to keep their doors open when the state could not pay its bills due to the economic downturn. Many folded or shifted their strategy, much like Bethel New Life. Meanwhile, rural prison employees were successful in keeping correctional facilities open despite consistently falling crime rates, illustrating the power of justice system actors to resist reforms or threats of prison depopulation.

Illinois' recent and unprecedented budget impasse, an ideological fight resulting in no budget passed in fiscal years 2015 to 2017, led to many consequences that have rippled across state agencies, nonprofit agencies, higher education institutions, and businesses in ways that impact nearly every sector. No other state has gone such a length of time without an official budget. The most disadvantaged populations, including the elderly, racial and ethnic minorities, children, and those with mental and physical health needs, have all paid a steep price. But the erosion of the social safety net has had the greatest consequences in areas that were already characterized by high disadvantage and high levels of inequality.

The political battle waged in Illinois provides a clear example of how the aforementioned political and economic forces converge to create roadblocks to deep justice system reform. The state's Republican governor, Bruce Rauner, took office on the promise to massively cut and privatize human and social services in the name of making the state more competitive to business—a brash embodiment of the same neoliberal ideology that has helped create and maintain high-incarceration neighborhoods throughout the entire period of US prison population growth. It is the idea that any government investment, other than in law enforcement and punishment, will crowd out private-sector investment and job creation. Governor Rauner's entire platform was based on drastically shrinking government investment and cutting taxes for individuals and corporations, which will hypothetically attract businesses. Notably, these principles have been fiercely contested and there is scant evidence that this approach will produce the promised savings and economic growth.[25]

Regardless of the deep political divisions between Illinois Republicans and Democrats, there is some bipartisan agreement on justice system reform, precisely because of how costly it is to lock up so many people. Although there have been some bipartisan discussions on reducing the prison population in Illinois, little if any have included strategies for improving high-incarceration neighborhoods. Rauner followed through on his promise to refuse the passage of any budget that did not include a wish list of reforms such as greater privatization, weakening of public-sector unions, and large spending cuts to all areas, including health, human, and social services so desperately needed in neighborhoods such as Austin. What resulted was a full two years without a state budget, the longest of any state since at least the Great Depression. This resulted in a self-imposed austerity that has only made disadvantaged places—both urban and rural—worse.[26]

At the core of this fight is a question about the role of government in improving the lives of people and neighborhoods, with one side seeing state investment as crucial and the other seeking drastic cuts that make way for the private sector and a profit motive. Yet, as has been demonstrated, the private sector has not served urban neighborhoods of color well, instead contributing to their demise through deindustrialization, predatory lending, and later, reckless subprime lending that led to foreclosed homes and lost wealth.[27]

Figure 9 shows areas across the state that have been most affected by health and human services spending that was cut as a result of the stalemate. The biggest budget cuts are in counties that have higher levels of income inequality, where income is concentrated among high-income earners as opposed to the majority of low-wage earners. These state investments equate to better health services, job training, and education, to name just a few areas. Without them, neighborhoods like Austin and towns like Pontiac are both left even worse off.

This ideological fight is ultimately a massive barrier to justice system reform in that it has decimated the state's proven cost-effective alternatives

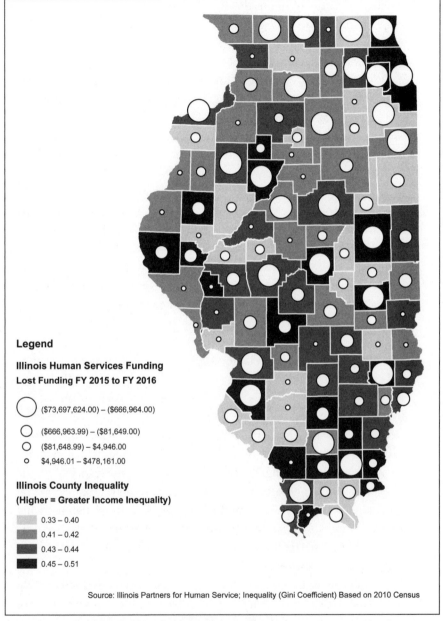

Legend

Illinois Human Services Funding
Lost Funding FY 2015 to FY 2016

○ ($73,697,624.00) – ($666,964.00)

○ ($666,963.99) – ($81,649.00)

○ ($81,648.99) – $4,946.00

○ $4,946.01 – $478,161.00

Illinois County Inequality
(Higher = Greater Income Inequality)

▢ 0.33 – 0.40

▢ 0.41 – 0.42

▢ 0.43 – 0.44

▢ 0.45 – 0.51

Source: Illinois Partners for Human Service; Inequality (Gini Coefficient) Based on 2010 Census

Figure 9: State Map of Budget Cuts and County Inequality

to incarceration—programs that build offender skills and capacity while keeping individuals out of prison. One such positive reform—Adult Redeploy Illinois (ARI)—provides state grants to local jurisdictions to implement less expensive and more effective community-based alternatives such as substance abuse and mental health treatment, cognitive behavioral therapy, and education and employment training provided by a network of local providers. State investment in these local service providers results in lower incarceration rates and less money committed to the prison system.[28]

Unfortunately, the delayed or nonexistent payments to the program's local sites have meant that service levels dropped sharply during the two fiscal years in which the state had no approved budget. Without any state funds, counties and judicial circuits had to search for temporary "bridge" funding. What's more, the uncertainty about receiving payments for services resulted in many providers cutting staff or dropping out of the program entirely. Ultimately, the program was unable to meet its goal of reducing prison sentences and state spending on incarceration during the first full year of the budget impasse, where data are available.[29] Ironically, or perhaps predictably, the ideology of reducing government spending on human and social services has only resulted in more spending on incarceration.[30]

The misguided rationale for keeping prisons open is deeply entrenched and pervasive. In the fight to keep the Pontiac Correctional Center operating, little if any of the public debate noted the steep human and neighborhood costs of incarceration to places like Austin. Rural jobs trumped human suffering. But this is a profoundly false choice. With the right intervention, high-poverty communities in both urban and rural areas can find stability. From producing renewable energy and restoring organic farming to building new infrastructure for the twenty-first century, both types of communities can experience an economic resurgence with the right investments.

But, like a lie that necessitates a web of subsequent lies to cover up the original, brighter economic horizons are being obscured by the false premise that crime and disorder are the main causes of urban disadvantage. Other lies have spawned and become entrenched: that prison jobs are more important than human lives and thriving neighborhoods; that alternatives to punishment are weak and risky; that black neighborhoods are filled with more bad potential than good; that status quo policing needs to be protected and not questioned; and that disadvantaged urban neighborhoods and rural prison towns are locked in a zero-sum game with no possible alternative economic development strategy but prisons.

We cannot shift an entire ecosystem by pushing for piecemeal reforms. Just as one Austin organization demanding its check from the government did not result in greater community investment in high-incarceration neighborhoods, piecemeal approaches always run the risk of leaving failing patterns intact. The only way to move beyond the massive web of false assumptions, beliefs, and untruths is to build an alternative belief system that makes connections between education, community development, and public safety and continues to create a movement around the whole rather than the parts. If such a movement is to succeed, it requires dreaming big and not settling for small.[31]

CHAPTER 8

LIMITS TO REFORM

OUR RESPONSE TO CRIME must be put on trial: the ways we invest tax dollars, the opportunities we have not created for youth, the harm we do to families, the jobs programs that lack the funding they need to make a difference in people's lives. Our policies must be held liable, as must the institutions charged with implementing them. If convicted, we may find that the guilt of public officials is greater than that of any individual offender, for it is through society's failed responses that so many other harms continue.

From 2015 through 2017, amid Illinois's budget impasse, violence escalated in the very Chicago neighborhoods that have been crippled by reduced funding for basic human needs. It is no coincidence that the places affected most by reduced funding for education, health, social services, and workforce development are areas with the highest concentrations of people of color, disadvantage, and violent crime (figure 10). As this correlation implies, austerity measures are likely to increase inequality and disadvantage, and erode public safety.[1]

In the Illinois capital, many elected officials are open to criminal justice reform. They recognize that the current system has deep flaws. But for some, the openness to change is highly conditional. It is tempered by a larger push to dismantle the public sector's role in improving people's lives. Not only do these officials want to reduce the scale of the criminal justice system, they would like to broadly slash public investments, including systems as central as public schools. Their arguments are often supported by a rosy optimism about the private sector's ability to provide

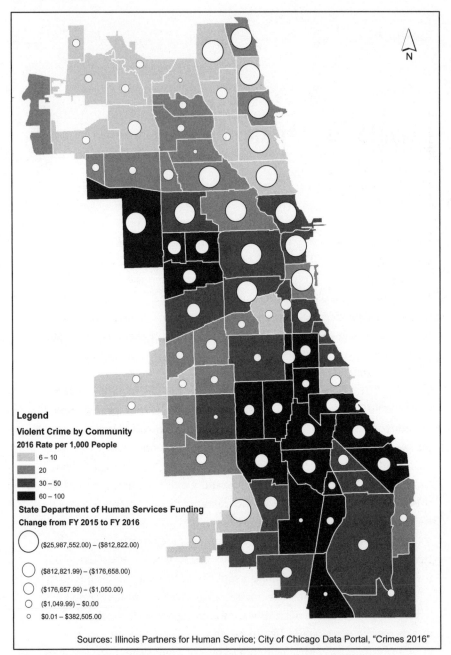

Figure 10: *Map of Human Service Cuts and Neighborhood Violence in Chicago*

for all people, to efficiently meet needs and tackle problems. Meanwhile, deeper public investments in places like Austin are off the table.

This is the neoliberal policy approach known as government austerity. It is by no means limited to Illinois. Austerity thinking has taken many different forms in institutions around the world but always features cuts in public expenditures, regardless of the impacts on everyday people. What makes this thinking attractive? Why do some government leaders believe that government itself has little role to play in improving people's lives?

We explore answers to these questions throughout this chapter, showing how austerity thinking prevents the deep criminal justice reforms that are so desperately needed. To uproot concentrated punishment, new platforms for reducing violence are needed. Those platforms require major investments in areas like Austin, investments that cannot be controlled by prosecutors or probation officials. Rather, the new public-safety paradigm should directly engage neighborhood residents, support victims, uplift the surrounding community, and challenge offenders to grow beyond established patterns of behavior. Achieving this will require that policymakers go beyond their own established behavior patterns, moving well beyond the current comfort zone of bipartisan politics.

INEQUITY AND INACTION

Today, trust in government is at an all-time low.[2] Consequently, the very idea of government is unappealing to many voters. Under this reality, austerity policies have gained widespread support, even when they are against the best interest of the people supporting them.[3] The reasons for distrust of government range from corruption to the belief that government does not represent the interests of ordinary people, a range that is fully represented in Illinois. When Austin residents live in fear of police officers' abuse of power, they share these concerns, albeit in a more immediate way than most.

But the diagnosis rarely matches the prescription. Rather than systematically improve the transparency and efficiency of government, most attempted fixes attack the foundations of human development and well-being. Illinois prisons continue to swell, but Chicago public schools have been closed across communities. Accountability for police-involved shootings remains elusive, but teachers are demonized and held to impossible standards. Hard-earned pensions are under threat, but massive tax breaks are given to already massively profitable companies.[4] All the while, campaign finance remains broken. Wealthy individuals and institutions have outsized influence on elections. Even basic steps like online voter registration can face fierce resistance.[5] Consequently, inequality continues to grow.

Inequality itself is one of the main drivers of distrust of government.[6] Historically, when income inequality increases, people lose faith in government more so than other institutions. But, when digging deeper, today's distrust of government is also linked to a distrust of corporate and other special influences. Nearly 75 percent of the US general public believes the federal government is run by big special interests, as opposed to 19 percent who believe it is run for the benefit of all people.[7] Paradoxically, while people are concerned about the role of corporate influence in government decisions, it is the public sector that takes the reputation hit. The private sector is still presented as the optimal societal force.[8]

What's more, over the course of modern history, economic crises similar to the Great Recession have been followed by increases in right-wing extremism.[9] Nationally, these links may help to explain the election of an antigovernment billionaire president whose core message claimed to be protecting the little guy. They also shed light on Illinois governor Bruce Rauner, another extremely wealthy individual who blocked a state budget from being adopted for two years straight in the name of austerity while promoting tax breaks to other billionaires and, at the same time, pandering to prison unions in an effort to win downstate votes.

Since 1980 in the United States, the share of annual income going to the top 1 percent of households has more than doubled and continues to increase, due in large part to the returns wealthy households receive from lightly taxed investments. Those dollars might otherwise have supported job creation or other economic outputs.[10] Similar gains have been seen across the top 20 percent of households, which has seen a $4 trillion–plus increase in pretax income since 1979.[11] Those raised within these wealthy families start off with undeniable advantages. Consequently, children who grow up in top 20 percent households are very likely to stay in that bracket throughout their lives or drop down only slightly.[12] In contrast, the bottom 80 percent of US households have seen their incomes remain flat or even decline.[13] Since these incomes did not keep pace with the rate of economic growth since 1980, they lost out on an estimated $750 billion in additional income that instead went to the very top income-earning households.[14] And it is black households that have missed out the most on income and wealth building. Since 1980, the average wealth of white households has grown by 84 percent, which is three times more than the growth rate of black households. If black wealth continues to grow at the same rate as it did during the previous three decades, it would take 228 years to accumulate as much as white families have today.[15] All of these underlying dynamics impose substantial limits to building a more just public-safety system. Chiefly, to rebuild areas like Austin it will be vital to move beyond austerity thinking. Not every public dollar spent will be effective. Inevitably, some programs, efforts, and organizations do not succeed. But those occurrences cannot be used as an excuse to disinvest in our most disadvantaged urban areas. After all, massive tax breaks to corporations don't always succeed in providing the promised jobs to citizens. Sometimes those corporations fail or move to another city. Yet we have not questioned the logic of continuing to incentivize businesses. To hold investment in human and community development to a different standard would only ensure that inequality becomes further entrenched across Illinois and beyond, and would weaken the tools available for helping society climb out of that hole.

SURFACE-LEVEL REFORM

In the summer of 2015, Barack Obama became the first sitting US president to visit a prison when he toured the El Reno Federal Correctional Institute in Oklahoma. In a speech to the NAACP, he made the case that our country's criminal justice system isn't smart, isn't keeping us safe, and isn't fair.[16] He called for reduced sentences for nonviolent drug offenses, greater focus on job training for successful prisoner reentry, and early childhood education and other efforts to prevent crime.

A similar focus defined Obama's administration.[17] His most well-known attorney general, Eric Holder, amplified criticisms of disparities in sentencing for crack versus powder cocaine. In so doing, Holder joined a long line of war-on-drugs detractors, noting how this disparity (whereby users of crack cocaine receive longer sentences than those using the powdered form) has served as a primary mechanism in sentencing African Americans to longer prison sentences.[18] With the support of advocates like Holder, the Fair Sentencing Act was passed in 2010, reducing this disparity from 100:1 to 18:1 but nonetheless leaving a major disparity in place. A key part of Holder's public messaging was the notion that this act would reduce sentences for low-level and nonviolent drug offenders.[19] While advocating for the reduction in disparate cocaine sentences, Holder recommended that violent and gun offenders be excluded. At the state level, there are abundant examples of lawmakers embracing the low-hanging fruit of sentencing reform for drug and nonviolent offenses while ignoring or increasing penalties for others. The state of Illinois recently released recommendations for reducing the prison population by 25 percent that ultimately ignored violent and property offenses.[20]

Other drug reform efforts have echoed this dichotomy between acceptable reforms for nonviolent, nontrafficking offenses and unacceptable violent and trafficking offenses. Several states have passed drug sentence reforms while leaving stiff penalties for other offenses in place or, in some cases, even increasing them. For example, in 2010 South Carolina implemented new reforms that reduced sentencing disparities for crack cocaine and increased the use of diversion for some drug offenses. At the same time, the state reclassified new offenses as violent and expanded the list of offenses eligible for life without parole. A more punitive stance was also enacted for repeat offenders.

Similar scenarios have played out across the country. In 2012, Massachusetts passed legislation that reduced some drug-related offenses while also enacting new three-strikes penalties for other offenses. A common theme seems to be the desire to appear balanced in the approach to prison reform while maintaining a perception of being "tough on crime." Even California's recent Proposition 47, hailed as a uniquely promising statewide reform due to its reinvestment of funds into drug treatment and other forms of prevention, largely targeted low-level drug and property offenses for reduced sentences.

Meanwhile, a recent substance abuse trend has emerged in the United States: an opiate epidemic with a white face. The life experiences of people like Michael, the suburban heroin addict, have grown much more common. Recent bipartisan unity on reducing drug sentences coincides with the rising number of white people abusing drugs and getting sent to prison for it. Since 1990, the fastest-growing prison population has been white people over the age of forty, with a growth rate of over 350 percent.[21] In 1990, approximately three thousand white Americans over forty died from a drug overdose; by 2013, that number had increased by over 600 percent to twenty-two thousand.[22] Substance abuse and resulting prison sentences are likely affecting more white families than ever before. To be clear, the rates of incarcerated black and brown people remain well above those of the white population; however, there is now a greater chance that white people are personally affected by drug-related incarceration. These trends have caused some to speculate that bipartisan interest in criminal justice reform has grown in recent years due to the increased impact on white people.[23] But those living in a high-incarceration neighborhood like Austin, where heroin sales are inextricably linked with disadvantage and lack of opportunity, experience no such sympathetic policy push. The war on neighborhoods rages on.

Reducing "recidivism" has been another issue at the leading edge of criminal justice reform. The Second Chance Act, which funds state and local governments to reduce recidivism through improved programming, was passed in 2008 with bipartisan support. It continues to be refunded amid fights over nearly every other federal line item. In no small part, this broad support exists because the need to support people returning from prison is so dramatic. But recidivism rates in most states remain alarmingly high. For example, in Illinois approximately 50 percent of those released from prison will return within three years.[24] A quick interpretation of this is that prisons don't rehabilitate offenders— or, worse yet, that incarceration may actually lead to more criminal behavior. A more nuanced examination reveals major questions and issues with the concept of recidivism and the resources dedicated to it.

Recidivism is almost exclusively viewed as a function of individual behaviors, attitudes, and choices. Efforts to reduce it typically focus on predicting the risk level of the individual—based on factors such as offense history, antisocial attitudes, association with criminal peers, and substance abuse history—and tailoring programming to meet those risks and needs.[25] Many corrections departments and other branches of the justice system use risk-assessment tools that have been validated by research studies in order to make probation and programming decisions. Courts, juvenile detention centers, and police departments also use risk assessments to make decisions about whether to divert or to incarcerate individuals. More and more, "evidence-based decision making" is becoming a mandatory condition for reentry funding and is considered the best practice in working to reduce recidivism.

There are several problems with current approaches to reducing recidivism. First and foremost, recidivism does not necessarily have a universal definition. In some cases it could mean re-arrest and in others reconviction. The length of time over which recidivism is considered also varies, but one-year and three-year time periods are most commonly discussed. These differences are very important, for reasons we will explain shortly. However recidivism is defined, it almost exclusively considers the individual, ignoring many contextual factors associated with a re-offense or parole violation. The underlying assumption is that if an individual returns to prison or is arrested again, it is due only to his or her actions and behaviors.

But some former prisoners—roughly 10 percent—end up back in prison due to a technical violation of parole, rather than the perpetration of new punishable offenses.[26] Such violations include missing appointments with a parole officer or a court date, testing positive for drugs like marijuana if remaining substance free is a condition of parole, and getting arrested for any reason. Although many states are attempting to reduce technical violations, a person can easily end up back in prison for something minor at the discretion of a parole officer. In turn, the actions, motivations, and biases of parole officers can have more bearing on recidivism rates than those of former prisoners.[27]

Parole violation policies ignore broader factors in a person's life after prison, such as neighborhood context. People who return to high-incarceration neighborhoods like Austin are more likely to come into contact with law enforcement by virtue of living in an area that is disproportionately policed. Police contact increases the likelihood of a parole violation, irrespective of individual behaviors. Those living in high-incarceration neighborhoods are also more likely to face neighborhood-level barriers such as unemployment, limited healthcare, minimal access to transportation, and longer commute time, all of which may contribute to difficulty in making appointments with a parole officer.[28] In these ways, concentrated punishment is reproduced simply because of long-standing neighborhood disadvantage, police enforcement, and subsequent parole decisions.

Moreover, although many policies have gone all-in on the use of risk assessments and so-called evidence-based decision making, such tools are not settled science. Risk-assessment tools can be inherently biased toward those who come from and return to high-incarceration neighborhoods. For example, association with others with a criminal background is a dimension measured by many risk-assessment tools.[29] Thus, black and brown people may necessarily be labeled as higher risk simply because they live in a historically segregated neighborhood with high concentrations of criminal records.

Finally, one of the biggest limitations of prisoner reentry efforts is that they are still controlled by corrections departments that view success through a singular criminal justice lens. As such, recidivism reduction efforts operate through institutions that still believe uncritically in the necessity and efficacy of punishment. Treating reentry as a function of behaviors and actions, as opposed to a healthy integration into society—family, neighborhood, health, and employment, for example—blames extremely vulnerable individuals for returning to prison, all the while turning a blind eye to responsible institutions. In reality, much recidivism programming provides another path for the criminal justice system to sustain itself. Moreover, private corrections companies are increasingly competing for contracts to provide reentry programs and services. In reentry services, unlike other business domains, profit is best when the customer is wrong. Conflicts of interest abound.

Without question, people returning from prison need support. But the current strategies fall well short of providing it. Although there are success stories—programs and practices that have reduced recidivism rates—these corrections-based approaches are flawed by design. As such, they will not dramatically lower the prison population. They often reinforce rather than disrupt the war on neighborhoods, expanding the role of the criminal justice system in people's lives. Meanwhile, other strategies that could reduce disadvantage and foster better human outcomes struggle for resources.

FACING VIOLENCE

Reducing the number of people sentenced to prison for nonviolent and drug offenses may provide grounds for consensus among policymakers, but it will not drastically reduce the number of people under correctional control. Neither will a narrow focus on reducing recidivism. We must build bold new platforms for reducing violence, or current incarceration trends will largely continue.

The majority of people sent to state prison over the past several decades were incarcerated not for drug offenses but for violent or property offenses.[30] Whereas the drug war initially contributed to the explosive growth of the prison population, in more recent years such growth has come from stiff sentences for a range of violent, property, and other so-called serious offenses. Approximately 17 percent of people in prison in the United States were sentenced for a drug offense. Nearly two-thirds were sent there for a violent or property-related offense, in part because these sentences typically are much longer.[31]

Though there is political will to look sympathetically at drug users, this sympathy only extends to what political scientist Marie Gottschalk refers to as the "non, non, nons"—or nonviolent, non-serious, and nonsexual offenders.[32] But major reductions in the number of people who are incarcerated in the United States cannot be achieved by continuing to draw a dichotomy between so-called low-level and serious offenses. The percentage of unambiguously low-level drug offenders in prison is very low and a matter of interpretation. One study even puts that number at 6 percent of state prisoners and only 2 percent of federal prisoners.[33] The Urban Institute illustrates this point with an interactive web application that allows the user to set the type of reform desired to see what effect it would have in reducing the prison population by the year 2021. If all states were successful in reducing new drug sentences by 25 percent, it estimates that the total US prison population would fall by 3 percent by 2021.[34]

At the same time, many urban neighborhoods of color are still witnessing large disparities in prison sentences for drug offenses, including the lowest categories of felonies. Justice systems are not always transparent, and current data for cities are often hard to come by. But according to Cook County Circuit Court data on convictions issued between 2005 and 2009, the majority of Chicago residents sent to prison were sentenced for drug offenses. And the majority of these offenses were for possession, though drug sentences have likely decreased in more recent years.[35] Austin has its share of violence, as noted previously. But the vast majority, as illustrated in figure 11, of prison sentences given to its residents are for drug offenses. Its rate is higher than the City of Chicago average.[36] Thus, a drastic reduction in drug sentences would be a meaningful starting place for reform in Austin. However, such a reduction would not be enough to address broader drivers of incarceration, crime, and neighborhood disadvantage.

After launching the website Chicago's Million Dollar Blocks, one of the authors was invited to shoot a local news segment in Austin along with a community development professional from the neighborhood. As that author chatted with the story's reporter prior to the shoot, the reporter expressed dismay at the amount of money being spent to combat drug crimes. But he then very quickly asserted that serious criminals should be incarcerated, as if he instinctively understood there is an unwritten rule where one should qualify any call for justice reform with a reaffirmation of harsh punishment for so-called serious offenders. The segment later aired with the reporter professing his belief that serious criminals unquestioningly needed to be behind bars. This journalist was a sympathetic ally of decriminalizing neighborhoods yet also sensed the political infeasibility of going on record supporting reduced punishment for violent offenses. He clearly struggled to imagine that alternatives were even possible.

This anchor's worldview is far from isolated. In the book *Locked In: The True Causes of Mass Incarceration and How to Achieve Real Reform*, John Pfaff makes it clear that high incarceration rates will not end unless long sentences for violent crime also end. He is equally clear that advocating for shorter sentences for violent offenders is a difficult road.[37] For politicians elected on the promise to reform the way we sentence individuals, there is always the risk of political blowback if ever a person who is not given a stiff sentence commits a serious crime. In the words of a senior researcher at the Charles Koch Institute, "For very serious violent offenders, the sentences are going to be long and probably need to be long." Pfaff, on the other hand, would rather see the extra money now spent on long sentences invested in proven violence-reduction programs.[38]

The view that serious offenders need long punishments is a norm deeply ingrained within our politics and culture, no matter where one

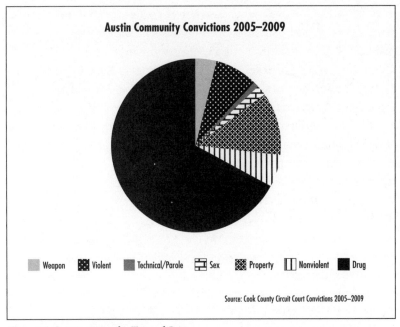

Figure 11: Incarceration by Type of Crime

falls on the political spectrum. This narrative shows up in political debates, often when a violent offender who was released commits another offense. It is used to brand politicians as weak and irresponsible on public safety.[39] Yet, there is evidence that those with the most stake in punishment decisions—the victims of offenses—don't necessarily feel that incarceration is the best approach. In a public poll of state residents, Californians for Safety and Justice found that victims of violent crimes were twice as likely to believe that the state should put its resources into rehabilitation and probation rather than incarceration.[40] This same group favored investment in health and drug treatment services over jail and incarceration by a six-to-one margin. These percentages were similar for victims of any type of crime. Perhaps the closer you are to the harm, the more likely you are to want solutions that actually work.

But victims' voices have not been leading reform conversations. Driven by policymakers who are often disconnected from areas like Austin, the focus has been on the "low-hanging fruit," on the people held in jails and sentenced to prison for drug and nonviolent offenses.

Most of these policymakers do not understand the depths of Chicago's divisions. There is a distinctly separate reality for many black families. This reality, created over generations, is one where shootings, stop-and-frisk policing, failing schools, and vacant lots are commonplace, in stark contrast to the low crime rates and abundant businesses found in white neighborhoods. Surface-level reforms will not uproot concentrated punishment, or the division and instability it fosters. Violence will continue until new platforms for supporting the most vulnerable are developed, until policymakers can move away from human containment strategies and move toward a focus on human capital and capacity.

A PROSECUTORIAL PARADIGM

Punitive state and federal policies play a key role in the war on neighborhoods, incentivizing the disparate policing and enforcement witnessed in high-incarceration areas. However, prosecutors and judges—district and state's attorneys in particular—are also a crucial component of concentrated punishment's machinery. The propensity of district attorneys to embrace tough-on-crime approaches is something that is largely untouched by legislative reform efforts. District attorneys are key decision-makers in how harsh the sentence a person receives is, setting the tone for what offenses are deemed "serious." They often do so with impunity. The US Sentencing Commission found that, for all crimes, black men received sentences that were 20 percent longer than those for whites.[41] But this finding has led to no substantive reforms governing prosecutorial behavior.

Prosecutors' decisions are often based on ideology as much as evidence. Their recommendations to judges are rarely guided by objective public-safety assessments. Lengthy sentences are not related to a reduced likelihood of reoffending.[42] In addition, many violent offenders "age out" of such behavior, making lengthy sentences superfluous and unnecessary from a reoffending perspective. In fact, those convicted of murder have lower recidivism rates compared to many other crimes.[43] And in many cases, spending time in prison actually increases the likelihood of reoffending after release.[44]

States' and district attorneys in cities across the United States have gotten elected largely on a tough-on-crime platform. This platform protects the status quo of disproportionate policing and enforcement in neighborhoods of color. It both drives and maintains the high-incarceration neighborhood. It embraces a narrative of fear, of superpredators, and reinforces the assumption that punishment of arbitrarily defined serious offenses is just and fair. Chicago's former state's attorney, Anita Alvarez, illustrates this point. For years she was accused by activists of handing out disproportionately punitive sentences and steep bond payments to people of color, while at the same time protecting law enforcement from prosecution, ensuring that enforcement went unabated in high-incarceration neighborhoods. She was unseated in 2016 by Kim Foxx, a black woman who rejected the tough-on-crime narrative and talked instead about the damage caused by mass incarceration.

In Chicago, this status quo may have carried on had it not been for the court-ordered release of the police video of the shooting of the black youth Laquan McDonald. Alvarez had declined to prosecute the officer who had shot McDonald sixteen times while the teenager was walking away from him—circumstances that contradict the official statement from the Chicago Police Department that McDonald had been lunging toward the officer. After a judge ordered the video released and the public witnessed the graphic footage, the state's attorney's office rushed to file charges against the officer, over a year after the shooting had happened. The protests, led largely by youth of color, that ensued over the months that followed led to Alvarez's loss in the Democratic primary to Foxx, a challenger who articulated a distinct vision of holding police accountable and dismantling the mass incarceration of black and brown people. Were it not for the graphic video, it is questionable whether the state's attorney—that is, the status quo—would have been challenged.

Prosecutors play an important role in maintaining the high-incarceration neighborhood by pushing for lengthy, punitive sentences. Yet even prosecutors who see this problem and want to change it have limited options. Their ability to divert cases away from prosecution often hinges on the presence or absence of reliable community supports. When violence is at stake, both state's attorneys and judges need partners in neighborhoods who can help mitigate the risk of their decisions. Whether or not those supports exist can make the difference between a continued dependence on punishment or a whole new paradigm.

JUSTICE REINVESTMENT IN AN AGE OF GOVERNMENT AUSTERITY

In Chicago, 2016 was one of the most violent years in recent history. The year ended with 762 homicides, the highest in more than twenty years. Given such a rise, why not move corrections dollars into violence prevention programs? The idea is not new. Known as "justice reinvestment," it has been selectively tried around the country.

The concept of justice reinvestment arose alongside the original "million dollar blocks" projects in the early 2000s.[45] Reform advocates produced visually compelling maps to illustrate just how much money was being spent on locking up people in New York neighborhoods. Laura Kurgan and Eric Cadora, innovators of the method, were instrumental in using these maps to call for shifting money from prisons into high-incarceration neighborhoods to improve employment, education, infrastructure, and other conditions. This early vision of justice reinvestment involved giving community stakeholders, rather than corrections and law enforcement, more control over the use of such funds. The idea of re-investing justice funds into community development is what drew both of the authors to work on criminal justice issues. For those interested in equitable neighborhoods, it is a compelling idea: we can reallocate money from a bloated justice system toward community development solutions that the state typically funds at miserly amounts. Unfortunately, as the concept of justice reinvestment grew and formalized, its implementation almost entirely abandoned this original vision.

Currently, the term "justice reinvestment" is most commonly associated with funding distributed to states by Pew Charitable Trusts and the Council on State Governments Justice Center. The funding is used to incentivize so-called evidence-based decision making by judges and corrections departments in the handling of offenders. It is referred to as the Justice Reinvestment Initiative, which aims to reduce state prison populations. In JRI, the notion of diverting resources away from corrections and into other sectors to improve neighborhood environments has been replaced by an overarching goal of cost savings and the achievement of a better return on investment through evidence-based diversion programs. Further, the savings created by reduced incarceration are almost exclusively shifted from one form of correctional control (prison) to another (community corrections). A main metric of success for JRI is reduced recidivism, and the alternatives to incarceration are mostly correctional programs that use an individual-focused risk assessment and case management response.

What are the limits of this approach? The focus on recidivism necessarily shifts sole responsibility of mass incarceration back onto individual attitudes and behaviors, while ignoring neighborhood determinants. It fails to build the kinds of reliable community-based referral sources that judges and prosecutors need to make better sentencing decisions. It also fails to think generationally, offering no supports to the children of the incarcerated who are at risk of following their parents' path. The war on neighborhoods, with its durable disadvantage and aggressive police enforcement, remains completely intact. Another limiting feature of JRI is top-down decision making. A condition of funding is support from high-level executives at different government agencies. For example, a state-level intervention is expected to have support and decision making input from the governor, as well as corrections leadership. This has led JRI initiatives into conflicts of interest. A top-down effort controlled by corrections departments, tasked with reducing the prison population, should not be counted on to divert its own money into other sectors, particularly to communities of color that make up much of its prison population. Limiting the initiative's focus to recidivism reduction controlled by corrections officials does little to dismantle mass incarceration and nothing to address the war on neighborhoods.

JRI's track record in reducing incarceration, with some states having participated for more than ten years, is mixed. Overall, the eight states that have participated in the program the longest have seen a slightly slower reduction in the prison population than non-JRI states. However, a few JRI states, such as California, Michigan, New Jersey, and New York, witnessed larger reductions in the prison population than those not participating in the program, although their projected rate of incarceration growth may not have been as high as those states targeted by JRI.[46]

Overall, JRI has not lived up to its potential. The Great Recession of the early twenty-first century left many governments strapped for cash, which, coupled with a previously existing ideological climate favoring limited government, produced an openness to reduce spending on imprisonment. Without question, this larger environment influenced the trajectory of JRI. By abandoning the idea of spending money to improve neighborhoods, and instead focusing largely on the fiscal goal of reducing government spending, JRI lost the crucial focus of helping to build human and community capacity. This limitation cannot be overstated. In theory, JRI's struggles are a result of the complexity of the operations involved, but they may have much more to do with a lack of political clarity. In many ways, the justice reinvestment movement fell victim to austerity thinking.

Outside of JRI, there are case studies that reveal some noteworthy attempts to invest resources outside of correctional programming. The state of Kansas funded a local development council to create a revitalization plan for high-incarceration neighborhoods that comprised stakeholders across sectors outside criminal justice. Plans were created to develop affordable housing for those reentering from prison. However, the Great Recession ultimately put the plans and development on hold.[47] The state of Connecticut also proposed innovative ways of investing in high-incarceration neighborhoods by funding local community development corporations (CDCs) to aid in the creation of affordable housing. During the implementation phase, however, this was abandoned in favor of general housing placement support rather than in targeted geographies.[48] Recently, California's jail and prison population was far beyond the capacity of facilities. This, coupled with high state debt at the height of the recent recession, facilitated policy changes to depopulate jails and prisons and search for more cost-effective public-safety alternatives.[49] These cases are still unfolding.

Our analysis might seem, at first glance, to reveal a cynicism about the possibility of progressive reforms. But we must scrutinize current solutions in order to arrive at better ones. Successful reform will require state investments to improve high-incarceration neighborhoods. The tidal wave of austerity thinking must be stopped, before it further harms public-safety reform and, ultimately, entire metropolitan regions.

THE BIPARTISAN MIRAGE

In addition to the divides that define cities such as Chicago, pronounced divides are also rife in national politics. On the surface, justice system reform appears to have emerged as one of the few consensus issues enjoying some degree of bipartisan support. Prominent political figures on both the left and the right have acknowledged the need to reduce the number of people in prison.[50] Perhaps because such moments of political coalescence are few and far between, it is tempting to see bipartisanship as a feel-good story of common sense trumping politics. Unfortunately, that is often a mirage.

The reforms we've reviewed focus on important yet minimally impactful policy changes. They also fail to address neighborhood disadvantage, the conditions in which each new generation of Austin youth struggles to soar. Although there is some agreement about sentencing reform and investment in prisoner reentry, there is little bipartisan agreement to increase funding for foundational supports like violence prevention, public education, affordable housing, or job creation—the very programs that can change the calculus of risk when judges are making sentencing decisions.

It is impossible to end mass incarceration and the war on neighborhoods without expanding positive government investments in racial equity. But under the Trump administration, even limited reforms are contested. Donald Trump was elected after running a campaign that signaled a return to tough-on-crime, law-and-order approaches to urban policy. For example, in the fall of 2016, during a presidential debate, he specifically referenced violence in Chicago to signal the type of approaches he favored. He called for the use of stop-and-frisk policing and more law and order to save the city from its current state—what he called a more dangerous place than Afghanistan. The stop-and-frisk approaches that Trump references as successful took place in New York City under Mayor Rudy Giuliani. They were found to be both unreliable and unconstitutional and are also an important basis for the Black Lives Matter movement.

Since Trump took office and appointed Jeff Sessions as the US attorney general, there has been a clear call for harsher sentencing and reversals in police accountability efforts, making reformers nostalgic for the gains of even a couple of years ago.[51] Meanwhile, the names of black men and women killed by sanctioned police officers who've faced no conviction continue to mount: Philando Castile. Terence Crutcher. Eric Garner. Mike Brown. Rekia Boyd. Sean Bell. Tamir Rice. Freddie Gray. Danroy Henry. Oscar Grant III. Kendrec McDade. Aiyana Jones. Ramarley Graham. Amadou Diallo.

Just when racial justice, police reform, and justice system reform were gaining popular momentum, the Trump administration has attempted to turn back the clock and stake out a more punitive position. Indeed, the election of Trump immediately emboldened the Fraternal Order of Police to release a statement calling for the rollback of many Obama administration reforms, including police oversight, the reduction in funding for police access to military-grade weapons, and Deferred Action for Childhood Arrivals, which has allowed many young immigrants to avoid deportation.

The sharp, vengeful return to harsh criminal justice approaches presents major obstacles to progress. In the short term, advocates are working tirelessly just to hold on to basic measures like the Second Chance Act. But we must do more than just hold the line. Those who want to uproot concentrated punishment, once and for all, must also lead with vision. Any politician's insistence that more punitive, law-and-order policies in Chicago will reduce violence must be called into question. To move backward is to double down on racially unjust, expensive, and ineffective safety strategies, reinforcing the war on neighborhoods.

Throughout this book, you've seen how these strategies play out in Judge J's courtroom, with Harold's journey, and with the struggles faced by Fifthteenth District police officers. By keeping residents in a downward spiral of disadvantage, regressive approaches lead to more crime and violence, not less.[52] This spiral was set in motion years ago through discriminatory housing policies, accelerated by deindustrialization and mass incarceration policies, and continued through the constant removal of resources. Harmful government misinvestments make things worse, for all involved. To reverse the momentum, it will take more than surface-level reforms.

THE ROAD TO RACIAL EQUITY

Though justice system reform is a rare area of bipartisan agreement, lawmakers treat it as separate from the larger fight over austerity policies. But these policies are decimating high-incarceration neighborhoods and negatively influencing public safety. As discussed earlier, forced austerity in Illinois has made the goal of reducing prison populations nearly impossible.[53]

The stakes are high. They involve the future of entire cities. Not just Chicago but also Louisville, Baltimore, Cleveland, Milwaukee, Detroit, and many others, all with neighborhoods defined by long-standing disadvantage. These cities need strong and intentional investments to ensure that every young person and every family have the supports they need to thrive. But amid Chicago's extended violence crises, policymakers, civic leaders, and philanthropic organizations typically search for simple, silver-bullet solutions without taking action to change the underlying dynamics of neighborhood disadvantage.

Both mass incarceration and broader citywide inequality are holding cities back—stalling or reversing gains in population growth, economic output, poverty reduction, violence reduction, and social cohesion. Chicago's population grew by only twenty-three thousand residents between 2010 and 2015, which is the slowest growth of all the top-ten US cities.[54]

More recently, with the rise in violence, Chicago has seen net losses in residents, a fact that nearly ensures Houston will surpass Chicago as the third-largest city within the next decade.[55] Much of Chicago's population decline results from the loss of black residents. Not only were these residents disproportionately removed from communities by criminal justice policies, but these same high-incarceration neighborhoods were decimated by predatory lending and foreclosures during the Great Recession, which resulted largely because of long-standing patterns of racial segregation.[56] In turn, black residents with options have moved away by the thousands.

Stagnant population growth has very real consequences for all residents, not the least of which is billions in lost income, income that would translate to tax revenue for making investments in improving the city. A recent study found that metropolitan areas with greater levels of segregation witnessed slower economic growth than others, including slower income growth and slower property value appreciation.[57]

Meanwhile, the cycles of criminalization, removal, and reentry in high-incarceration neighborhoods combine to reinforce long-standing segregation, increase poverty rates, and cripple the growth and productivity of entire cities and regions. In the words of scholars Robert DeFina and Lance Hannon, "The evidence indicates that growing incarceration has significantly increased poverty, regardless of which index is used to gauge poverty. Indeed, the official poverty rate would have fallen considerably during the [last forty years] had it not been for mass incarceration."[58]

Despite the political momentum behind austerity arguments, spending on suppression and punishment has since the early 1980s been seen as a necessary and good form of government intervention. Throughout this book, we have provided arguments for and examples of how punishment-focused investments are faulty and structurally racist. When viewed alongside the rise of austerity, these investments are particularly troubling. They highlight a willingness to invest heavily in suppression when people fail, but no such willingness when people are merely on a path to possible failure. To uproot the problem of violence, we must also uproot this limited logic.

As inequality has risen, cities and states alike have become more divided. So too have people's ideas about what kinds of reforms are needed to create meaningful change. Today's policy landscape is marked by wildly different ideas about the role of public policies and budgets. People are frustrated with government, but they are frustrated because they do not believe government is working for ordinary people and, by extension, their neighborhoods and their cities. This means that the potential exists to recapture the trust of people by articulating ways that policies *can* work to improve our neighborhoods and build the capacity of community institutions.

The various reforms we have discussed in this chapter have positive elements with the potential to make some progress in reducing the prison population. However, they fall short of dismantling the paradigm of mass incarceration because they leave the corrections-based system intact and ignore the neighborhood-level damage of years of unjust policies. The constant cycling of prisoners in and out of neighborhoods with high incarceration rates has actually perpetuated more crime and disorder.[59] This, in turn, limits private investment and blunts community development. Incarceration damages individuals, families, and whole neighborhoods, producing the opposite of what is intended. The ripple effects of our decades-long policies of disproportionately incarcerating people from urban neighborhoods of color include many of our biggest problems today: poor health outcomes, unemployment, and disinvestment, to name just a few.

To uproot concentrated punishment and end structural racism within areas like Chicago's West Side, it is vital to reclaim the role of public investment in fostering public safety. To really create peace and end concentrated punishment, we must see past austerity politics. Increased investment is essential. It is important to see concentrated punishment as a misallocation of government resources. But it is also necessary for all of us to know that much wiser allocations are possible. Rather than abandoning public-sector responsibilities, public-sector responsibilities must be rethought and revitalized. Only then can policymakers surpass the surface-level reforms that have, so far, dominated the discussion.

THE PATH TO PEACE

FROM NEW PRIUSES to ailing SUVs, cars of all makes and models drive the Eisenhower Expressway. Behind the wheels, some drivers have grown familiar with the term "mass incarceration." They may have heard about the "new Jim Crow," thanks to both the writing and public education efforts of Michelle Alexander.[1] Some have started to understand that police officers cannot end addiction, that state's attorneys cannot provide work alternatives to street-level dealers, and that judges have disturbingly little influence over the anger, pain, and trauma that flows into their courtrooms daily. Many other drivers still lack this awareness. As they pass West Side exits, they may give little thought to life in those neighborhoods, or their thinking may be misinformed, shaped by antiblack narratives presented in shallow news accounts and "tough on crime" policies.[2]

The expressway itself is a testament to how Chicago has grown more divided. Built in the decades immediately preceding mass incarceration, it helped lay the groundwork for the hypersegregation of African American communities on the West Side and the concentrated punishment that ensued. Today, in the early decades of the twenty-first century, where you live along the expressway shapes your destiny.

Babies born into neighboring Oak Park homes have a significantly longer life expectancy than babies born into Austin homes. This inequity cannot be explained away by bad individual choices. As the stories of West Side residents and workers have shown, concentrated punishment plays a central role in preserving social disorder. It ensures disparate outcomes by condemning individuals for their poverty, their race, their homelessness, their mental illness, and their home address. In so doing, the punishment paradigm imprisons people's potential, ignores their pain, and misdirects vast resources.

These patterns must change. America can no longer displace responsibility for dire neighborhood conditions onto a punitive system that is incapable of having a positive transformative effect. The habit of embracing failed solutions must be broken.

In order to create lasting peace in cities like Chicago, we must shift popular thinking around what produces safety. We are told that safety is the result of positive individual behaviors and that when people's behavior is seriously out of alignment, when they cause harm to others, then safety can be reclaimed simply by removing them from the environment. When people are released, it is assumed they have learned their lesson and are now more hesitant to commit wrongdoing. But there are fatal flaws in this logic.

At the individual level, being locked up has questionable effects on people's beliefs about the world, about how they see the causes and effects of their actions. It also weakens the resources available to them upon their release. At the collective or neighborhood level, where thousands of people are forcibly removed from a place like Austin, the effects are only amplified. The line between cause and effect grows blurry. The most precious resource of all—the love of family and friends—is drained over time, causing the larger environment to suffer. All the while, safety remains a distant goalpost.

We will never create safer neighborhoods by continuing to punish disadvantage. Challenges like addiction, mental illness, and unemployment cannot be dismissed as criminal concerns. The temporary removal of residents is no magic spell that ends violence or drug sales. It is precisely that delusion that has fed the rise and resilience of mass incarceration, with more than two million people in US prisons at any given time.[3]

As we saw with Harold, who was pulled away from his children while battling his own ghosts, one person's imprisonment can become a multigenerational sentence. But responses that dig deeper, that actually help people to face their ghosts, have more potential to break the cycle of harm that now plagues so many high-incarceration areas. To some observers, it may sound radical to give an underemployed addict the supports they need to change the course of their life. Yet, the stories of many Austin residents and leaders suggest this is exactly what is needed.[4]

How society responds to harmful behaviors—from selling heroin or stealing cars to attacking others with fists or guns—will determine the scale on which those behaviors continue. If we want drug sales to stop, economic desperation should be met with opportunity. If we aim to end addiction, suffering should be countered with abundant opportunities to heal. If we really want to create peace, then jobs, healing, and conflict-resolution resources must become commonplace. But, as we have plainly seen over the last four decades of public-safety policymaking, responses that hinge on broken logics will continue to get broken results.

To end our addiction to punishment, to stop both violence and mass incarceration, it is vital that everyone play a role. How you might contribute depends largely on where you live, who you know, what resources you have available, and how you approach the world. But many contributions are possible. Leaders across the city must be more strongly aligned and pull in the same direction to provide opportunities for marginalized young people. All residents of urban places need to be advocates of deep reform, because a strong economy hinges on strong neighborhoods and population growth. Even suburban dwellers, or other concerned citizens across and outside urban regions, can educate their peers about the dangers of concentrated punishment. They too stand to benefit when cities are safer and less divided. Working together, a diverse coalition of stakeholders can achieve the sweeping changes that are needed, including major investments in areas like Austin.[5]

FROM AWARENESS TO ACTION

No matter where you live or work, or what your network looks like, you have a role to play in creating a safer, more just future. That work will not be easy. Hopefully it will be deeply joyful and socially rewarding, but that is not guaranteed. However you contribute, your voice matters. The more you can integrate humility and boldness, the greater your impact will be.

The work begins with recognizing your limits, even as you push society to change its own. No matter how long you labor to support disadvantaged neighborhoods, if you are an outsider, you will remain minimally exposed to the realities lived by residents. This has undoubtedly been true in our own journeys. We have spent years working for and with social change efforts rooted on the West Side, directing violence prevention programs, strengthening community development efforts, and assisting restorative justice experiments. Through this work, we've gotten to know incredible community residents, organizational leaders, and visionaries. And we've been honored to provide them modest supports. Still, we don't personally know the pressures of having to feed one's children under difficult financial circumstances or to defend one's block from warring factions of youth. Nor do we know what it's like to be a police officer on night patrol, routinely responding to danger.

However, we do know that these pressures are lived daily, whether by residents coming back from fragile places to reclaim their peace or by police officers unable to forge justice with broken tools. We have seen how their stories fit together, like pieces in a complex puzzle. When you are involved in the work of community building, peacemaking, criminal justice reform, or police accountability, you realize no single voice or approach will solve the entrenched challenges facing high-incarceration areas. It will take unified efforts—among different leaders and across various sectors—to make these places whole again.

The first key to participating in this work is to check the assumptions you bring to the table. We have all been saturated with the idea that neighborhoods like Austin are perilous. From media coverage to movies, desperate images of the city's peripheries have been implanted in our minds. Whether you grew up watching *Adventures in Babysitting* and *Candyman*, seeing fights posted on Facebook and Snapchat, or just paying attention to any news about Chicago, you've seen images that reduce places like the West and South Sides to violence, drugs, danger, and intimidating young men portrayed as criminals and gang members.[6] In turn, these images support the idea that whatever law enforcement is happening in these areas is well justified. They keep us from asking deeper questions or taking more meaningful actions.

Meanwhile, the prevailing public-safety response to violence has not changed. Policymakers and elected officials have not checked their own assumptions. Arrest, detention, prosecution, and imprisonment remain the dominant strategies for pursuing peace. Befitting the definition of insanity—repeating the same mistakes while expecting different results— these dominant strategies have not shifted the city's trajectory. Not only has there been a resurgence in violence but addiction rates also remain high across the Chicago region, and the drug trade continues to expand. Meanwhile, systemic police brutality has gone unchecked and police-community relations have little ground to stand on.

Why have violence, addiction, and illicit drug sales proven to be such difficult problems for policymakers to tackle? We've argued that it is because they have misunderstood the underlying dynamics. Official equations for public safety have not accounted for people's ability to find housing, jobs, healing, and healthy food.[7] The math has been far too focused on aggressive policing and prison cells, even though those formulas are undeniably limited—they assume that poverty is caused by crime and violence, rather than the other way around.

Consequently, policymakers fuel the punishment of disadvantage, the secret engine of mass incarceration. They remain so focused on re-moving "problem" people that they've failed to build systems that can uproot the very real problems that people face. As a result, the efforts of even the best community leaders are like a pail of water thrown against a wave. They cannot turn the tide. As long as policymakers support the broken laws and skewed budgets that enable concentrated punishment, this pattern will continue. Prison budgets will swell, year after year, while schools and proven social programs will struggle to remain open.

If narrow discussions of "law and order" remain dominant, if root causes are ignored for another two or three decades, if people's capacity continues to be stripped away in the name of safety, then conditions will only get worse. Violence will intensify. The drug trade will expand. Addiction will take even more lives. The children of the incarcerated will face their own days in court. And for millions of Americans, the very forces that are supposed to keep people safe will continue func-tioning as another type of threat. If this happens, the blame should fall squarely on those in power—all political parties—who refuse to change our course.

Though imminently possible, such a future is not preordained. If so-ciety can learn from its recent past, gathering up as much wisdom and perspective as possible, then a new world might indeed be born. To-ward that end, we hope everyone can see mass incarceration with eyes wide open, how its injustices and dangers go hand in hand. Recognizing this reality is essential for anyone wishing to be a part of the solution.

Equipped with great awareness—of both oneself and the challenge at hand—every single person can indeed make real contributions. This is true whether you are a legislator, a funder, a peacemaker, an employer, an organizer, a clinician, or an everyday citizen.

NO-ENTRY NEIGHBORHOODS

We envision a future where the law is only one element of a much broader public-safety strategy, where 911 is not the only number residents of areas like Austin can call for help, where young people no longer feel they have to take matters of justice into their own hands, and where police officers are not the only leaders empowered to create safety. We envision a future where neighbors, community leaders, faith partners, and other grassroots forces all help to carry the weight of creating peace, and the criminal justice system is not the first, second, third, and fourth line of intervention.

Key elements of this future are already emerging on Chicago's West Side. In the North Lawndale neighborhood, very near to Austin, the Trauma Response and Intervention Movement (TRIM) is working to build up resident capacity to uproot community violence within an eight-block area. Nearby, the Lawndale Christian Legal Center is one of several Chicago organizations building restorative justice programs for justice-involved youth. Both groups are also helping to launch the nation's first community-based restorative justice court, for young adult offenders between the ages of eighteen and twenty-four, in partnership with reform-minded systems leaders like Judge Colleen Sheehan.[8]

With adequate resources, models such as these can nurture the kinds of leaders needed to address conflicts before they get out of hand. They can help peace prevail. Though not all would admit it, police officers desperately need these public-safety partners who can actually connect to people on the verge of committing crimes, as well as to those who have already broken the law and are at risk of doing it again. These models help talk people off the edge, away from the trigger, and toward a better version of themselves. To be effective, community-based peacemakers need their own high-quality training, lines of accountability, and a platform for communicating with residents, independent of the criminal justice system. Within Austin, a new organization called the Institute for Nonviolence Chicago is working to build precisely this vision, with support from a larger citywide effort called READI Chicago.[9]

By supporting leadership within communities, households and blocks have more available supports when seeking to resolve issues or uproot long-standing tensions. If this direction is well led and fully funded, every school could have an active peace room, where student trauma is safely processed. Every block-club captain and faith leader could be trained in psychological first aid. And anyone who witnesses a violent incident could have a nearby place to come together, share stories of resilience, and repair relationships.[10] This is intricate but necessary work, with the necessity of building trust at its very center. Because of the centrality of trust in making solutions like these work, restorative processes—such as peacemaking circles—should be used to develop and maintain shared values and guidelines among all key stakeholders.

When done right, such efforts can create "no-entry" neighborhoods, places where robust supports ensure that no young person ends up behind bars, no matter the obstacles they face or the hurdles they must overcome. Entry into prison can be removed as an option. The most vulnerable youth can be supported. Jobs can be created at scale. New forms of collaboration and coordination can be advanced.[11] And special attention can be paid to those who have endured the heaviest blows from concentrated punishment.[12]

"Second-generation incarceration" is the term for when a child whose parent was imprisoned is ultimately put behind bars. In cities such as Chicago, second- and even third-generation incarceration has become increasingly common. The solutions created by policymakers in previous decades set the stage for entire generations of youth to be raised without robust family supports. Policymakers can no longer make that mistake. They can no longer wait around until the next generation is imprisoned, until today's children are shipped downstate in ten or twenty years. In the years it takes to build out a community-based safety paradigm, incarceration should be treated as a last resort, and when people are put behind bars, the state should ensure that the imprisoned person's children have the necessary family resources, quality healthcare and education, and mentoring. Otherwise, public officials are kicking the can down the road and neglecting their central duty of building working solutions to challenges faced by those they serve.[13]

Real progress will occur only when we think generationally about how safety is created and, alternatively, how social disorder is spread in disadvantaged neighborhoods. For decades, American politicians have campaigned on overly simple strategies for reducing violence. They've promised to sweep the streets, to lock up offenders and throw away the keys. And they've done this in isolation from community-based efforts, often operating from the kinds of short-term horizons that drive political campaigns for election and reelection. Along the way, they've failed to think about the implications for the children and families of those locked away.

Our vision entails a much deeper commitment to human and community development in high-incarceration neighborhoods. Change agents must work across systems, both empowering local leaders and using data-driven approaches to collaboration. They must see how residents, schools, hospitals, foster homes, faith communities, and government leaders at all levels have leading roles to play in creating peace. Working together, they can uproot all the excuses that allow the greatest resources to be poured into the punishment paradigm, rather than one that actually positions people to thrive, no matter what vulnerabilities they face.

FROM THE GROUND UP

Having long faced overwhelming odds, Austin leaders are strongly committed to community building. As in other neighborhoods across the country, long-term residents create gardens, public officials collaborate with nonprofits to better coordinate services, senior citizens team up with police officers for prayer vigils, and neighbors work with youth to clean up the streets.

Austin also has a powerful history of organizing for structural and community change. Well-known organizers have included Gale Cincotta and Shel Trapp, from the 1960s to the 1980s, and Jackie Reed and Elce Redmond from the 1990s to the present. Viewed together, their efforts show how Austin residents can unite to improve their reach and influence, thereby protecting the interests of neighborhood residents and helping bend broken policies into practices that better support everyday life.

In addition to leading campaigns in Austin, Cincotta and Trapp co-founded National People's Action, one of the strongest community-based organizing coalitions of the late twentieth century. Cincotta was known for her work to advance two pieces of federal legislation that helped protect residents in places like Austin from fraudulent banking practices. The Home Mortgage Disclosure Act of 1975 forced banks to be more transparent about their lending decisions, thereby making any refusal to lend to some areas more visible. The Community Reinvestment Act of 1977 went beyond just data transparency. It encouraged banks to actually make investments in low-income areas. Compliance with the act is monitored and enforced through regulations on any financial institutions that seek to grow their branches or to merge.[14] Without this legislation, countless urban neighborhoods would have been hit even harder by predatory lending and the foreclosure crisis.

Jackie Reed, who founded the Westside Health Authority in 1990, has also been a tremendous voice for community investment in Austin. She helped grow dozens of block clubs in the area, built on the idea that "it takes a village" to create positive change. Her victories include successfully campaigning to redevelop a local hospital that was closing and building a modern wellness center on a vacant lot. In addition to the Westside Health Authority, several other organizing groups were formed in Austin in the middle and late twentieth century, including the now defunct Northwest Austin Neighborhood Council and the still active South Austin Coalition Community Council.[15] At the SACCC, Elce Redmond has been consistently active on the dual problem of violence and incarceration. He has helped both to lead prayer vigils after shootings and to organize downtown marches protesting the war on drugs.

This organizing history extends to other pressing issues as well, from environmental racism to the all-too-recent foreclosure crisis. For more than twenty years there was a waste incinerator in the neighborhood, a major threat to air quality on Chicago's West Side. The facility diverted garbage from Chicago's landfill and pumped pounds of lead into the air. It took a heavy toll on the health and well-being of residents in surrounding communities, with effects that are still not fully understood.[16] In the mid-1990s, led in part by the SACCC, a coalition was formed called the Westside Alliance for a Safe and Toxic-Free Environment.

Through a high-energy campaign, WASTE was able to permanently shut down the incinerator.[17]

More recently, the SACCC, the Westside Health Authority, and others actively tried to mitigate the impact on Austin households of the foreclosure crisis. They've pressured key banks that own foreclosed properties to provide modification relief, create property-maintenance jobs for unemployed residents, and transfer ownership of distressed properties so that community organizations can help to stabilize the residential blocks through ties with residents and block clubs.

Coalitions like these provide a sorely needed line of defense for residents, helping battle against some of the injustices that commonly find a home in disadvantaged areas. In Austin, similar multiagency efforts have been working on a brighter future, hustling to attract the outside resources needed to implement proactive visions. From recruiting corporate and university partners for economic development to applying for major federal grants to strengthen the educational landscape, they have tried to bring in the resources needed to expand opportunities for residents. But despite heroic efforts by organizers and nonprofit organizations, outside investors have come up short. While the supply of dollars for incarcerating Austin residents has been nearly unlimited, any other major investments have been few and far between.[18]

In recent years, a collective impact network called Austin Coming Together has attempted to align the planning efforts of leading institutions in the area. ACT began through the combined effort of local leaders, a major research university, and a large bank seeking to make a targeted investment in Austin. Although outside groups like the bank provided initial capital for the network, ACT is now driven by local partners, directed by a long-term resident, and governed by a robust board of directors that features influential neighborhood leaders.[19]

The network's purpose is to bring together local and outside experts to create a comprehensive strategy for economic development and educational improvement in Austin. This focus is crucial. Oftentimes the ability of local stakeholders to coalesce around issues hinges on whether or not they share a common vision. A group like ACT has the potential to work with its members to facilitate that common vision, guiding people through their diverse and sometimes diverging perspectives on how Austin's future should unfold. Through its education and economic development committees, ACT seeks to implement long-term improvement plans and lift up small-scale collaborations in ways that match community assets with outside resources, in the hope of growing its scale.

ACT is rooted in a collective impact model. A simple definition of collective impact, taken from leaders at the Foundation Strategy Group, is "the commitment of a group of actors from different sectors to a common agenda for solving a complex social problem." Rather than agencies trying to achieve lofty missions in isolation, collective impact is built on the idea that "no single organization can create large-scale, lasting social change alone."[20] Though strong organizations and programs are an essential part of effective social change, such initiatives are not enough to shift deeply entrenched patterns that warrant more complex, multi-dimensional solutions. Ongoing, well-coordinated, and clearly defined partnerships between residents, government, civil society, and business are necessary for building stronger community connections and achieving a deep impact.[21]

As criminal justice reform projects seek to work in concert with community leaders, multistakeholder collaborations are essential. When locally driven networks like ACT are prioritized, these strategies can be used to make no-entry neighborhoods real. They can guide place-based investments for reducing crime and violence, improving community development outcomes in the process. But the investment has to actually materialize, and that means the state must shift from investing in incarceration to investing in human and community development.

A NEW MARSHALL PLAN

After World War II, the United States invested billions of dollars to help rebuild Europe. It did so to ensure peace and long-term stability amid the regions most affected by the war. When strategizing about how to end violence in Chicago, a local business leader took this period of intense investment as a model. In a 2014 article in *Chicago Business Magazine*, businessperson Jim Reynolds wrote, "We have a serious problem, and philanthropy or government subsidies won't, by themselves, reverse the tide. We need jobs. We need commerce. We need to bring economic vitality into the communities that are the breeding grounds of such hopelessness that the typical teenage male resident does not expect to live past the age of 25."[22]

Drawing inspiration from past National Urban League president John Jacobs, Reynolds called for a domestic Marshall Plan. When the United States gave $13 billion to sixteen European nations in 1947 for fuel, food, and machinery, there were major declines in postwar poverty. Reclaiming this idea as a solution for ending violence, Reynolds asserts that the economic revitalization of areas like Austin is key to creating peace. With this article, he became one of a handful of observers calling for heavy investments that do more than temporarily suppress the problem of violence.

In addition to being a business leader and social observer, Reynolds is also one of the founders of Get IN Chicago, a fund that rallied large segments of the business community to invest in violence prevention. The premise of Get IN Chicago was to use data about school performance and disciplinary incidents to predict which youth had the highest risk of being involved in violence. Then, through a rigorous evaluation design, these identified youth would be assigned to evidence-based programs for support, from mentoring to cognitive behavioral therapy. It is one of several major efforts in Chicago seeking to help youth navigate the toxic and traumatic stress they face.

At the individual and small-group level, trauma-informed approaches to youth development have shown promise in reducing re-offense rates and instilling positive social and emotional skills in participants. Chicago has many examples of such programs, including Quiet Time, Urban Warriors, and Becoming a Man. Each of these has unique logic models, but all have been shown to increase adolescent well-being among youth with high levels of exposure to violence. In Quiet Time, students are taught basic meditation techniques that help them to calm their minds, freeing them from old reactionary patterns. In Urban Warriors, military veterans who have processed their own trauma from wartime experiences are paired in a mentoring relationship with youth who've encountered combat in their communities. In Becoming a Man, a highly skilled facilitator leads a series of workshops and rites of passage for young men that help to expand their definition of masculinity. In both of the latter examples, youth are connected with adults who can serve as mentors and role models, a critical factor for ensuring school success and lessening contact with the criminal justice system.[23]

Although programs like these use rigorous research designs, and have shown positive outcomes, scaling them up to all the youth in need has yet to happen. The Get IN Chicago fund has raised and invested more than $34 million in its first few years of operating—a figure that pales in comparison to what we invest in removing and imprisoning residents of Austin. Meanwhile, every hour in Chicago, youth are arrested without receiving the supports they need to prevent such arrests from happening again. Reynolds knows that greater investment strategies are needed.[24] He has provided leadership on two fronts: leveraging private wealth and calling for public investment.

More two-fronted leadership is needed. When LeBron James pledged $87 million to ensure that students from his hometown of Akron could attend college, it was an incredible gift.[25] But not even James can carry the weight of entire communities on his shoulders. Students are in need all across the country. Given the size of today's inequities, business and philanthropic leaders must join the chorus that is demanding robust, solutions-driven public investments—not into the existing infrastructure of the criminal justice system (those investments are all too firmly established) but into the types of community-based supports that can actually move society beyond suppression, confinement, and control.

Moreover, no matter how influential, well-funded, or well-designed, no single intervention has the power to shift the community contexts in which violence occurs. And as we have argued, context has an incredible shaping influence on individual actors, often determining whether or not those individuals will stay out of prison. Meanwhile, the most disadvantaged neighborhoods have been stripped of both financial and social assets by market and political forces, raising hurdles for each new life born into a high-incarceration area.

Righting these wrongs will take more than a handful of signature evidence-based programs. Even the best curriculums and program leaders in the world cannot rebuild widespread job opportunities or make housing more affordable. Those are systems-level goals. They require greater resources and coordination, which is why we advocate for a collective impact approach with a strong commitment to community investment.

A powerful vision of such investment was advanced by Chicago journalist Chip Mitchell. Working with a local economic development specialist, he estimated that it would take thirty thousand new jobs to make a major reduction in Chicago's violence problem, with those jobs being given to disconnected young men between the ages of sixteen and thirty-four across the city. Employment strategies would include a mix of job placement, wage subsidies, job creation incentives, and direct employment by relevant institutions, such as nonprofits. Another key element of Mitchell's proposal is social service supports to ensure that newly employed workers succeed in their positions. In essence, he lays out a blueprint for what an antiviolence Marshall Plan might look like. The total cost of this intervention would be $1.1 billion, roughly the amount provided to restore Union Station in Chicago's downtown. Local leaders who could help design the details of implementing such a plan already exist. In Austin, the organization Manufacturing Renaissance is working toward bold economic development goals along these lines.[26]

To reverse the long-standing war on neighborhoods and reduce the prison population across all offense categories, something like a new and comprehensive Marshall Plan is indeed needed. If it comes to pass, the potential rewards are massive: not only peace but all that comes with it, from lowered hurdles to success for children to greater economic growth for all areas of cities.[27]

TOWARD AN EQUITABLE CITY

Chicago has long been portrayed as treacherous terrain. In recent decades, the annual tally of homicides has risen, fallen, and risen again. As the charts fluctuate, some neighborhoods have grown safer while others have been caught in cycles of harm spanning generations, with young people learning to take cover early. But for large swaths of the general public, violence is just on the news; it is replayed on screens rather than seen through living-room blinds. As often happens in urban centers across the country, huge gaps exist in the ways these parts of the city understand one another.

Without the government as a fully invested partner, we will struggle to create change at the scale required to transform places like Austin. At the same time, if public investments do grow significantly yet organizations lack winning strategies for building the community-level leaders needed to create peace, those efforts, too, will come up short. In order to transform the justice system, we propose the following approaches:

1. Use justice mapping as a mandatory mechanism for reinvesting justice dollars in high-incarceration neighborhoods
2. Ensure human-capital investments through policies that shift resources away from incarceration spending to education, job creation, and healing
3. Train and support everyday leaders and organizations within high-incarceration areas to respond to conflict in restorative ways
4. Build and strengthen local collective impact networks to support these leaders, piloting new communications technologies where appropriate
5. Coordinate programs, services, and supports to ensure that children and youth stay out of the justice system

These strategies will help to build an "equitable city," one where high-incarceration neighborhoods are prioritized with targeted investments that help create interconnected community, organizational, and economic leadership, and where the explicit goal is to overcome persistent patterns of division, racial segregation, and economic isolation. To nurture peace, resources must be diverted from the justice system directly into the areas that the system has laid to waste with years of unjust policies. This is how equitable cities can be created: by acknowledging past failures and working to rebuild neighborhoods that have been the sites of concentrated punishment.

Within high-incarceration areas, youth must be connected to positive supports outside of the school and home, mentors and peacemakers must be trained and supported in dynamic, trackable ways, and adults who are struggling must have the resources and opportunities they need to rebuild their lives. Across the larger region, high-incarceration areas must be supported by major employers to grow labor market options for residents, by civic leaders who can coordinate financial investment in community development projects, and by citizens at large who can sustain the political will that these projects will need to succeed. Through these strategies, Chicago can indeed build a more vibrant city for all residents.[28]

This is an equity-based public-safety strategy. It has the potential to reverse entrenched patterns of racial injustice, so that areas like Austin foster opportunity rather than reinforce poverty. Overcoming these structural barriers is the central objective of the equitable-city lens. And while neighborhood leaders and community-based organizations have a core leadership role to play, so too do professional allies outside of the criminal justice system, for example, by using justice mapping to guide strategies for reinvesting corrections dollars.

Importantly, incarceration is just one form of disadvantage, and one driver of inequality. Working with residents, planning agencies, public health departments, foundations, and nonprofit organizations need to develop plans for addressing each neighborhood's top priorities, from creating jobs and improving health outcomes to solving housing and education challenges. This is what equitable development looks like: diverting resources into economic development in areas with few businesses and job opportunities; coordinating affordable housing development where options are lacking; and coordinating mental health services where major gaps exist.

Historically, urban planners bring expertise to this work, helping to coordinate successful long-term strategies. Meanwhile, public health professionals are well versed in using local data to identify problems and plan for equitable solutions.[29] By linking such professionals with community leaders, a new paradigm can be nurtured: local, neighborhood planning that connects all issues—health, employment, education, transportation, crime, violence—and delivers detailed strategies for their improvement, with the full range of resources required to ensure implementation.

Success in this strategy, which entails dual reductions in violence and incarceration, could be the new mode of competition among cities. Lowered incarceration rates would feature prominently in such competitions, alongside other positive indicators such as business growth, school performance, population increases, transportation access, and housing development.

An important breakthrough in US public health in recent years has been the use of county health rankings. The Center for Population Health at the University of Wisconsin created a website with county-level maps that rank each US county on different domains of health. The charge is for states and public health departments to target funding and create strategies for improving the overall health rankings of each county. In other words, counties are in competition with one another, within and across states, to have the healthiest areas across all relevant indicators. We believe that something similar could be used for high-incarceration neighborhoods.[30]

It is unlikely that all of these investments will be made to improve high-incarceration neighborhoods without a legislative mandate. The living ecosystem that is the justice system fights to maintain the status quo. It will be dismantled only by passing legislation that reduces prison sentences and shifts investment away from corrections and into human and community development efforts. Proposition 47 in California is an example of an important first step in making this a reality. The Reimagine Justice campaign in Illinois also drafted legislation—SB 2295—that would go deeper in mandating reinvestment into alternatives to incarceration. Amid mounting evidence that the current paradigm is unacceptable, such legislation will be essential to mandating the types of reforms that will actually begin to dismantle it.

A HIGHER ORDER

We live in a time of great disrepair: divided and toxic leadership, historically unprecedented natural disasters, and almost permanent conflict in some parts of the world. But much of our country's pain is far closer to home. It is not far away in Washington, coastal areas, or the Middle East. It is in neighborhoods across the country, often just down the street. Because it exists miles away from well-resourced towns and suburbs, this pain can be difficult to see, hard to feel, and sometimes even harder to accept. It is too near to touch, or so it seems, as even neighboring communities can appear worlds apart.

Though the exits of the Eisenhower Expressway take their drivers into starkly different social and economic realities, these realities are deeply intertwined. They are a part of a single city, of an indivisible region, of one political and historical journey with punishment at its very core. Through pushing out pain and punishing disadvantage, policymakers have avoided the deep work of helping communities recover from deindustrialization. Instead, aggressive criminal justice policies have been stacked on top of the legacies of racial injustice and exclusion.

The victims of this work avoidance have not just been those shipped to prisons, packed into steel closets in downstate towns. The victims are also future generations. The children and youth who, even as you read this, are bearing the legacies of lockdown and nearing their own time of disappearance into violence or the criminal justice system. And all of us suffer as well, as our cities and regions are held back by the division and disadvantage that mass incarceration has furthered.

That which is predictable should also be preventable. If we know that a train is about to crash for the fourth time in as many days, then we should be able to stop it. But each new decade of urban policies is another wreck-bound train. To reroute the tracks, it is not just policymakers who must respond. And not just voters, either, though voting for restorative public servants is essential.[31] To truly shift the world, we must all become sharper and more connected. We must think through the consequences of not only our ballots but also our investments, our free time, and even our long-held beliefs about right and wrong.[32] Justice is not made only in courtrooms. The gavel is struck every time we stay within our comfort zones, fail to look beyond the surface, or ignore the voices and movements of those whose lives have been far more difficult than our own.

Though we are now well into the twenty-first century, decades after the invention of space travel, the internet, and nanotechnology, our justice system seems to be stuck in a medieval paradigm. Our hearts have not evolved with our science. Incredible breakthroughs have been made in our understanding of trauma, addiction, and harmful behavior, but still we unfairly ask men and women in blue uniforms to go out every day and sweep away those who might otherwise benefit from these scientific breakthroughs.[33] The time for emotional evolution is long past due. A higher order is needed.

We must fully enter the current century, building the infrastructure needed to bring opportunity to scale, to make healing a habit. Only then will peace take root. If we keep reinforcing narrow laws that have little to do with helping people change, then we are indeed the greatest offenders. Tomorrow's addicts and murder victims will be our responsibility, as we will have failed to act.

We cannot spend another generation talking about reentry and reform while elementary classrooms remain overcrowded and their teachers overextended. When parents in high-incarceration areas lack the supports they need for their babies and toddlers, are we not stacking the deck yet again? If youth have nowhere supportive to go after school lets out, then how can we still be surprised when they wander into deep trouble?

Hope is not a pipe dream. It is not a playground for liberals nor a foolish curiosity for naive idealists. It is a core responsibility of being alive. But it cannot simply be felt; it must actually be constructed. If we stand around and applaud millions of dollars going into violence prevention programs, while billions flow into a broken approach that grows the conditions in which violence takes place, then who can really be surprised when little changes?

The flow of investments into neighborhoods like Austin must be switched over, from that which dooms the future to that which makes it possible for future generations to thrive. Anything less is a betrayal.

ACKNOWLEDGMENTS

IDEAS DO NOT EXIST IN ISOLATION. They are inherently interpersonal. Each thought is a gathering ground for truths and the people who've inspired them, especially in qualitative research, where arguments are constructed directly from the life experiences of others. First and foremost, we are grateful to the people who shared their stories with us, allowing us to enter their lives, even as many of them struggled to overcome mountainous obstacles.

We have been powerfully shaped by our mentors, both formal and informal. Key figures in our studies include Nik Theodore, Beth Richie, Dave Stovall, Rachel Weber, Janet Smith, Jamie Peck, Deborah Gould, Douglas Perkins, Paul Speer, and Phil Ashton. Not only did they pour their best thinking into ours, they modeled socially responsible scholarship in powerful ways. In particular, Nik helped Ryan to make the transition from concerned citizen to disciplined analyst without sacrificing his underlying commitment to creating a better world.

Our families are the foundation for everything we do. That certainly includes this book. Ryan is forever grateful to his wife, Michelle, and daughter, Olivia, for their patience with the process, their unconditional support and unbound brilliance, and their daily reminders that real life is lived outside the word processor. While Olivia endured the writing journey largely unwittingly, Michelle consciously and graciously stood in the gap, enabling the project to move forward at each key turn. Ryan's parents, Vicki and Les, and siblings, Rachel and Steven, as well as his extended family, Ellam, Freddy, Tom, and Paige, have all helped him to stay strong, sharp, and connected. Les, Vicki, and Michelle—if only the larger world could share your heart, such books would not be needed.

Daniel would like to thank friends and family whose help made his contributions to this book possible. Elena, Brad, Judah, Romeo, Tram, John, Jim, Zara, James, Matt, Jon, and Linda: *thank you.* The many meals, miles, and stories shared have added up to precisely the supports he needed.

We both are forever indebted to the restorative justice community of Chicago, as well as the larger web of change makers who keep the flames of hope burning, despite the fierce headwinds. Cheryl Graves, Ora Schub, Elena Quintana, Eddie Bocanegra, Mariame Kaba, Tracy Siska, Paul Hannah, Dave Stovall, Nancy Michaels, Andy Born, Cliff Nellis, Kathryn Bocanegra, Juliana Stratton, Chuy Garcia, Colleen Sheehan, John Ziegler, Barbara Engel, Peter Newman, Alice Kim, Erica Meiners, Lynn Cohn, Darnell Shields, Ana Mercado, Vinay Ravi, Harish Patel, Illana Walden, Charity Tolliver, Amisha Patel, Malcom London, LaCreshia Birts, Chris Huff, Eve Ewing, Forrest Greg, Derek Eder, Meg Helder, Richard Malone, Paula Wolff, Era Laudermilk, Fanny Diego Alvarez, Cosmos Boekell, Tiffany Childress Price, Sonia Matthews, Mildred Wiley, and Theodore Richards: you all carry the torch with extraordinary grace. Thanks also to the individuals and organizations of the Right on Justice Coalition, and special thanks to Grace Hou, Hina Mahmood, Elena Quintana, Jenny Arwade, and Raul Botello for your leadership and dedication.

Finally, thank you to the word warriors who've helped us sharpen our craft. Will Myers, Jill Petty, and Susan Lumenello, you've made this book possible and, at least at times, pleasurable to write. Sheila Black, Jeff Cowart, Michelle Lugalia-Hollon, Larry McEnerny, Daniel Tucker, Vicki and Rachel Hollon, Romeo Oros, James Manos, John Breland, Eula Biss, Sue Avila, Linda Murray, Katie Hill, Mildred Williamson, and Matt Barrington, you've helped make it one of the great learning experiences of our lives. Your investments will long be with us.

NOTES

INTRODUCTION: THE HEROIN HIGHWAY

1. Alexia Elejalde-Ruiz, "Chicago's Racial Employment Gaps among Worst in Nation," *Chicago Tribune*, May 25, 2016, http://www.chicagotribune.com /business/ct-brookings-disconnected-youth-report-0525-biz-20160524 -story.html.

2. "In two Chicago neighborhoods, Burnside and Fuller Park, the homicide rate eclipsed 100 per 100,000 residents last year [in 2015], more than five times the Chicago average, and more than 25 times the typical New York neighborhood." Daniel Hertz, "The Debate Over Crime Rates is Ignoring the Metric that Matters Most: "Murder Inequality," *Trace*, July 25, 2016.

3. Robert J. Sampson, *Great American City: Chicago and the Enduring Neighborhood Effect* (Chicago: University of Chicago Press, 2012), 113.

4. Nearly 40 percent of Chicago's operating budget goes to its police department. "Chicago Police Spending Budget Strip," American Friends Service Committee, June 16, 2016, https://www.afsc.org/resource/chicago-police-spending-budget -strip. Started under Richard M. Daley, Chicago has a decades-long history of using a tool called Tax Increment Financing to redirect general tax dollars to downtown investments. As mayor, Rahm Emmanuel has continued this regressive tradition. Ben Joravsky has covered this trend in great detail. For a recent piece, see Joravsky, "Who Wins and Loses in Rahm's TIF Game?," *Chicago Reader*, March 26, 2015.

5. This campus, just southwest of downtown, is known for its Brutalist architecture. It was originally lauded for its efficiency. "U. of I. Campus Seen as Model Urban College," *Chicago Tribune*, February 15, 1965; Jill Zarlenga and Robert Loerzel, "Displaced: When the Eisenhower Expressway Moved In, Who Was Forced Out?," Curious City series, WBEZ Chicago, August 28, 2016.

6. Marc Doussard, Jamie Peck, and Nik Theodore, "After Deindustrialization: Uneven Growth and Economic Inequality in 'Postindustrial' Chicago," *Economic Geography* 85, no. 2 (2009): 183–207, doi:10.1111/j.1944–8287.2009.01022.x.

7. Heather Ann Thompson, "Inner-City Violence in the Age of Mass Incarceration," *Atlantic*, October 30, 2014; Jonathan Simon, *Governing Through*

Crime: How the War on Crime Transformed American Democracy and Created a Culture of Fear (Oxford, UK: Oxford University Press, 2007).

8. Authors' analysis, 2015 American Community Survey, Median Household Income. https://factfinder.census.gov.

9. Rex W. Huppke, "Oak Park, Do You Think You're Sexy? Well, One Author Does, Putting You Up There with La Jolla, Calif., and Coral Gables, Fla.," *Chicago Tribune*, July 24, 2005.

10. Ta-Nehisi Coates, "The Case for Reparations," *Atlantic*, June 2014, https://www.theatlantic.com/magazine/archive/2014/06/the-case-for-reparations/361631.

11. John Komlos, "In America, Inequality Begins in the Womb," PBS *NewsHour*, May 20, 2015, http://www.pbs.org/newshour/making-sense/america-inequality-begins-womb.

12. John A. Powell, "Structural Racism: Building upon the Insights of John Calmore," *North Carolina Law Review* 86, no. 3 (2007): 791–816.

13. Patrick Sharkey, *Stuck in Place: Urban Neighborhoods and the End of Progress Toward Racial Equality* (Chicago: University of Chicago Press, 2013).

14. The year 2014 saw 10,574 deaths related to heroin. This data reflects "two distinct but interrelated trends," the CDC notes: a long-term increase in overdose deaths due to prescription opioids and a surge in illicit opioid overdose deaths, mostly related to heroin. CNN Wire, "Drugs Now Kill More People Than Cars and Guns," 5newsonline KFSM, September 2, 2016, http://5newsonline.com/2016/09/24/drugs-now-kill-more-people-than-cars-and-guns.

15. Jen Christensen and Sergio Hernandez, "This Is America on Drugs: A Visual Guide," *CNN*, June 23, 2017, http://www.cnn.com/2016/09/23/health/heroin-opioid-drug-overdose-deaths-visual-guide.

16. Josh Katz, "Drug Deaths in America Are Rising Faster Than Ever," *New York Times*, June 5, 2017.

17. Jonathan Rothwell, "How the War on Drugs Damages Black Social Mobility," Brookings Institute, September 30, 2014, https://www.brookings.edu/blog/social-mobility-memos/2014/09/30/how-the-war-on-drugs-damages-black-social-mobility.

18. Peter Wagner, "Incarceration Is Not an Equal Opportunity Punishment," Prison Policy Initiative, August 28, 2012, https://www.prisonpolicy.org/articles/notequal.html.

19. Public Safety Performance Project, "Federal Drug Sentencing Laws Bring High Cost, Low Return," issue brief, Pew Charitable Trusts, August 27, 2015, http://www.pewtrusts.org/en/research-and-analysis/issue-briefs/2015/08/federal-drug-sentencing-laws-bring-high-cost-low-return.

20. Sara Wakefield and Christopher Wildeman, *Children of the Prison Boom: Mass Incarceration and the Future of American Inequality* (New York: Oxford University Press, 2014).

21. For decades now, US drug policy has attempted to uproot drug addiction by punishing the frontline workers of the drug market, a fact that forever changed

the life of Harold, his family, and millions like him. These joint disparities—
in how people are treated based on their skin color and resources as well as
in what counts as a serious crime—help to explain why, although African
Americans are significantly less likely to abuse hard drugs, they "are disproportionately incarcerated for drug crimes." Leah J. Welty et al. "Health Disparities
in Drug- and Alcohol-Use Disorders: A 12-Year Longitudinal Study of Youths
after Detention," *American Journal of Public Health* 106, no. 5 (2016): 872–80.

22. Sampson, *Great American City*, 113.

23. Author's tabulation of Circuit Court of Cook County convictions between
2005 and 2009. Data made available by Chicago Justice Project, "Convicted in
Cook," Chicago Justice Project, http://convictions.smartchicagoapps.org.

24. Todd R. Clear et al., "Predicting Crime Through Incarceration: The Impact of
Rates of Prison Cycling on Rates of Crime in Communities," document no.
247318, National Institute of Justice, 2014, https://www.ncjrs.gov/App
/Publications/abstract.aspx?ID=269418.

25. Mark L. Hatzenbuehle et al. "The Collateral Damage of Mass Incarceration: Risk of Psychiatric Morbidity Among Nonincarcerated Residents of
High-Incarceration Neighborhoods," *American Journal of Public Health* 105,
no. 1 (2015): 138–43.

26. Peter Wagner and Bernadette Rabuy, "Mass Incarceration: The Whole Pie,"
press release, Prison Policy Initiative, March 14, 2017, https://www.prison
policy.org/reports/pie2017.html.

27. Authors' calculations, using data from Circuit Court of Cook County convictions and global incarceration rate comparisons from the International Centre
for Prison Studies. See the World Prison Brief website, at http://www.prison
studies.org/world-prison-brief-data. For more on international data, see Michelle Y. Hee Lee, "Yes, U.S. Locks People Up at a Higher Rate Than Any Other
Country," *Washington Post*, July 7, 2015, https://www.washingtonpost.com
/news/fact-checker/wp/2015/07/07/yes-u-s-locks-people-up-at-a-higher-rate
-than-any-other-country.

28. Lise McKean and Jody Raphael, *Drugs, Crime, and Consequences: Arrest and
Incarceration in North Lawndale* (Chicago: North Lawndale Employment Network and Center for Impact Research, 2002), http://www.saferfoundation.org
/files/documents/northlawndaleincarceration.pdf.

29. Christopher Muller and Christopher Wildeman, "Geographic Variation in the
Cumulative Risk of Imprisonment and Parental Imprisonment in the United
States," *Demography* 53, no. 5 (2016): 1499–509.

30. Robert J. Sampson and Charles Loeffler, "Punishment's Place: The Local
Concentration of Mass Incarceration," *Daedalus* 139, no. 3 (2010): 20–31. As
a technical term, "concentrated disadvantage" is a marker of relative poverty
across neighborhoods and is taken as a composite variable of "welfare receipt,
poverty, unemployment, female-headed households, racial composition (percentage black), and density of children." See Sampson, *Great American City*,

100. Relatedly, "cumulative disadvantage theory emphasizes how early advantage or disadvantage is critical to how cohorts become differentiated over time. Not only do the early risk factors shape trajectories in the short-term outcomes but in the long-term outcomes as well. The effects of risk factors accumulate over the life course, thereby increasing heterogeneity in later life." Kenneth Ferraro and Jessica Kelley-Moore, "Cumulative Disadvantage and Health: Long-Term Consequences of Obesity?," *American Sociological Review* 68, no. 5 (2003): 708.

31. Christopher Muller states that "criminal offending cannot be measured directly." Muller, "Northward Migration and the Rise of Racial Disparity in American Incarceration," *American Journal of Sociology* 118, no. 2 (2012): 283.

32. Analyses derived from Cook County Circuit Court data made available by Chicago Justice Project, "Convicted in Cook," http://convictions.smartchicagoapps.org.

33. Todd R. Clear, *Imprisoning Communities: How Mass Incarceration Makes Disadvantaged Neighborhoods Worse* (New York: Oxford University Press, 2009).

34. Loic Wacquant, *Deadly Symbiosis: Race and the Rise of Neoliberal Penalty* (Oxford, UK: John Wiley & Sons, 2015).

35. Cyndi Banks, *Criminal Justice Ethics: Theory and Practice* (Los Angeles: SAGE, 2017).

36. Retribution is rooted in vengeance. It is a moral position that says punishment provides an end all by itself. From the lens of retribution, incarceration creates pain for offenders by isolating them from everyone and everything they know and love. In contrast, incapacitation, deterrence, and rehabilitation are more practical positions, claiming that incarceration can prevent future wrongdoing. If someone is no longer allowed in society, then they can no longer pose a threat, their absence will serve as a warning to others, and their time away may be instructive for them. See Robert Nozick, *Philosophical Explanations* (Cambridge, MA: Harvard University Press, 1983), 366–68.

37. For example, in the bail-bonds industry. Shawn Carter, "Jay Z: For Father's Day, I'm Taking On the Exploitative Bail Industry," *Time*, June 16, 2017, http://time.com/4821547/jay-z-racism-bail-bonds.

38. Alicia R. Riley, "Neighborhood Disadvantage, Residential Segregation, and Beyond: Lessons for Studying Structural Racism and Health," *Journal of Racial and Ethnic Health Disparities* (June 1, 2017, advance online publication), doi:10.1007/s40615-017-0378-5. Detailed sociological accounts of neighborhoods like Austin often fail to capture the structural racism at play. Far too often, systemic racial bias is ignored and is explained away through an ahistorical concept called "neighborhood disadvantage." This concept functions as a catchall, referring to the predominance of dark-skinned residents, single-parent households, high unemployment and/or low-income salaries, and low education levels. In turn, these characteristics are associated with low

levels of human, social, and/or fiscal capital. While they include a long list of characteristics, most definitions of neighborhood disadvantage are ahistorical and fail to capture how many of these characteristics are a product of policy choices and structural violence.

39. To see the local concentration of incarceration across cities, see the Justice Atlas of Sentencing and Corrections (http://www.justiceatlas.org), which reveals the "place-based dimension of incarceration, re-entry, and community supervision in states around the country."

40. Aaron Marks, "These 5 Neighborhoods Supply Over a Third of NYC's Prisoners," *Gothamist*, May 1, 2013, http://gothamist.com/2013/05/01/these _interactive_charts_show_you_w.php.

41. Matthew R. Durose, Alexia D. Cooper, and Howard N. Snyder, *Recidivism of Prisoners Released in 30 States in 2005: Patterns from 2005 to 2010*, special report (Washington, DC: Bureau of Justice Statistics, April 2014), https://www .bjs.gov/content/pub/pdf/rprts05p0510.pdf.

42. For more on this idea and pattern, see We Are All Criminals, http://www.we areallcriminals.org.

43. DataMade, "Million Dollar Blocks," Chicago's Million Dollar Blocks, http:// chicagosmilliondollarblocks.com.

44. For more on the technical history of community areas, see Ann Durkin Keating's introduction, "Chicago Neighborhoods: Building Blocks of the Region," to her edited volume *Chicago Neighborhoods and Suburbs: A Historical Guide* (Chicago: University of Chicago Press, 2008).

45. See map "Seventy Statistical Areas of Chicago, Percentage Distribution of Committee of Fifteen Cases for 1910 to 1929," originally published in Walter C. Reckless, *Vice in Chicago* (Chicago: University of Chicago Press, c. 1933).

46. To the east is the Belt Railway line, which cuts across the city, hauling freight for many of the major railroad companies. The northern border is marked by a commuter-train line, transporting workers downtown from the northwestern suburbs. The southern border is marked by Roosevelt Road, which, since being named after President Theodore Roosevelt in 1919, has become a major artery connecting Chicago.

47. Jean Davidson, "Island Neighborhood Still Troubled by Image," *Chicago Tribune*, May 6, 1985, http://articles.chicagotribune.com/1985-05-06/news /8501270911_1_neighborhood-racial-predominantly-white-community.

48. Ibid.

49. Two striking features of Austin's life were his passion for prohibition and his strong disinclination toward foreclosures. Elected to the Illinois legislature in 1870, he was the champion of the Illinois Temperance Law, which aimed to curb not just alcoholism but also the domestic violence, neglect of children, and economic struggles commonly associated with it. Meanwhile, as a businessman, he had a reputation for never having the heart to foreclose a

mortgage on one of his properties. Over one hundred years later, both foreclosure and substance abuse proved to be issues that would heavily impact family
life in Austin. "Sudden Death of Henry W. Austin," *Chicago Tribune*, December
25, 1889.

50. For another perspective on how drugs impacted the neighborhood and the
dearth of policy responses, see Ben Joravsky, "Lost in Austin: Fighting Drugs,
Decay, and the City Bureaucracy on the Far West Side," *Chicago Reader*, June
30, 1988, http://www.chicagoreader.com/chicago/lost-in-austin-fighting-drug
s-decay-and-the-city-bureaucracy-on-the-far-west-side/Content?oid=872435.

51. Amanda I. Seligman, *Block by Block: Neighborhoods and Public Policy on Chicago's West Side* (Chicago: University of Chicago Press, 2005).

52. Simon, *Governing Through Crime*; US Department of Justice, "Investigation
of the Ferguson Police Department," Civil Rights Division, US Department of
Justice, Washington, DC, March 4, 2015, https://www.justice.gov/sites/default
/files/opa/press-releases/attachments/2015/03/04/ferguson_police_department
_report.pdf.

CHAPTER 1: HISTORY OF THE WAR

1. Sendhil Mullainathan, "A Top-Heavy Focus on Income Inequality," *New York
Times*, March 8, 2014, https://www.nytimes.com/2014/03/09/business/a-top
-heavy-focus-on-income-inequality.html; Whet Moser, "Chicago Isn't Just Segregated, It Basically Invented Modern Segregation," *Chicago Magazine*, March
31, 2017, http://www.chicagomag.com/city-life/March-2017/Why-Is-Chicago
-So-Segregated.

2. Corporation for Enterprise Development, *Racial Wealth Divide in Chicago*
(Washington, DC: Corporation for Enterprise Development, January 2017).

3. Richard Wilkinson and Kate Pickett, *The Spirit Level: Why Greater Equality
Makes Society Stronger* (New York: Bloomsbury Press, 2010).

4. Joint Center for Political and Economic Studies Health Policy Institute, *Place
Matters for Health in Cook County: Ensuring Opportunities for Good Health for All*
(Washington, DC: Joint Center for Political and Economic Studies, July 2012).

5. Alan Berube, *All Cities Are Not Created Unequal* (Washington, DC: Brookings
Institute, February 20, 2014).

6. Of these cities, San Francisco has the smallest African American population.
The neighborhood of Bayview–Hunters Point is rare as a majority African
American community and has been home to both intensive law enforcement
strategies and overt environmental racism. See Jaron Browne, "Court Blocks
Hunters Point Shipyard Redevelopment until Navy Completes Toxic Cleanup,"
San Francisco Bay View National Black Newspaper, September 16, 2011.

7. Reema Amin and Mario Lekovic, "School Closings in Austin to Impact Nearly
2,000 Students," *Austin Talks*, March 22, 2013.

8. For drug crimes, see We Are All Criminals. For more on the scale and scope of
white-collar crimes, see Rodney Huff, Christian Desilets, and John Kane, *The*

2010 National Public Survey on White Collar Crime (Fairmont, WV: National White Collar Crime Center, 2010), https://www.nw3c.org/docs/research/2010 -national-public-survey-on-white-collar-crime.pdf.

9. Odis Johnson Jr., "Is Concentrated Advantage the Cause? The Relative Contributions of Neighborhood Advantage and Disadvantage to Educational Inequality," *Urban Review* 45, no. 5 (2013): 561–85, doi:10.1007/s11256-013-0242-9.

10. Michelle Alexander, *The New Jim Crow: Mass Incarceration in the Age of Colorblindness* (New York: New Press, 2010); Loic Wacquant, "The Penalisation of Poverty and the Rise of Neo-Liberalism," *European Journal on Criminal Policy and Research* 9, no. 4 (2001): 401–12.

11. Coates, "The Case for Reparations."

12. Zarlenga and Loerzel, "Displaced."

13. Seligman, *Block by Block*. Oak Park has a unique history as a suburb that fought white flight. See Steven Jackson, "Integrated Solutions: How Oak Park, Illinois, Fought White Flight," *BackStory*, http://backstoryradio.org/blog/integrated -solutions.

14. Muller, "Northward Migration."

15. Sonia Benson, Daniel E. Brannen Jr., and Rebecca Valentine, *UXL Encyclopedia of US History* (Detroit: Gale, 2009), s.v. "Suburbanization"; Leah P. Boustan, "Was Postwar Suburbanization 'White Flight'? Evidence from the Black Migration," *Quarterly Journal of Economics* 125, no. 1 (2010): 417–43; "Austin: A Neighborhood in Trouble. Fiery Civic Group Fights 'Panic Peddlers,'" *Chicago Daily News*, December 16, 1967.

16. Zarlenga and Loerzel, "Displaced."

17. Here's how *Chicago Tribune* reporter William Mullen summed up the Eisenhower Expressway's impact in a 1985 article: "The destruction of neighborhoods by the construction of the inner-city expressways sent many people to the suburbs forever. Construction of the Eisenhower Expressway, for example, destroyed long-established, flourishing, seemingly permanent Italian and Jewish communities on the West Side, robbing the city of part of its ethnic diversity." Quoted in Zarlenga, "Displaced."

18. Beryl Satter, *Family Properties: How the Struggle over Race and Real Estate Transformed Chicago and Urban America* (New York: Picador, 2009), ch. 1.

19. Eric R. Avila, *The Folklore of the Freeway: Race and Revolt in the Modernist City* (Minneapolis: University of Minnesota Press, 2014); Adam Doster, "Could a New Plan Fix the Circle Interchange?" *Chicago Magazine*, April 24, 2013, http://www.chicagomag.com/Chicago-Magazine/The-312/April-2013/Illinois -department-of-transportation. Originally named the Congress Expressway, because it ran over what was once Congress Avenue, the road's moniker was changed by the Chicago City Council in 1964 to recognize the man who had guided the passage of the Federal Aid Highway Act in 1956. Famous Chicago news columnist Mike Royko later joked that this was Chicago's only Republican expressway.

20. Zarlenga and Loerzel, "Displaced."

21. Satter, *Family Properties*.

22. Khalil Gibran Muhammad, *The Condemnation of Blackness: Race, Crime, and the Making of Modern Urban America* (Cambridge, MA: Harvard University Press, 2010).

23. Muller, "Northward Migration."

24. Ibid., 283.

25. Ibid., 294–96. This issue is also explored in Noel Ignatiev, *How the Irish Became White* (New York: Routledge, 2009).

26. Ibid. See also "Chicago and the Great Migration, 1915–1950," Newberry, Digital Collections for the Classroom, http://dcc.newberry.org/collections/chicago-and-the-great-migration, retrieved October 5, 2017.

27. Seligman, *Block by Block*; Leah Platt Boustan, *Competition in the Promised Land: Black Migration and Racial Wage Convergence in the North, 1940–1970* (Cambridge, MA: National Bureau of Economic Research, 2008).

28. "Austin: A Neighborhood in Trouble." Indicating the racial fears at play among this network, one observer stated: "Negroes are moving in, whites are moving out, and the issues of how to keep Austin from becoming another black ghetto is dividing residents and setting one well-meaning civic group against the other."

29. Ibid.

30. Thomas Buck, "CTA Shutting Down 7 Rapid Transit Stations Today," *Chicago Tribune*, September 2, 1973.

31. David K. Fremon, *Chicago Politics, Ward by Ward* (Bloomington: Indiana University Press, 1988).

32. Jaime Fuller, "The 2nd Most Memorable SOTU: LBJ Declares War on Poverty," *Washington Post*, January 27, 2014; "Timeline: The War on Poverty," *Education Week*, January 23, 2015, http://www.edweek.org/ew/section/multimedia/war-on-poverty-timeline.html.

33. At the time, this fact entered public discussion through the work of the Sentencing Project and was echoed by President Bill Clinton and by most major national news outlets. Marc Mauer, *The Crisis of the Young African American Male and the Criminal Justice System*, report prepared for US Commission on Civil Rights (Washington, DC: Sentencing Project, April 15–16, 1999).

34. See Emily Dufton, "The War on Drugs: How President Nixon Tied Addiction to Crime," *Atlantic*, March 26, 2012.

35. See Todd Clear and Natasha Frost, *The Punishment Imperative: The Rise and Failure of Mass Incarceration in America* (New York: New York University Press, 2013).

36. Dan Baum, "Legalize It All: How to Win the War on Drugs," *Harper's Magazine*, April 2016, https://harpers.org/archive/2016/04/legalize-it-all; Tom LoBianco, "Report: Nixon Aide Says War on Drugs Targeted Blacks, Hippies," *CNN Politics*, March 24, 2016, http://edition.cnn.com/2016/03/23/politics/john

-ehrlichman-richard-nixon-drug-war-blacks-hippie/index.html; Julianne Escobedo Shepherd, "Nixon Policy Advisor Admits He Invented War on Drugs to Suppress 'Anti-War Left and Black People,'" *Jezebel*, March 22, 2016, http://jezebel.com/nixons-policy-advisor-admits-he-invented-war-on-drugs-t-1766359595.

37. See Andrew B. Whitford and Jeff Yates, *Presidential Rhetoric and the Public Agenda: Constructing the War on Drugs* (Baltimore: Johns Hopkins University Press, 2009), 57.

38. See James Austin and Aaron David McVey, "The 1989 NCCD Prison Population Forecast: The Impact of the War on Drugs," *NCCD Focus*, National Council on Crime and Delinquency, December 1989, https://www.ncjrs.gov/pdffiles1/Photocopy/122794NCJRS.pdf.

39. Whitford and Yates, *Presidential Rhetoric*, 58.

40. For an overview of "tough on crime" legislation across presidential administrations, see Arit John, "A Timeline of the Rise and Fall of Tough on Crime Drug Sentencing," *Atlantic*, April 22, 2014.

41. Human Rights Watch, *Targeting Blacks: Drug Law Enforcement and Race in the United States* (New York: 2008).

42. Daniel Burton-Rose, ed., *The Celling of America: An Inside Look at the US Prison Industry* (Monroe, ME: Common Courage Press, 1998), 246–47.

43. Human Rights Watch, "Punishment and Prejudice: Racial Disparities in the War on Drugs," accessed February 3, 2010, https://www.hrw.org/legacy/campaigns/drugs/war/key-facts.htm; Becky Pettit and Bruce Western, "Mass Imprisonment and the Life Course: Race and Class Inequality in U.S. Incarceration," *American Sociological Review* 69, no. 151 (2004): 151–69.

44. Pettit and Western, "Mass Imprisonment and the Life Course."

45. Riley, "Neighborhood Disadvantage, Residential Segregation, and Beyond."

46. Marie Gottschalk, *Caught: The Prison State and the Lockdown of American Politics* (Princeton, NJ: Princeton University Press, 2016).

47. Julilly Kohler-Hausmann, "Welfare Crises, Penal Solutions, and the Origins of the 'Welfare Queen,'" *Journal of Urban History* 41, no. 5 (2015): 756–71, doi: 10.1177/0096144215589942.

48. Tom Pelton, "Hawthorne Works' Glory Now Just So Much Rubble," *Chicago Tribune*, April 18, 1994, http://articles.chicagotribune.com/1994-04-18/news/9404180047_1_factory-taco-bells-hawthorne-works.

49. Ron Grossman, "Flashback: Sears Was the Amazon.com of the 20th Century," *Chicago Tribune*, May 12, 2017, http://www.chicagotribune.com/news/opinion/commentary/ct-sears-roebuck-homan-catalog-flashback-perspec-0514-jm-20170512-story.html; "Sears, Roebuck and Co.," Homan Square website, accessed June 4, 2017, http://www.homansquare.org/history/sears-roebuck-and-co. Over the years, Sears enlarged the Merchandise Building numerous times. These expansions helped make the building at one time the second-largest business structure of its kind in the world. The electricity supplied by the

powerhouse operated the ventilating system, escalators, and transmission belts for carrying merchandise between the stock departments and the shipping departments. Over nine miles of pneumatic tubing quickly transported letters and other papers from one department to another. "Store History—Chicago, Illinois," *Sears Archives*, 2012, http://www.searsarchives.com/stores/history _chicago_first.htm.

50. Jamie Peck and Nik Theodore, "Carceral Chicago: Making the Ex-Offender Employability Crisis," *International Journal of Urban and Regional Research* 32, no. 2 (2008): 6.

51. Healthcare employers include nursing homes and hospitals, namely, Loretto Hospital, West Suburban Hospital, and Shriner's Children's Hospital.

52. Compared to the manufacturing jobs of years past, these businesses generate little new income within the community. Instead, as local service industries with no real export function, these businesses typically cycle dollars outside Austin.

53. *Black Work Matters: The Fight for $15*, shot and edited by Terrence Thompson, Black Youth Project, 2015, online video, https://vimeo.com/124835182.

54. James Forman, *Locking Up Our Own: Crime and Punishment in Black America* (New York: Farrar, Straus and Giroux, 2017).

55. Robert D. Crutchfield, *Get a Job: Labor Markets, Economic Opportunity, and Crime* (New York: New York University Press, 2014).

56. Devah Pager, *Marked: Race, Crime, and Finding Work in an Era of Mass Incarceration* (Chicago: University of Chicago Press, 2007).

57. Peck and Theodore, "Carceral Chicago."

58. In 2010, the Illinois Department of Corrections had an operating budget of $1.22 billion and a recidivism rate of 51 percent. Of that money, only two community-based programs were being funded. Outside of these two minor exceptions, the entire corrections budget in Illinois was—and is—being spent to punish or supervise approximately 75,000 people every year.

59. "Justice Atlas of Sentencing and Corrections," Justice Mapping Center, http:// www.justiceatlas.org/, accessed June 1, 2017.

60. Research briefs and maps illustrating this concept can be found on Columbia University's Center for Spatial Research (formerly the Spatial Information Design Lab) website (http://c4sr.columbia.edu). See, for example, Eric Cadora et al., *Architecture and Justice* (New York: Spatial Information Design Lab, Columbia University Graduate School of Architecture, Planning and Preservation, 2006), http://www.spatialinformationdesignlab.org/MEDIA/PDF_04.pdf.

61. Assuming that individuals serve the minimum of the range of time for which they are sentenced. In Illinois, prisoners are required to serve at least 50 percent of their sentence, meaning some could be paroled earlier than this minimum sentence amount. It also assumes an average annual cost of $22,000, which is the average cost per prisoner based on the Illinois Department of Corrections annual budget for 2012, rather than a marginal cost of each additional

prisoner. Analyses derived from Cook County Circuit Court data made available by Chicago Justice Project, "Convicted in Cook," December 15, 2014, https://chicagojustice.org/2014/12/15/convicted-cook-release.

62. Author's tabulation of data obtained and released by Illinois Partners for Human Services, http://www.illinoispartners.org.

63. See note 63.

64. Angela Caputo, "Cell Blocks," *Chicago Reporter*, March 1, 2013, http://chicagoreporter.com/cell-blocks. According to Caputo, the Adams block in Austin had the highest incarceration costs in the city from 2000 to 2011.

65. "Ending the Schoolhouse to Jailhouse Track," Advancement Project website, 2012, http://www.advancementproject.org/issues/stopping-the-school-to-prison-pipeline.

66. Congressional Budget Office, "Trends in the Distribution of Household Income between 1979 and 2007," Pub. No. 4031, US Congress, Congressional Budget Office, October 25, 2011.

67. Noreen S. Ahmed-Ullah, John Chase, and Bob Secter, "CPS Approves Largest School Closure in Chicago's History," *Chicago Tribune*, May 23, 2013.

68. Steve Bogira, "Deadly Poverty," *Chicago Reader*, August 22, 2012, https://www.chicagoreader.com/chicago/poverty-and-segregation-cause-health-mortality-disparities/Content?oid=7256286.

69. Wacquant, *Deadly Symbiosis*.

70. Elvia Malagon, "Nearly 40 Shot in Chicago over Weekend, but Gun Violence Still Behind Last Year," *Chicago Tribune*, May 22, 2017; Ryan S. King, Marc Mauer, and Malcolm C. Young, *Incarceration and Crime: A Complex Relationship* (Washington, DC: Sentencing Project, 2005); Marc Mauer and Nazgol Ghandnoosh, "Fewer Prisoners, Less Crime: A Tale of Three States," policy brief, Sentencing Project, Washington, DC, 2014.

71. Tim Dickinson, "Why America Can't Quit the Drug War," *Rolling Stone*, May 5, 2016, http://www.rollingstone.com/politics/news/why-america-cant-quit-the-drug-war-20160505.

72. Bruce Western et al., "Stress and Hardship after Prison," *American Journal of Sociology* 120, no. 5 (2015): 1512–47.

73. Alex Nitkin, "50 Years Ago MLK Lived In, Led Fair Housing Fight from Chicago's West Side," *DNA Info*, January 25, 2015.

74. David Bernstein, "The Longest March," *Chicago Magazine*, August 2016, http://www.chicagomag.com/Chicago-Magazine/August-2016/Martin-Luther-King-Chicago-Freedom-Movement.

75. Frank James, "Martin Luther King Jr. in Chicago," *Chicago Tribune*, 2017, http://www.chicagotribune.com/news/nationworld/politics/chi-chicagodays-martinlutherking-story-story.html.

76. Ibid.

77. As covered in the PBS documentary *Black America Since MLK: And Still I Rise* (2016), the movement had helped black people come out of the shadows.

78. Steve Bogira, "A Dream Unrealized for African-Americans in Chicago," *Chicago Reader*, August 21, 2013, http://www.chicagoreader.com/chicago/african-american-percentage-poverty-unemployment-schools-segregation/Content?oid=10703562.
79. Ibid.
80. Douglas Martin, "Gale Cincotta, 72, Opponent of Biased Banking Policies," *New York Times*, August 17, 2001.
81. Once known as the West Side's worst high school, the Austin High School campus has been broken up into three smaller schools, including the Austin Business and Entrepreneurship Academy and the Austin Polytechnical Academy. The second of these was started by Manufacturing Renaissance, a West Side organization working to build bridges between the Austin workforce and high-end manufacturing, often found in the suburbs. "Argie Seizes Austin High: The Shocking Story," *Austin Voice*, March 21 & March 28, 1995; Melissa Espana, "Trumpet Mouthpiece Business Helps Austin Students Show Their Mettle," *Chicago Sun-Times*, June 15, 2014.

CHAPTER 2: ADDICTED TO PUNISHMENT

1. Illinois Consortium on Drug Policy, "Timeline: Historical Drug Policy Changes and Number of Illinois Individuals Incarcerated for Drug Offenses from 1984 to 2002," May 2007.
2. Nicole D. Porter, *The State of Sentencing 2013: Developments in Policy and Practice* (Washington, DC: Sentencing Project, 2013), http://sentencingproject.org/wp-content/uploads/2015/11/State-of-Sentencing-2013.pdf.
3. Caputo, "Cell Blocks."
4. Ibid.
5. See Allen Feldman, *Formations of Violence: The Narrative of the Body and Political Terror in Northern Ireland* (Chicago: University of Chicago Press, 1991).
6. See Ruth Wilson Gilmore, *Golden Gulag: Prisons, Surplus, Crisis, and Opposition in Globalizing California* (Berkeley: University of California Press, 2007).
7. Lauren Weber, "More American Workers Are Testing Positive for Drugs," *Wall Street Journal*, May 16, 2017; Chad Brooks, "Employee Drug Use Continues to Rise," *Business News Daily*, May 19, 2017.
8. "Questions and Coincidences Arise in Fire Killing Big Tom," *Austin Voice*, 1994.
9. For an overview of heroin's impact on the West Side, see Kathleen Kane-Willis and Scott Metzger, *Hidden in Plain Sight: Heroin's Impact on Chicago's West Side*, report conducted for the West Side Heroin Task Force, Illinois Consortium on Drug Policy, August 2016. As this report documents, the publicly funded treatment options for users have been declining. For a deeper dive into these reductions, see Kathleen Kane-Willis et al., "Diminishing Capacity: The Heroin Crisis and Illinois Treatment in National Perspective," Illinois Consortium on Drug Policy, August 2015.

10. "West Side Neighborhoods Rank in the City's Top 10 for Violent Crime," *Austin Voice*, 1993. This violence persisted despite major drug busts. An example of such an operation is Project Triggerlock, a three-year investigation that targeted Vice Lords with stiff federal gun and drug laws in 1991. More than sixty members of the Vice Lords were arrested on narcotics and weapons charges, including thirty-eight who were indicted on federal charges. "Cops Smash Vice Lords!" *Austin Voice* 7, no. 3 (1991).

11. "The Cheese Stands Alone! Policeman Rick Miller Pleads Guilty to All Drug Charges," *Austin Voice* 5, no. 13 (1990).

12. "Mario Guilty! Faces 10 Years without Parole, $159,000 Fine, Feds Seize Store," *Austin Voice* 5, no. 16 (1990). Lettieri was convicted for being affiliated with the drug operation.

13. Matt O'Connor, "Austin Cops Sent to Prison," *Chicago Tribune*, October 19, 2001, http://articles.chicagotribune.com/2001-10-19/news/0110190048_1 _federal-sentencing-laws-prison-term-police-officers.

14. Angela Caputo, "Road to ruin," *Chicago Reporter*, March 1, 2013 http://chicago reporter.com/road-ruin/; Gloria Casas, "Heroin Highways Between Kane and Chicago Thriving, Officials Say," *Chicago Tribune*, March 30, 2017, http://www .chicagotribune.com/suburbs/aurora-beacon-news/news/ct-abn-aurora-heroin -st-0330-20170329-story.html.

15. John Lippert, Nacha Cattan, and Mario Parker, "Heroin Pushed on Chicago by Cartel Fueling Gang Murders," *Bloomberg*, September 16, 2013.

16. Kathleen Kane-Willis et al., "Understanding Suburban Heroin Use: Research Findings from the Reed Hruby Heroin Prevention Project at the Robert Crown Center for Health Education," Illinois Consortium on Drug Policy, 2011.

17. Kane-Willis and Schmitz-Bechteler, "A Multiple Indicator Analysis of Heroin Use in the Chicago Metropolitan Area: 1995 to 2002," Illinois Consortium on Drug Policy, 2004.

18. Kathleen Kane-Willis et al., "Heroin Use: National and Illinois Perspectives (2008–2010)," Illinois Consortium on Drug Policy, 2012.

19. Jack Houston, "Mayor Fires Shot in War on Drugs," *Chicago Tribune*, November 7, 1986. See also Deborah J. Vagins and Jesselyn McCurdy, *Cracks in the System: Twenty Years of the Unjust Federal Crack Cocaine Law* (New York: American Civil Liberties Union, October 2006).

20. John Kass, "Daley Enlists US in War on Drugs, Gangs," *Chicago Tribune*, October 23, 1992.

21. Muller and Wildeman, "Geographic Variation"; Alexia Elejalde-Ruiz, "Nearly Half of Young Black Men in Chicago Out of Work, Out of School: Report," *Chicago Tribune*, January 25, 2016. For more national context, see Bruce Western and Becky Pettit, "Incarceration and Social Inequality," *Daedalus* 139, no. 3 (2010): 8–19; and Craig Haney and Philip Zimbardo, "The Past and Future of U.S. Prison Policy: Twenty-Five Years After the Stanford Prison Experiment," *American Psychologist* 53, no. 7 (1998): 709–27.

22. Mick Dumke, "Heroin, LLC," *Chicago Reader*, December 4, 2013, http://www .chicagoreader.com/chicago/heroin-arrests-sales-dealers-west-sideeconomics /Content?oid=11722393.

23. Sarah Stillman, "Taken," *New Yorker*, August 12 and 19, 2013, http://www.new yorker.com/magazine/2013/08/12/taken.

24. Linda Greenhouse, "Supreme Court Roundup: Justices Uphold Civil Forfeiture as Anti-Drug Tool," *New York Times*, June 25, 1996, http://www.nytimes.com /1996/06/25/us/supreme-court-roundup-justices-uphold-civil-forfeiture-as -anti-drug-tool.html; John Burnett, "Cash Seizures by Police Prompt Court Fights," NPR, June 16, 2008, http://www.npr.org/templates/story/story.php ?storyId=91555835.

25. John R. Emshwiller and Gary Fields, "Federal Asset Seizures Rise, Netting Innocent with Guilty," *Wall Street Journal*, August 22, 2011, https://www.wsj.com /news/articles/SB10001424053111903480904576512253265073870.

26. Steven D. Levitt and Sudhir Alladi Venkatesh, "An Economic Analysis of a Drug-Selling Gang's Finances," *Quarterly Journal of Economics* 115, no. 3 (2000): 755–89.

27. Dan Immergluck, *Foreclosed: High Risk Lending, Deregulation, and the Undermining of America's Mortgage Market* (Ithaca, NY: Cornell University Press, 2009).

28. Johann Hari, "The Likely Cause of Addiction Has Been Discovered, and It Is Not What You Think," *Huffington Post*, January 20, 2015, http://www.huffingtonpost .com/johann-hari/the-real-cause-of-addicti_b_6506936.html.

29. US Department of Health and Human Services, *The Health Consequences of Smoking—50 Years of Progress: A Report of the Surgeon General* (Atlanta: US Department of Health and Human Services, Centers for Disease Control and Prevention, National Center for Chronic Disease Prevention and Health Promotion, Office on Smoking and Health, 2014); Centers for Disease Control and Prevention, *Alcohol-Related Disease Impact (ARDI)* (Atlanta: CDC, 2014). Given this discrepancy, one question is raised: Why was a war declared on illegal drugs that focused on such a small percentage of the culprits for American deaths? That is, why were the leading killers—tobacco and alcohol—not the leading targets? Notably, tobacco has a mighty political lobby behind it, one that has been working in overdrive ever since the lethal impacts of smoking started to become public record. Meanwhile, alcohol had already survived a domestic war, known as Prohibition, and had come out the clear winner.

30. Katz, "Drug Deaths in America."

31. Kane-Willis et al., "Diminishing Capacity."

32. Maia Szalavitz, *Unbroken Brain: A Revolutionary New Way of Understanding Addiction* (New York: Picador, 2016).

33. Maia Szalavitz, interview by Terry Gross, *Fresh Air*, KQED Public Radio, July 7, 2016, http://www.npr.org/sections/health-shots/2016/07/07/485087604 /unbroken-brain-explains-why-tough-treatment-doesnt-help-drug-addicts.

34. See Vincent J. Felitti et al., "Relationship of Childhood Abuse and Household Dysfunction to Many of the Leading Causes of Death in Adults: The Adverse Childhood Experiences (ACE) Study," *American Journal of Preventive Medicine* 14, no. 4 (1998): 245–58.

35. Gabor Maté, "Fixing Fentanyl Means Treating Trauma that Creates Addicts," *CBC News*, February 23, 2017, http://www.cbc.ca/news/canada/british-columbia /fixing-fentanyl-means-treating-trauma-that-creates-addicts-1.3966361; Jane Stevens, "Substance-Abuse Doc Says: Stop Chasing the Drug! Focus on ACEs," *ACEs Connection*, May 1, 2017, http://www.acesconnection.com/blog/substance -abuse-doc-says-stop-chasing-the-drug-and-focus-on-the-aces.

36. See "New Poll Suggest Surprising Support for Criminal Justice Reforms Among Trump Voters," Charles Koch Institute (blog), https://www.charleskochinstitute .org/news/new-poll-suggests-surprising-support-criminal-justice-reforms -among-trump-voters/, accessed October 5, 2017.

37. Ekow Yankah, "There Was No Wave of Compassion When Addicts were Hooked on Crack," interview by Judy Woodruff, *PBS News Hour,* March 29, 2016, http://www.pbs.org/newshour/bb/there-was-no-wave-of-compassion -when-addicts-were-hooked-on-crack.

38. Harold Pollack, "The Most Embarrassing Graph in American Drug Policy," *Wonkblog* (blog), *Washington Post*, May 29, 2013, https://www.washingtonpost .com/news/wonk/wp/2013/05/29/the-most-embarrassing-graph-in-american -drug-policy.

39. Author analysis of data from Cook County Circuit Court, 2005–2009.

40. Jason McGahan, "Why Mexico's Sinaloa Cartel Loves Selling Drugs in Chicago," *Chicago Magazine*, September 17, 2013; Steven Reinberg, "Heroin Epidemic Expands Its Grip on America," *Chicago Tribune*, March 30, 2017.

41. The idea that "we are asking police to do too much" has also been advanced by David Brown, former police superintendent of Dallas. Michael J. Mooney, "The Empathy of David Brown," *Texas Monthly*, May 2017, http://features.texas monthly.com/editorial/the-empathy-of-david-brown.

42. Ronald A. Heifetz and Donald L. Laurie, "The Work of Leadership," *Harvard Business Review* (January–February 1997); Ronald A. Heifetz and Marty Linsky, *Leadership on the Line: Staying Alive Through the Dangers of Leading* (Boston: Harvard Business School Press, 2002).

43. David Downs, "Oakland Green Lights Drug War Reparations, Passes Marijuana Equity Program," *East Bay Express*, May 17, 2016, https://www.eastbay express.com/LegalizationNation/archives/2016/05/17/oakland-green-lights -drug-war-reparations-passes-marijuana-equity-program.

CHAPTER 3: A CYCLE UNBROKEN

1. There are major differences in the number of total homicides across these periods, as articulated by Andrew Papachristos in his op-ed "Chicago Is Safer Now, but You Can't Tell," *Chicago Tribune*, September 18, 2014. However, as we

argue, the safety gains he references are only temporary in nature, built upon a flawed approach that fails to address root causes.

2. Heather Cherone, "New $95 Million Police, Fire Training Academy Planned for Garfield Park," *DNA Info*, July 3, 2017, https://www.dnainfo.com/chicago /20170703/garfield-park/new-police-fire-academy-training-first-responder -department-mayor-rahm-emanuel.

3. For evidence on the relationship between concentrated disadvantage and youth-on-youth homicide in urban cities, see John M. MacDonald and Angela R. Gover, "Concentrated Disadvantage and Youth-on-Youth Homicide: Assessing the Structural Covariates over Time," *Homicide Studies* 9, no. 1 (2005): 30, 40–44. For more on the relationship between inequality and violence, see Jeffrey D. Morenoff, Robert J. Sampson, and Stephen W. Raudenbush, "Neighborhood Inequality, Collective Efficacy, and the Spatial Dynamics of Urban Violence," *Criminology* 39, no. 3 (2001): 517–58.

4. City of Chicago, "Executive Summary," *Chicago Violence Prevention Strategic Plan* (Chicago, 1996), 1–37, https://www.cityofchicago.org/dam/city/depts /cdph/chron_dis/general/Office_Violence_Prevention/OVP_Chicago_Violence _Prevention_Strategic_Plan.pdf. For a more recent example—in which the stated goal is "making Chicago the safest big city in America by 2020"—see City of Chicago and Cook County, *Community Anti-Violence Restoration Effort: City-County Action Plan* (Chicago, 2015), http://www.ccachicago.org/wp-content /uploads/2015/08/CARE4Community-Action-Plan.pdf.

5. Ryan Marx, "Chicago Homicide Data since 1957," *Chicago Tribune*, March 2, 2016, http://www.chicagotribune.com/news/local/breaking/ct-chicago-homicides -data-since-1957-20160302-htmlstory.html.

6. Matt Ford, "What's Causing Chicago's Homicide Spike?," *Atlantic*, January 2017. See also "Chicago Murders," *DNA Info*, https://www.dnainfo.com /chicago/2017-chicago-murders, accessed October 5, 2017.

7. Even in the relatively peaceful times, some neighborhoods experience very low levels of violent crime while others have disturbingly high rates of incidents. Noah Berlatsky, "How Chicago Points to a Growing Inequality of Urban Violence," *Atlantic Cities*, October 3, 2013, http://www.theatlanticcities.com/neighborhoods /2013/10/how-chicago-points-growinginequality-urban-violence/7103; Daniel Hertz, "We've Talked about Homicide in Chicago at Least One Million Times, but I Don't Think This Has Come Up," *City Notes*, August 5, 2013, https://daniel kayhertz.com/2013/08/05/weve-talked-about-homicide-in-chicago-at-least-one -million-times-but-i-dont-think-this-has-come-up/.

8. Many individual, school, and community-level factors shape the context for violence. See Prevention Institute, *Preventing Violence: A Primer* (Oakland, CA: October 2009); and, on the role of community context in better understanding crime, Robert J. Sampson, "The Place of Context: A Theory and Strategy for Criminology's Hard Problems," *Criminology* 51, no. 1 (2013): 1–31. See also Esther Franco Payne and Paula Wolff, "Overcrowding Our Prisons Is a Failed

Policy," *Chicago Tribune*, January 31, 2014, http://articles.chicagotribune.com
/2014-01-31/news/ct-perspec-violence-0131-20140131_1_illinoisprisons-state
-youth-prisons-domestic-violence; and, on how incarceration complicates
economic challenges for already poverty-stricken communities, National
Research Council, "U.S. Should Significantly Reduce Rate of Incarceration;
Unprecedented Rise in Prison Population 'Not Serving the Country Well,' Says
News Report," press release, National Academies of Sciences, Engineering, and
Medicine, April 30, 2014, http://www8.nationalacademies.org/onpinews/news
item.aspx?RecordID=18613.

9. Duncan Campbell, "Nothing Stops a Bullet Like a Job," *Guardian*, November,
November 23, 1999.

10. There is, however, a growing number of research articles focused on trauma.
See National Center for PTSD, "PILOTS Update: Eitinger Classic Selected as
10,000th PILOTS Record," *PTSD Research Quarterly* 7, no. 6 (1996): 8, which
notes that the Published International Literature on Traumatic Stress (PILOTS)
database contained citations to 1,950 papers in 1991. Despite a well-established
understanding of how trauma exposure shapes antisocial behaviors, the
juvenile justice system has failed to address the experiences of trauma in those
that it serves. See Robert L. Listenbee Jr. et al., *Report of the Attorney General's
National Task Force on Children Exposed to Violence* (Washington, DC: US
Department of Justice, 2012), 171–91.

11. See Felitti et al., "Childhood Abuse and Household Dysfunction." The ACEs
study found a strong "relationship between the breadth of exposure to abuse or
household dysfunction during childhood and multiple risk factors for several
of the leading causes of death in adults" (251).

12. Jennifer N. Shaffer, "The Victim-Offender Overlap: Specifying the Role of Peer
Groups" PhD diss., Pennsylvania State University, 2003, 7, 30, https://www.ncjrs
.gov/pdffiles1/nij/grants/205126.pdf.

13. Beth Richie, *Arrested Justice: Black Women, Violence, and America's Prison
Nation* (New York: New York University Press, 2012).

14. Ibid.

15. Jeremy Gorner, "Gang Factions Lead to Spike in City Violence," *Chicago Tribune*, October 3, 2012; David Schaper, "Chicago 'Heroin Highway' Bust Shows
a 'New Face of Organized Crime,'" National Public Radio, June 2014; Leon
Neyfakh, "How Did Chicago Get So Violent?," *Slate*, September 2016.

16. "Harper High School: Part One," February 15, 2015, in *This American Life*, produced by Ira Glass, podcast, https://www.thisamericanlife.org/radio-archives
/episode/487/harper-high-school-part-one; Jenna Marie Stupar, "Gangsta's Paradise? How Chicago's Antigang Loitering Ordinance Punishes Status Instead of
Behavior," *DePaul Law Review* 64, no. 3 (2015), http://via.library.depaul.edu
/cgi/viewcontent.cgi?article=3947&context=law-review.

17. Ted Cox, "Rahm Avoids Criticizing 'Absentee Fathers' In Anti-Violence
Speech," *DNA Info*, September 2016.

18. See Michelle Lugalia-Hollon, "Black Lives Matter—A Call for Empathy," Praxis Center, Kalamazoo College, December 8, 2015, http://www.kzoo.edu/praxis /black-lives-matter.

19. For an extreme example of this argument, see S. Randall Humm, "Criminalizing Poor Parenting Skills as a Means to Contain Violence," *University of Pennsylvania Law Review* 139, no. 4 (1991): 1123–61.

20. Amanda Chan, "Police Sleep: Officers on Night Shift 14 Times More Likely to Be Sleep Deprived," *Huffington Post*, 2012, http://www.huffingtonpost.com /2012/07/21/police-sleep-shift-work-_n_1686727.html.

21. An important exception to this is the crisis-intervention training that has been implemented in the Chicago Police Department. See Rebecca Skorek and Christine Devitt Westley, "Evaluation of Chicago Police Department's Crisis Intervention Team for Youth Training Curriculum: Year 2," Illinois Criminal Justice Information Authority, Chicago, July 16, 2016. This exception is part of a larger national trend toward trauma-informed care. A leading city in this movement is San Antonio, Texas; see Troy Blevins, "SAPD's Crisis Intervention Training Program to Be Recognized," KSAT, October 2016, http://www.ksat .com/news/sapds-crisis-intervention-training-program-to-be-recognized.

22. Importantly, power is never restored directly to the survivor. See Danielle Allen, "Democratic Dis-ease: Of Anger and the Troubling Nature of Punishment," in *The Passions of Law*, ed. Susan Bandes (New York: New York University Press, 1999), 191–214.

23. Patrick J. Carr, Laura Napolitano, and Jessica Keating, "We Never Call the Cops and Here Is Why: A Qualitative Examination of Legal Cynicism in Three Philadelphia Neighborhoods," *Criminology* 45, no. 2 (2007): 445–80; Muller, "Northward Migration," 283.

24. Kay Pranis, Barry Stuart, and Mark Wedge, *Peacemaking Circles: From Conflict to Community* (St. Paul, MN: Living Justice Press, 2003).

25. Trauma is often transmitted across generations. Caregivers who have profound experiences of trauma can struggle to react appropriately to children's needs, and those maladaptive strategies can be taken on by their children. See Molly Castelloe, "How Trauma Is Carried Across Generations," *Psychology Today*, May 28, 2012, http://www.psychologytoday.com/blog/the-me-in-we/201205 /how-trauma-is-carried-across-generations; and "Multigenerational Trauma," Ranch website, October 6, 2010, http://www.recoveryranch.com/articles /trauma-and-ptsd-articles/multigenerational-trauma/.

26. Yana Kunichoff, "Should Communities Have a Say in How Residents Are Punished for Crime?," *Atlantic* (2017), https://www.theatlantic.com/politics/archive /2017/05/chicago-restorative-justice-court/524238.

27. The leading provider of this training has been the Community Justice for Youth Institute, directed by Cheryl Graves and Ora Schub. Major contributions have also been made by Project Nia, led by Mariame Kaba, and the Mansfield Institute at Roosevelt University, with trainings led by Nancy Michaels.

28. For more on First Nations traditions, see Wanda D. McCaslin, *Justice as Healing: Indigenous Ways* (St. Paul, MN: Living Justice Press, 2005).
29. Daniel J. Siegel, *Pocket Guide to Interpersonal Neurobiology: An Integrative Handbook of the Mind* (New York: W. W. Norton, 2012).
30. See M. G. Vaughn, M. O. Howard, and L. Harper-Chang, "Do Prior Trauma and Victimization Predict Weapon Carrying among Delinquent Youth?," *Youth Violence and Juvenile Justice* 4, no. 4 (2006): 314–27.
31. Maia Szalavitz and Bruce Perry, *Born for Love: Why Empathy Is Essential—and Endangered* (New York: William Morrow Paperbacks, 2011). As the book demonstrates, people exposed to extreme threats respond to the world differently, often developing faster reaction times and more impulsive reactions.
32. Esther Armah has developed the concept of "emotional justice" to shed light on this blind spot. See Dalila-Johari Paul, "Emotional Justice: What Black Women Want and Need," *Guardian*, December 3, 2015.
33. Richie, *Arrested Justice.*
34. John Bacon, "More Than 100 Wounded, 14 Killed in Chicago over July 4th Weekend," *USA Today*, July 5, 2017.

CHAPTER 4: THE SPACE BETWEEN

1. Emily Von Hoffman, "How Incarceration Infects a Community," *Atlantic*, March 2015.
2. Dana Ford, Rosa Flores, and Ed Payne, "Chicago's Homan Square Police Complex under Fire," *CNN*, December 22, 2015, http://www.cnn.com/2015/12/15/us/chicago-homan-square-hearing/index.html.
3. Fifty-seven people received a total of $5.5 million in torture reparation. As so often happens in Chicago, no progress would have been made in acknowledging this history of torture without the work of extremely committed activists. See Flint Taylor, "How Activists Won Reparations for the Survivors of Chicago Police Department Torture," *In These Times*, June 26, 2015; Merrit Kennedy, "Decades Later, Victims of Chicago Police Torture Paid Reparations," National Public Radio, January 5, 2016, http://www.npr.org/sections/thetwo-way/2016/01/05/462040444/decades-later-victims-of-chicago-police-torture-paid-reparations.
4. "Citizens Forcing Cops to Make Community Policing Work," *Austin Voice*, 1993; Ted Cox, "Rahm Rails against Gangbangers in Tavon Tanner Shooting: 'No Moral Remorse,'" *DNA Info*, (2016), https://www.dnainfo.com/chicago/20160810/west-town/rahm-rails-against-gangbangers-tavon-tanner-shooting-no-moral-remorse. Also, "More than simply a remnant of the southern environment they left behind, African Americans' distrust of the criminal justice system sprang from early evidence that they could not rely on police—even in the promised land—to protect or process them impartially." Muller, "Northward Migration," 312–13.
5. The Supreme Court struck down this law in a 6–3 vote. In her opinion, Justice Sandra Day O'Connor wrote, "There remain open to Chicago reasonable

alternatives to combat the very real threat posed by gang intimidation and vio-lence." See Linda Greenhouse, "Loitering Law Aimed at Gangs Is Struck Down by High Court," *New York Times*, June 11, 1999.

6. Richard Dvorak, assistant public defender, quoted in Eric Ferkenhoff, "Newly Written Anti-Loitering Code Faces Test," *Chicago Tribune*, February 27, 2002, http://articles.chicagotribune.com/2002-02-27/news/0202270045_1_gang -members-anti-gang-loitering.

7. Ferkenhoff, "Newly Written Anti-Loitering Code."

8. George L. Kelling and James Q. Wilson, "Broken Windows: The Police and Neighborhood Safety," *Atlantic*, March 1982.

9. Bernard Harcourt, *Illusion of Order: The False Promise of Broken Windows Policing* (Cambridge, MA: Harvard University Press, 2005), 161.

10. For a deep dive on this school of thought, see Anthony A. Braga and David L. Weisburd, *Policing Problem Places: Crime Hot Spots and Effective Prevention* (New York: Oxford University Press, 2010).

11. Jeremy Travis, "But They All Come Back: Rethinking Prisoner Reentry," *Sentencing and Corrections* 7 (May 2000), https://www.ncjrs.gov/pdffiles1/nij/181413.pdf.

12. For example, at the dawn of the millennium, the commanders of Austin's Fifteenth and Twenty-Fifth Districts said they wanted to rid Austin of all public drug sales by the end of 2000, a goal they pursued by targeting ten priority lo-cations. See "Drug Area Shut-Down Project Launched with Praise from Austin Leaders and Police," *Austin Voice*, 2000.

13. As such, these zones perpetuate the false idea that punishment, and the surveil-lance that often precedes it, leads to safety. Strategies like this always fall short. This particular effort has been strangely separate from the CPD's official com-munity policing strategy. Mick Dumke, "The Mayor Doesn't Know Who We Are," *Chicago Reader* (2012), http://www.chicagoreader.com/Bleader/archives /2012/03/29/the-mayor-doesnt-know-who-we-are.

14. This model was developed by David Kennedy, now at the John J. College of Criminal Justice. See Kennedy, *Don't Shoot: One Man, a Street Fellowship, and the End of Violence in Inner-City America* (New York: Bloomsbury USA, 2012).

15. Authors' tabulation of publicly available crime data set: "Crimes 2012" data set, *Chicago Data Portal*, City of Chicago, accessed June 5, 2017, https://data.city ofchicago.org.

16. "Citizens Forcing Cops to Make Community Policing Work," *Austin Voice*, 1993.

17. Even Harold Washington, Chicago's only African American mayor, was no exception. See Toussaint Losier, "'The Public Does Not Believe the Police Can Police Themselves': The Mayoral Administration of Harold Washington and the Problem of Police Impunity," *Journal of Urban History* (May 26, 2017, advance online publication), doi:10.1177/0096144217705490.

18. Joel Rose, "Despite Laws and Lawsuits, Quota-Based Policing Lingers," NPR, April 4, 2015, http://www.npr.org/2015/04/04/395061810/despite-laws-and -lawsuits-quota-based-policing-lingers.

19. Leon Neyfakh, "No Deal," *Slate*, April 2015.

20. Dana Bartholomew, "Cops Claim Harassment for Speaking Up against Alleged LAPD Arrest Quotas," *Los Angeles Daily News*, May 3, 2016, http://www.daily news.com/general-news/20160503/cops-claim-harassment-for-speaking-up -against-alleged-lapd-arrest-quotas; Sarah Wallace, "I-Team: NYPD Lieutenant Latest Cop to Say Department Enforces Quota," *NBC New York* (2016), http:// www.nbcnewyork.com/investigations/NYPD-Lieutenant-Says-There-Are -Quotas-I-Team-Wallace-374307721.html.

21. Mick Dumke and Ben Joravsky, "The Grass Gap," *Chicago Reader*, July 7, 2011. See also Katherine Beckett, Kris Nyrop, and Lori Pfingst, "Race, Drugs, and Policing: Understanding Disparities in Drug Delivery Arrests," *Criminology* 44, no. 1 (2006): 105–37.

22. Kathleen Kane-Willis et al., "Patchwork Policy: An Evaluation of Arrests and Tickets for Marijuana Misdemeanors in Illinois," Illinois Consortium on Drug Policy, May 2014.

23. Harcourt, *Illusion of Order*.

24. Progress has since been made toward this end. See Steve Schmadeke, "Arrestees to Get Access to Lawyers Free of Charge at Chicago Police Stations," *Chicago Tribune*, May 14, 2017.

25. Since the time of our interview, Elizabeth's organization has built serious momentum toward realizing this vision. See Erica Demarest, "Free Attorneys Coming to Police Stations, Chief Judge Says," *DNA Info*, March 14, 2017, https:// www.dnainfo.com/chicago/20170314/little-village/free-attorneys-coming -police-stations-chief-judge-says.

26. Andrew Cohen, "Eric Holder: A 'State of Crisis' for the Right to Counsel," *Atlantic*, March 15, 2013, https://www.theatlantic.com/national/archive /2013/03/eric-holder-a-state-of-crisis-for-the-right-to-counsel/274074; Alexa Van Brunt, "Poor People Rely on Public Defenders Who Are Too Overworked to Defend Them," *Guardian*, June 17, 2015, https://www.the guardian.com/commentisfree/2015/jun/17/poor-rely-public-defenders-too -overworked.

27. Daniel T. Coyne, "A Report on Chicago's Felony Courts," Chicago Appleseed Fund for Justice Criminal Justice Project, December 2007, member of advisory board, unpublished report, January 2007, http://scholarship.kentlaw.iit.edu/ fac_schol/189.

28. Merrit Kennedy, "Chicago Police Respond to Domestic Disturbance, Shoot and Kill Teen, Neighbor," National Public Radio, December 26, 2015, http:// www.npr.org/sections/thetwo-way/2015/12/26/461119329/chicago-police -respond-to-domestic-disturbance-shoot-dead-teen-and-neighbor; Mariame Kaba, "All of Chicago—Not Just Its Police—Must See Systemic Change to Save Black Lives," *Guardian*, December, 28, 2015, https://www.theguardian .com/commentisfree/2015/dec/28/all-chicago-not-just-police-systemic -change-save-black-lives.

29. Wesley Lowery et al., "Distraught People, Deadly Results," *Washington Post*, June 30, 2015, http://www.washingtonpost.com/sf/investigative/2015/06/30/ distraught-people-deadly-results.

30. "Laquan McDonald's Journey in Foster Care," editorial, *Chicago Tribune*, December 4, 2015.

31. David Matthews and Jane Sabella, "Dante Servin Quits, Set to Collect Pension 4 Years after Killing Rekia Boyd," *DNA Info* (2016), https://www.dnainfo.com /chicago/20160517/garfield-park/dante-servin-quits-four-years-after-killing -rekia-boyd.

32. "Final Charge Dropped Against Detroit Cop in Fatal Raid," *CBS News*, January 30, 2015.

33. Annie Sweeney and Jeremy Gorner, "Cop Who Quit in Face of Firing for Fatal Shooting Seeking Disability Pay," *Chicago Tribune*, October 27, 2016.

34. Paul O'Neal was also killed by CPD officers. After being shot at by an officer while driving, he was shot again during a chase and was then handcuffed while dying.

35. See Citizens Police Data Project, https://cpdb.co/findings.

36. In January 2017, Donald Trump tweeted that he "will send in the Feds!" if Chicago's violence continues to escalate (@realDonaldTrump, January 24, 2017, 7:25 p.m.). He was only the latest of commentators to make that call, though he was the first sitting president to do so. Mitch Smith, "Chicago Police and Federal Agents to Team Up on Gun Violence," *New York Times*, June 30, 2017, https:// www.nytimes.com/2017/06/30/us/chicago-guns-violence-atf-police.html.

37. Nick Bumberg, "How Chicago Police Department Can Address Suicide Rate Among Officers," *WTTW Chicago Tonight*, February 13, 2017, http://chicago tonight.wttw.com/2017/02/13/how-chicago-police-department-can-address -suicide-rate-among-officers.

38. Timothy Mclaughlin, "Chicago Police Department Struggles with Officer Suicide," Reuters, May 4, 2017, http://www.reuters.com/article/us-chicago-police -suicide-idUSKBN180149.

39. John Marx, "Focus on Officer Wellness: Building Community Trust Requires Supporting Healthy Officers," *FBI Law Enforcement Bulletin* (2016), https://leb. fbi.gov/2016/october/focus-on-officer-wellness-building-community-trust -requires-supporting-healthy-officers.

40. Tanveer Ali and Heather Cherone, "Full Report: Read Justice Department's Report on Chicago Police Departmnet," *DNA Info* (2017), https://www.dnainfo .com/chicago/20170113/bronzeville/department-of-justice-report-chicago -police-department-loretta-lynch-full-report.

41. To access the letter, go to "Open Letter from Former US Attorney Zachary Fardon," March 13, 2017, *Chicago Tribune*, http://www.chicagotribune.com /news/local/breaking/ct-open-letter-zachary-fardon-20170313-htmlstory.html. Sharing the perspective of one of the top-ranking law enforcement leaders

in the country, Fardon's letter called for five policy changes. First, he called for a consent decree to ensure that an independent federal monitor oversees reforms at the CPD, a move that reinforces the DOJ report. Accompanying this call, Fardon argued for substantial increases in the policing budget and a permanent funding stream for youth centers in neighborhoods with high levels of violence. Next, he called for expanded federal law enforcement, with a special consolidated task force focused on violence through traditional aggressive strategies. He went on to argue that the disease of violence is now spread through social media. Shortly after his appeal for more federal officers, he wrote, "Don't send in the National Guard, send in the tech geeks. If a gang member makes CPD's Strategic Subject List, find a way to curb or realtime monitor that gang member's social media accounts." Fardon recognized that his proposal would worry some defenders of the First Amendment but wrote, "Let's test those limits. Lives are at stake." His final two appeals were to create a new youth center and to end a bail bond system that allows accused gang members and repeat gun offenders to leave confinement before their trials.

42. Jeremy Gorner, "ACLU, Chicago Police Agree to Changes on Controversial Street Stops," *Chicago Tribune*, August 7, 2015.

43. Jeremy Gorner, "Chicago Violence, Homicides and Shootings Up in 2015," *Chicago Tribune*, January 2, 2016 , http://www.chicagotribune.com/news/local /breaking/ct-chicago-police-violence-2015-met1-20160101-story.html.

44. Josh Sanburn and David Johnson, "Violent Crime Is On the Rise in U.S. Cities," *Time*, January 30, 2017, http://time.com/4651122/homicides-increase-cities -2016/.

45. Matt O'Connor, "Austin Cops Sent to Prison," *Chicago Tribune*, October 19, 2001, http://articles.chicagotribune.com/2001-10-19/news/0110190048_1 _federal-sentencing-laws-prison-term-police-officers.

46. Ibid.

CHAPTER 5: MISSING PARENTS

1. Devin Dwyer, "Obama Reflects on Absent Father in Gun Violence Appeal," *ABC News*, February 13, 2013, http://abcnews.go.com/blogs/politics/2013/02 /obama-reflects-on-absent-father-in-gun-violence-appeal.

2. Fran Spielman and Frank Main, "In Addressing Violence, Mayor Plans to Confront Absentee Fathers," *Chicago Sun-Times*, September 15, 2016, http:// chicago.suntimes.com/politics/in-addressing-violence-mayor-plans-to -confront-absentee-fathers.

3. Authors' analysis of publicly available "Crimes 2016" data set, *Chicago Data Portal*, City of Chicago, https://data.cityofchicago.org, accessed May 15, 2017.

4. "Are African Americans Ignoring Collapse of the Family?," *The O'Reilly Factor*, Fox News, July 16, 2012, http://www.foxnews.com/transcript/2012/07/17/are -african-americans-ignoring-collapse-family.html.

5. Julie Bosman, "Obama Sharply Assails Black Fathers," *New York Times*, June 16, 2008, http://www.nytimes.com/2008/06/16/us/politics/15cnd-obama.html.

6. See Megan Comfort, *Doing Time Together: Love and Family in the Shadow of the Prison* (Chicago: University of Chicago Press, 2007).

7. Justin Wolfers, David Leonhardt, and Kevin Quealy, "1.5 Million Missing Black Men," *New York Times*, April 20, 2015, https://www.nytimes.com/interactive/2015/04/20/upshot/missing-black-men.html.

8. Ibid.

9. "Incarcerated Women and Girls," fact sheet, Sentencing Project, Washington, DC, November 30, 2015, http://www.sentencingproject.org/publications/incarcerated-women-and-girls/.

10. Elizabeth Swavola, Kristine Riley, and Ram Subramanian, *Overlooked: Women and Jails in an Era of Reform* (New York: Vera Institute of Justice, 2016), http://www.safetyandjusticechallenge.org/wp-content/uploads/2016/08/overlooked-women-in-jails-report-web.pdf.

11. Wakefield and Wildeman, *Children of the Prison Boom*.

12. Natasha J. Cabrera et al., "Low-Income Nonresident Father Involvement with Their Toddlers: Variation by Fathers' Race and Ethnicity," *Journal of Family Psychology* 22, no. 4 (2008): 643–47.

13. Jo Jones and William D. Mosher, "Fathers' Involvement with Their Children: United States 2006–2010," *National Health Statistics Reports* 71, US Department of Health and Human Services, Washington, DC, December 20, 2013, https://www.cdc.gov/nchs/data/nhsr/nhsr071.pdf.

14. This story was part of an interview series conducted by Kathryn Bocanegra and Grant Buhr, "22 Year Sentence," for *Two Sides of Justice*, prod. Kathryn Bocanegra, audio file, accessed June 25, 2017, https://soundcloud.com/2sidesofjustice/sets.

15. Wakefield and Wildeman, *Children of the Prison Boom*.

16. Bryan L. Sykes and Becky Pettit, "Mass Incarceration, Family Complexity, and the Reproduction of Childhood Disadvantage," *Annals of the American Academy of Political and Social Science* 654, no. 1 (2014): 127–49.

17. Wakefield and Wildeman, *Children of the Prison Boom*.

18. William Rohe, "Reexamining the Social Benefits of Homeownership after the Housing Crisis," in *Homeownership Built to Last: Lessons from the Housing Crisis on Sustaining Homeownership for Low-Income and Minority Families*, ed. Eric S. Belsky, Christopher E. Herbert, and Jennifer H. Molinsky (Washington, DC: Brookings Institution Press, 2014).

19. Bruce Western, *Punishment and Inequality in America* (New York: Russell Sage Foundation, 2006).

20. Authors' analyses derived from the 2010 American Community Survey five-year estimates and Cook County Circuit Court data made available by the Chicago Justice Project. See "Convicted in Cook," chicagojusticeproject.org, December 15, 2014, https://chicagojustice.org/2014/12/15/convicted-cook-release/.

21. Our estimate is for adults between the ages twenty-five and fifty-four. It aligns exactly with the estimates described in Wolfers, Leonhardt, and Quealy, "1.5 Million Missing Black Men."

22. Lauren E. Glaze and Laura M. Maruschak, "Parents in Prison and Their Minor Children," *Bureau of Justice Statistics Special Report*, August 2008, revised March 30, 2010, https://www.bjs.gov/content/pub/pdf/pptmc.pdf.

23. Beth Molnar et al., "Effects of Neighborhood Resources on Aggressive and Delinquent Behaviors among Urban Youths," *American Journal of Public Health* 98, no. 6 (2007): 1086–93.

24. Western, *Punishment and Inequality*.

25. William J. Sabol and James P. Lynch, "Assessing the Longer-Run Effects of Incarceration: Impact on Families and Employment," in *Crime Control and Social Justice: The Delicate Balance*, eds. Darnell Hawkins, Samuel Myers Jr., and Randolph Stine (Westport, CT: Greenwood, 2003).

26. Kathryn Edin, "What Do Low-Income Single Mothers Say about Marriage?," *Social Problems* 47, no. 1 (2000): 112–33.

27. Western, *Punishment and Inequality*.

28. Matthew Desmond, *Evicted: Poverty and Profit in the American City* (New York: Crown, 2016).

29. Ibid.

30. Martin H. Teicher et al., "Developmental Neurobiology of Childhood Stress and Trauma," *Psychiatric Clinics of North America* 25, no. 2 (2002): 397–426.

31. Felitti et al., "Childhood Abuse and Household Dysfunction."

32. Ibid.

33. Scott Menard, "Short- and Long-Term Consequences of Adolescent Victimization," *Youth Violence Research Bulletin* 12, Office of Juvenile Justice and Delinquency Prevention, US Department of Justice (February 2002).

34. David Finkelhor et al., "Violence, Abuse, and Crime Exposure in a National Sample of Children and Youth," *Pediatrics* 124, no. 5 (2004): 1411–23.

35. Betty Hart and Todd R. Risely, "The Early Catastrophe: The 30 Million Word Gap by Age 3," *American Educator* (Spring 2003): 4–9.

36. Curtis Lawrence, "Austin: Parents' Imprisonment Tough on Kids," *Chicago Reporter*, November 13, 2006, http://chicagoreporter.com/austin-parents-imprisonment-tough-kids/.

37. Susan F. Cole et al., *Helping Traumatized Children Learn: Supportive School Environments for Children Traumatized by Family Violence* (Boston: Massachusetts Advocates for Children, Trauma and Learning Policy Initiative, 2005).

38. See Laverne S. Williams, "Mental Health Challenges Facing African American Youth in Urban Communities," PowerPoint presentation, n.d., http://www.njmhi.org/presentations/MH%20Challenges%20with%20AA%20Youth%20-%20Laverne%20Williams.pdf, accessed July 5, 2017.

39. Western, *Punishment and Inequality*.

40. Sampson, *Great American City.*

41. Clear, *Imprisoning Communities.*

42. Douglas Perkins et al., "Participation and the Social and Physical Environment of Residential Blocks: Crime and Community Context," *American Journal of Community Psychology* 18, no. 1 (1990): 83–115.

43. Jacob S. Rugh and Douglas S. Massey, "Racial Segregation and the American Foreclosure Crisis," *American Social Review* 75, no. 5 (2011): 629–51.

44. Immergluck, *Foreclosed.*

45. Clear et al., "Predicting Crime Through Incarceration."

46. Kim Manturuk, Mark Lindblad, and Roberto Quercia, "Friends and Neighborhoods: Homeownership and Social Capital Among Low- to Moderate-Income Families," *Journal of Urban Affairs* 32, no. 4 (2010): 471–88.

47. Molnar et al., "Effects of Neighborhood Resources."

48. Ibid.

49. John Kania and Mark Kramer, "Collective Impact," *Stanford Social Innovation Review* (Winter 2011).

50. Crimesider Staff, "Chicago Saw More Murders Than NYC, LA Combined," CBSnews.com, January 2, 2017, http://www.cbsnews.com/news/chicago-murders-shootings-2016-more-than-new-york-city-los-angeles-combined/.

51. Erin E. Holmes et al., "Meta-Analysis of the Effectiveness of Resident Fathering Programs: Are Family Life Educators Interested in Fathers?," *Family Relations* 59, no. 3 (2010): 240–52.

CHAPTER 6: MISSING SYSTEMS

1. In his first campaign, Emanuel said nothing of where these youth should go, and he certainly did not name the reasons they may have started roaming the streets in the first place.

2. Marisa de la Torre, Molly F. Gordon, Paul Moore, and Jennifer Cowhy, *School Closings in Chicago: Understanding Families' Choices and Constraints for New School Enrollment* (Chicago: University of Chicago Consortium on Chicago School Research, January 2015), https://consortium.uchicago.edu/sites/default/files/publications/School%20Closings%20Report.pdf.

3. Max Kapustin, Jens Ludwig, Marc Punkay, Kimberley Smith, Lauren Speigel, and David Welgus, *Gun Violence in Chicago, 2016* (Chicago: University of Chicago Crime Lab, January 2017).

4. Caputo, "Cell Blocks."

5. Stephanie Stullich, Ivy Morgan, and Oliver Schak, "State and Local Expenditures on Corrections and Education," policy brief, US Department of Education, Policy and Program Studies Service, Washington, DC, July 2016, https://www2.ed.gov/rschstat/eval/other/expenditures-corrections-education/brief.pdf.

6. Ibid. For additional analysis of prison expenditures versus social welfare expenditures in Illinois during this period, see Peck and Theodore, "Carceral Chicago," 6.

7. Johanna Wald and Daniel Losen, "Defining and Redirecting a School-to-Prison Pipeline," paper presented at School-to-Prison Pipeline Research Conference, Harvard University, May 16–17, 2003.

8. Kari Lydersen and Javier Ortiz, "More Young People Are Killed in Chicago Than Any Other American City," *Chicago Reader*, January 25, 2012, http://chicagoreporter.com/more-young-people-are-killed-chicago-any-other-american-city/.

9. And as was previously known, race was a key risk factor in getting shot, the study noted. For every 100,000 people, an average of 1 white person, 28 Hispanics, and 113 blacks became victims of nonfatal shootings every year in Chicago over the six-year study period.

10. Andrew V. Papachristos and Christopher Wildeman, "Network Exposure and Homicide Victimization in an African American Community," *American Journal of Public Health* 104, no. 1 (2013): 143–50.

11. For an overview of the developmental relationships framework, see Eugene Roehlkepartain et al., *Relationships First: Creating Connections That Help Young People Thrive* (Minneapolis: Search Institute, 2017).

12. Ian Lambie and Isabel Randell, "The Impact of Incarceration on Juvenile Offenders," *Clinical Psychology Review* 33, no. 3 (2013): 448–59.

13. Rolf Loeber and David P. Farrington, *Young Homicide Offenders and Victims: Risk Factors, Prediction, and Prevention from Childhood* (New York: Springer, 2011).

14. Anna Aizer and Joseph J. Doyle Jr., "Juvenile Incarceration, Human Capital and Future Crime: Evidence from Randomly-Assigned Judges," NBER Working Paper No. 19102, National Bureau of Economic Research, Cambridge, MA, June 2013.

15. Neal Hazel, *Cross-National Comparison of Youth Justice* (London: Youth Justice Board, 2008), http://dera.ioe.ac.uk/7996/1/Cross_national_final.pdf.

16. The majority of youth who enter juvenile detention have survived family and/or community violence. See Janet Wiig, Cathy Spatz Widom, and John A. Tuell, *Understanding Child Maltreatment and Juvenile Delinquency: From Research to Effective Program, Practice and Systematic Solutions* (Washington, DC: Child Welfare League of America Press, 2003).

17. Mark W. Lipsey, "The Primary Factors That Characterize Effective Interventions with Juvenile Offenders: A Meta-Analytic Overview," *Victims and Offenders* 4 (2009): 124–47.

18. Authors' tabulation of data released by the Cook County Temporary Juvenile Detention Center.

19. Juan Perez Jr., "CPS Makes Cuts to Alternative Programs for Dropouts, At-Risk Children," *Chicago Tribune*, March 22, 2017, http://www.chicagotribune.com/news/local/breaking/ct-chicago-alternative-school-budget-cuts-met-20170321-story.html.

20. Terry Dean and Robert Felton, "Brach Site School Plan Submitted: Activists Publicize Proposal to Convert Brach Site to College-Prep Campus," *Austin*

Weekly News, June 25, 2008, http://www.austinweeklynews.com/News/Articles /6–25–2008/Brach-site-school-plan-submitted/.

21. For a deeper dive, see Laura Dwyer-Lindgren et al., "Inequalities in Life Expectancy Among US Counties, 1980 to 2014: Temporal Trends and Key Drivers," *JAMA Internal Medicine* 177, no. 7 (2017): 1003–11.

22. Adeshina Emmanuel, "Chicago's Black Unemployment Rate Higher Than Other Large Metro Areas," *Chicago Reporter,* November 16, 2014, http://chicagoreporter .com/chicagos-black-unemployment-rate-higher-other-large-metro-areas/.

23. Carl Hulse, "Unity Was Emerging on Sentencing. Then Came Jeff Sessions," *New York Times*, May 14, 2017, https://www.nytimes.com/2017/05/14/us /politics/jeff-sessions-criminal-sentencing.html.

CHAPTER 7: FROM URBAN TO RURAL AND BACK

1. Gregory Hooks et al., "Revisiting the Impact of Prison Building on Job Growth: Education, Incarceration, and County-Level Employment, 1976–2004," *Social Science Quarterly* 91, no. 1 (2010): 228–44.

2. Gwyneth Troyer, *2015 Monitoring Report Pontiac Correctional Center* (Chicago: John Howard Association of Illinois, 2015).

3. This story was part of an interview series conducted by Kathryn Bocanegra and Grant Buhr: "When's the Cycle Going to Break?," *Two Sides of Justice*, prod. Kathryn Bocanegra, audio file, https://soundcloud.com/2sidesofjustice/sets, accessed June 25, 2017. Carlos Miranda, "Save Pontiac Prison," *Pantagraph*, July 9, 2008.

4. Tony Sapchetti, "1000-Plus People Show Up for Giant 'Save Pontiac Prison' Photo," *Pantagraph*, June 21, 2008.

5. "COGFA Advisory Opinion on Pantiac Correctional Center Issued," *Pontiac Daily Leader*, September 25, 2008.

6. Amy K. Gladmeier and Tracey Farrigan, "The Economic Impacts of the Prison Development Boom on Persistently Poor Rural Places," *International Regional Science Review* 30, no. 3 (2007): 274–99.

7. Ryan S. King, Marc Mauer, and Tracy Huling, "Big Prisons, Small Towns: Prison Economics in Rural America," Sentencing Project, Washington, DC, Feburary 1, 2003.

8. Gladmeier and Farrigan, "The Economic Impacts of the Prison Development Boom on Persistently Poor Rural Places."

9. "Illinois Prison Overview," Illinois State Commission on Criminal Justice Sentencing Reform, http://www.icjia.org/cjreform2015/research/illinois-prison -overview.html, accessed July 2, 2016.

10. Elizabeth Hinton, *From the War on Poverty to the War on Crime: The Making of Mass Incarceration in America* (Cambridge, MA: Harvard University Press, 2016).

11. Peck and Theodore, "Carceral Chicago," 6.

12. National Research Council, *The Growth of Incarceration in the United States: Exploring Causes and Consequences* (Washington, DC: National Academies Press, 2014).

13. Alexander, *The New Jim Crow.*

14. Hinton, *From the War on Poverty to the War on Crime.*

15. Larry Bennett, Janet L. Smith, and Patricia A. Wright, eds., *Where Are the Poor People to Live? Transforming Public Housing Communities* (New York: Routledge, 2015).

16. National Research Council, *The Growth of Incarceration in the United States.*

17. Alexander, *The New Jim Crow.*

18. See also Simon, *Governing Through Crime.*

19. Alexander, *The New Jim Crow.*

20. Gilmore, *Golden Gulag.*

21. Alexander, *The New Jim Crow.*

22. Gilmore, *Golden Gulag.*

23. Chris Kirkham, "Private Prison Corporation Offers Cash in Exchange for State Prisons," *Huffington Post*, February 14, 2012, http://www.huffingtonpost.com /2012/02/14/private-prisons-buying-state-prisons_n_1272143.html.

24. Gottschalk, *Caught.*

25. Rich Miller, "Rauner's Turnaround Agenda Math Doesn't Add Up," *Crain's Chicago Business*, January 19, 2016, http://www.chicagobusiness.com/article/20160119 /NEWS02/160119822/rauners-turnaround-agenda-math-doesnt-add-up.

26. Illinois Partners for Human Services, *Human Services as an Economic Engine: How Human Services in Illinois Drive Jobs and Economic Benefits* (Chicago: Illinois Partners for Human Service, May 2016), https://www.scribd.com/doc /313584219/Economic-Impact-Report-Illinois-budget-impasse.

27. William Julius Wilson, *When Work Disappears: The World of the New Urban Poor* (New York: Vintage Books, 1997). See also Immergluck, *Foreclosed.*

28. Illinois Criminal Justice Information Authority, "Adult Redeploy Illinois Dashboard Report," August 4, 2016 http://www.icjia.org/redeploy/pdf /publications/Adult_Redeploy_Illinois_Dashboard_080416.pdf, accessed November 15, 2016.

29. Ibid.

30. Katherine Beckett and Bruce Western, "Governing Social Marginality: Welfare, Incarceration, and the Transformation of State Policy," *Punishment and Society* 3, no. 1 (2001): 43–59.

31. For example, the Movement for Black Lives policy platform calls for investment in economic justice and reparations for black neighborhoods, in addition to ending overpolicing and mass incarceration. "Policy," Movement for Black Lives, https://policy.m4bl.org/platform/, accessed October 10, 2017.

CHAPTER 8: LIMITS TO REFORM

1. Daniel Cooper and Tiffany McDowell, *The Downward Spiral: The Impact of Illinois' Year Without a Budget* (Chicago: Adler University Institute on Social Exclusion, June 1, 2016), http://www.adler.edu/resources/content/3/3/8/1 /documents/ISE_IllinoisReport_v06.pdf.

2. According to the Pew Research Center, only 19 percent of Americans believe government is working for the benefit of all people; this figure is an all-time low in the poll. See Pew Research Center, "Beyond Distrust: How Americans View Their Government," Washington, DC, November 23, 2015, http://www .people-press.org/files/2015/11/11–23–2015-Governance-release.pdf.

3. The Pew Research Center reports that 53 percent of Americans want a smaller government with fewer services, while 38 percent want a bigger government with more services. This gap was larger in the 1980s. See ibid.

4. For a common example of the narrative about attracting businesses through tax breaks and cutting pensions, see "Foxconn: How the Cookie Crumbles for Illinois Economy," editorial, *Chicago Tribune*, August 2, 2017, http://www .chicagotribune.com/news/opinion/editorials/ct-foxconn-illinois-wisconsin -jobs-edit-0803-jm-20170802-story.html.

5. Rick Pearson, "Rauner Vetoes Automatic Voter Registration Bill," *Chicago Tribune*, August 12, 2016, http://www.chicagotribune.com/news/local/politics/ct -bruce-rauner-veto-automatic-voter-registration-met-0813–20160812-story.html.

6. Eric M. Uslaner and Mitchell Brown, "Inequality, Trust, and Civic Engagement," *American Politics Research* 31, no. 10 (2003): 1–28.

7. The Pew Research Center finds that people identify "the influence of special interests" as the biggest problem with elected officials and that 76 percent of the public believe that money has a larger influence on politics now than at any time in the past. See Pew Research Center, "Beyond Distrust."

8. As trust in government declines, so does political participation. People tend to disengage and are less likely to do things like vote in elections when they believe government is not working for them. See Uslaner and Brown, "Inequality, Trust, and Civic Engagement."

9. Manuel Funke, Moritz Schularick, and Christoph Trebesch, "Politics in the Slump: Polarization and Extremism after Financial Crises," CESifo Working Paper No. 5553, 2015.

10. Thomas Piketty, *Capital in the Twenty-First Century*, trans. Arthur Goldhammer (Cambridge MA: Belknap Press of Harvard University Press, 2014).

11. Richard V. Reeves, "Stop Pretending You're Not Rich," *New York Times,* June 10, 2017.

12. As Gary Solon, one of the leading scholars of social mobility, put it recently, "Rather than a poverty trap, there seems instead to be more stickiness at the other end: a 'wealth trap,' if you will." Richard V. Reeves, "Stop Pretending You're Not Rich," *New York Times*, June 10, 2017.

13. Jacob S. Hacker and Paul Pierson, *Winner-Take-All Politics: How Washington Made the Rich Richer—and Turned Its Back on the Middle Class* (New York: Simon & Schuster Paperbacks, 2010).

14. Ibid.

15. Dedrick Asante-Muhammed, Chuck Collins, Josh Hoxie, and Emanuel Nieves, *The Ever-Growing Gap: Without Change, African-American and Latino Families*

Won't Match White Wealth for Centuries (Washington, DC: CFED, August 2016), http://www.ips-dc.org/wp-content/uploads/2016/08/The-Ever-Growing-Gap-CFED_IPS-Final-2.pdf.

16. Peter Baker, "Obama, in Oklahoma, Takes Reform Message to the Prison Cell Block," *New York Times*, July 16, 2015, https://www.nytimes.com/2015/07/17/us/obama-el-reno-oklahoma-prison.html.

17. The Obama administration also pushed for treating the issue as a matter of public health best treated through prevention. However, the willingness to take a more public health–oriented approach to drugs does not extend to drug sales.

18. Alexander, *The New Jim Crow.*

19. Eric Holder, "Remarks at the Annual Bar Association's House of Delegates," US Department of Justice, Washington, DC, August 12, 2013, https://www.justice.gov/opa/speech/attorney-general-eric-holder-delivers-remarks-annual-meeting-american-bar-associations.

20. Illinois State Commission on Criminal Justice and Sentencing Reform, *Final Report (Parts I & II)* (Chicago: Illinois Commission on Criminal Justice and Sentencing Reform, December 2016), http://www.icjia.org/cjreform2015/pdf/CJSR_Final_Report_Dec_2016.pdf.

21. See Keith Humphrys, "There's Been a Big Drop in the Black Incarceration Rate and Almost Nobody's Been Paying Attention," *Washington Post*, February 10, 2016, https://www.washingtonpost.com/news/wonk/wp/2016/02/10/almost-nobody-is-paying-attention-to-this-massive-change-in-criminal-justice. See also Mike Males, "A Modest Theory of Why Conservatives Suddenly Champion Criminal Justice Reform," Center on Juvenile and Criminal Justice, June 23, 2015, http://www.cjcj.org/news/9351.

22. Males, "A Modest Theory of Why Conservatives Suddenly Champion Criminal Justice Reform."

23. Ibid.

24. Illinois Sentencing Policy Advisory Council, "Illinois Results First: The High Cost of Recidivism," Summer 2015, http://www.icjia.state.il.us/spac/pdf/illinois_results_first_1015.pdf.

25. Christopher T. Lowenkamp and Edward J. Latessa, "Increasing the Effectiveness of Correctional Programming through the Risk Principle: Identifying Offenders for Residential Placement," *Criminology and Public Policy* 4, no. 2 (2005): 263–90.

26. Danielle Kaeble and Thomas P. Bonczar, "Probation and Parole in the United States, 2015," *Bureau of Justice Statistics Bulletin* NJ250230 (December 2016), revised February 2, 2017, https://www.bjs.gov/content/pub/pdf/ppus15.pdf.

27. Jesse Jannetta, Justin Breaux, and Helen Ho, *Examining Racial and Ethnic Disparities in Probation Revocation* (Washington, DC: Urban Institute, April 2014), http://www.urban.org/sites/default/files/publication/22746/413174-Examining-Racial-and-Ethnic-Disparities-in-Probation-Revocation.pdf.

28. Corina Graif, Andrew Gladfelter, and Stephen A. Matthews, "Urban Poverty and Neighborhood Effects on Crime: Incorporating Spatial and Network Perspectives," *Sociology Compass* 8, no. 9 (2014): 1141–55.

29. Edward J. Latessa et al., "Creation and Validation of the Ohio Risk Assessment System: Final Report," unpublished paper, School of Criminal Justice, University of Cincinnati, July 2009, http://www.uc.edu/content/dam/uc/ccjr/docs /reports/project_reports/ORAS_Final_Report.pdf.

30. E. Ann Carson and Elizabeth Anderson, "Prisoners in 2015," *Bureau of Justice Statistics Bulletin*, no. NCJ 250229 (December 2016), https://www.bjs.gov /content/pub/pdf/p15.pdf.

31. John F. Pfaff, *Locked In: The True Causes of Mass Incarceration and How to Achieve Real Reform* (New York: Basic Books, 2017).

32. Gottschalk, *Caught*.

33. Eric L. Sevigny and Jonathan P. Caulkins, "Kingpins or Mules: An Analysis of Drug Offenders Incarcerated in Federal and State Prisons," *Criminology and Public Policy* 3, no. 3 (2004): 401–22.

34. Ryan King, Bryce Peterson, Brian Elderbroom, and Elizabeth Pelletier, "Reducing Mass Incarceration Requires Far-Reaching Reforms," *Urban Institute*, http:// webapp.urban.org/reducing-mass-incarceration/, accessed February 10, 2016.

35. Cook County Circuit Court data made available by the Chicago Justice Project. See "Convicted in Cook," chicagojusticeproject.org, December 15, 2014, https://chicagojustice.org/2014/12/15/convicted-cook-release.

36. Authors' analysis of Cook County Circuit Court data made available by the Chicago Justice Project. See "Convicted in Cook," chicagojusticeproject.org, December 15, 2014, https://chicagojustice.org/2014/12/15/convicted-cook -release.

37. Pfaff, *Locked In*.

38. Ibid.

39. The most famous example is the case of Willie Horton, a man who received an early release work furlough in Massachusetts under Governor Michael Dukakis and later went on to commit additional violent offenses. George H. W. Bush continually hammered Dukakis, the Democratic nominee, about this during the 1988 presidential campaign.

40. Californians for Safety and Justice, *California Crime Victims' Voices: Findings from the First-Ever Survey of California Crime Victims and Survivors*, http:// libcloud.s3.amazonaws.com/211/72/d/228/2/VictimsReport_07_16_13.pdf, accessed March 27, 2016.

41. US Sentencing Commission, *Report on the Continuing Impact of* United States v. Booker *on Federal Sentencing*, report to Congress (Washington, DC: December 2012), https://www.ussc.gov/research/congressional-reports/2012-report -congress-continuing-impact-united-states-v-booker-federal-sentencing.

42. National Research Council, *The Growth of Incarceration in the United States*.

43. Gottschalk, *Caught*.

44. Christopher T. Lowenkamp and Edward J. Latessa, "Understanding the Risk Principle: How and Why Correctional Interventions Can Harm Low-Risk Offenders," *Topics in Community Corrections* Annual Issue (2004): 1–8.

45. Jennifer Gonnerman, "Million-Dollar Blocks," *Village Voice*, November 9, 2004; Cadora et al., *Architecture and Justice.*

46. Nancy LaVigne et al., *Justice Reinvestment Initiative State Assessment Report* (Washington, DC: Urban Institute/Bureau of Justice Assistance, January 2014), http://www.ajc.state.ak.us/acjc/sentencing%20reform/reinvest.pdf.

47. James Austin et al., "Ending Mass Incarceration: Charting a New Justice Reinvestment," Sentencing Project, Washington, DC, April, 2013, http://sentencing project.org/wp-content/uploads/2015/12/Ending-Mass-Incarceration-Charting -a-New-Justice-Reinvestment.pdf.

48. Ibid.

49. California voters approved Proposition 47 in 2014 in order to address the state budget crisis and prison overcrowding. For more information on the proposition, see "What You Need to Know about Proposition 47," California Department of Corrections and Rehabilitation, http://www.cdcr.ca.gov/news/prop47 .html, accessed September 7, 2017.

50. Illinois's Republican governor Bruce Rauner and Democrat senator Kwame Raoul coauthored an op-ed expressing support for criminal justice reform: "Dems and Republicans Can Reduce Illinois Prison Population," *Chicago Sun-Times*, June 24, 2016, http://chicago.suntimes.com/news/dems-and -republicans-can-reduce-illinois-prison-population/.

51. Colin Dwyer, "Sessions Tells Prosecutors to Seek 'Most Serious' Charges, Stricter Sentences," National Public Radio, May 12, 2017, http://www.npr.org /sections/thetwo-way/2017/05/12/528086525/sessions-tells-prosecutors-to -seek-most-serious-charges-stricter-sentences.

52. Oliver Roeder, Lauren-Brooke Eisen, and Julia Bowling, *What Caused the Crime Decline?* (New York: Brennan Center for Justice, New York University School of Law, 2015).

53. While incarceration rates fall nationwide, Illinois is lagging behind, and violent crime has climbed in Chicago.

54. 2016 American Community Survey Population Estimate, https://factfinder .census.gov/.

55. Marwa Eltagouri and Grace Wong, "Chicago Area Leads U.S. in Population Loss, Sees Drop for 2nd Year in a Row," *Chicago Tribune*, March 23, 2017.

56. Rugh and Massey, "Racial Segregation and the American Foreclosure Crisis."

57. Huiping Li, Harrison Campbell, and Steven Fernandez, "Residential Segregation, Spatial Mismatch and Economic Growth across US Metropolitan Areas," *Urban Studies* 50, no. 13 (2013): 2642–60.

58. Robert DeFina and Lance Hannon, "The Impact of Mass Incarceration on Poverty," *Crime and Delinquency* 59, no. 4 (2013): 562–86.

59. Clear et al., "Predicting Crime Through Incarceration."

CONCLUSION: THE PATH TO PEACE

1. Alexander, *The New Jim Crow*.
2. For more on antiblack racism in Chicago, see "A World Without Prisons: A Conversation with Mariame Kaba," *Lumpen Magazine*, April 7, 2016.
3. In failing to create reliable pathways for learning and growth, we have actively fueled prison cycling for decades. See Clear et al., "Predicting Crime Through Incarceration"; Adam Liptak, "Inmate Count in U.S. Dwarfs Other Nations," *New York Times*, April 23, 2008.
4. For an international example of this model, see Lauren Frayer, "In Portugal, Drug Use Is Treated as a Medical Issue, Not a Crime," National Public Radio, April 18, 2017.
5. Anyone near an organization involved in the Black Lives Matter (http://black livesmatter.com/) movement can lend their skills and expertise to its work, helping to meet existing needs and grow the scale of its influence.
6. In the movie *Adventures in Babysitting* (1987), a suburban babysitter ends up navigating the underbelly of Chicago's crime scene. *Candyman* (1992) is a supernatural horror film set in Cabrini Green, a once iconic public-housing development.
7. Mass incarceration and divestment from the social safety net in the US are conceptually intertwined policy moves. These links are also well covered in scholarship by Beth Richie, Loic Wacquant, Jill McCorkel, and others.
8. See Trauma Response and Intervention Movement (http://www.tr4im.org); Lawndale Christian Legal Center (http://lclc.net). For a leading example of community-based restorative justice in Chicago, see the Precious Blood Center for Reconciliation (http://www.pbmr.org). For details on the restorative justice community court, see Kunichoff, "Should Communities Have a Say in How Residents Are Punished for Crime?"
9. See Institute for Nonviolence Chicago (http://www.nonviolencechicago.org/). READI stands for Rapid Employment And Development Initiative. It is a project of Heartland Alliance for Human Needs and Human Rights.
10. See Melissa Harris-Perry, "'Peace Rooms' a Safe Space for Chicago Students," MSNBC, October 24, 2015. For a powerful article on responding to trauma exposure at scale, see Stevan E. Hobfoll et al., "Five Essential Elements of Immediate and Mid-Term Mass Trauma Intervention: Empirical Evidence." *Psychiatry* 70, no. 4 (2007): 283–315, doi:10.1521/psyc.2007.70.4.283, and the discussion that follows on pp. 316–69.
11. This coordination must be created both between residents and organizations, and between scales and sectors of government.
12. For a link between the idea of reinvestment and reparation, see the Movement for Black Lives policy platform. "Reparations," Movement for Black Lives, https://policy.m4bl.org/reparations, accessed September 7, 2017.
13. For more on effective supports, see "Supporting Children and Families of Prisoners," Child Welfare Information Gateway, https://www.childwelfare.gov /topics/supporting/support-services/prisoners, accessed September 7, 2017.

14. Martin, "Gale Cincotta, 72, Opponent of Biased Banking Policies."

15. Victoria Salinas, "Founder of Westside Health Authority honored," *Austin Talks*, December 14, 2011.

16. For the effects of lead exposure on violent crime, see Michael Hawthorne, "Studies Link Childhood Lead Exposure, Violent Crime," *Chicago Tribune*, June 6, 2015.

17. See Environment, Culture, and Conservation (ECCo), *Engaging Chicago's Diverse Communities in the Chicago Climate Action Plan: Community #8: Austin*, research report, Field Museum, 2012.

18. A recent example is the effort made to successfully complete an application to the US Department of Education to become one of its Promise Neighborhoods sites, a process that required the commitment of dozens of local agencies and schools, as well as key outside institutions. No grant was awarded.

19. Since its founding, ACT has been sustained with the support of well-established groups such as Bethel New Life, Good City, and Friendship Baptist Church.

20. John Kania and Mark Kramer, "Collective Impact," *Stanford Social Innovation Review* (Winter 2011), https://ssir.org/articles/entry/collective_impact.

21. ACT draws from multiple strategies for building strong neighborhood networks. One is the collective impact method, which is said to have five key conditions: (1) a common agenda, (2) shared measurement, (3) mutually reinforcing activities, (4) continuous communication, and (5) a backbone organization, which could be a public or private entity so long as it is respected and trusted by all key stakeholders. Each of these components helps foster healthy inter-organizational relationships and, in so doing, facilitates long-term success. Kania and Kramer, "Collective Impact."

22. James Reynolds Jr., "Another Weekend, Another Shooting? Chicago Needs a Marshall Plan," *Chicago Business Journal*, July 2014, http://www.chicagobusiness .com/article/20140714/OPINION/140719946/another-weekend-another -shooting-chicago-needs-a-marshall-plan.

23. See "Reducing Toxic Stress to Help Students Succeed," Urban Labs, University of Chicago, https://urbanlabs.uchicago.edu/projects/quiet-time, accessed September 7, 2017; Audie Cornish, "Chicago Teens and Combat Veterans Join Forces to Process Trauma," National Public Radio, January 25, 2016; Ulrich Boser, "The Youth-Counseling Program Helping to Curb Chicago's Violence," *Atlantic*, June 13, 2017. At the adult level, there is also much evidence supporting more cost-effective and efficacious alternatives to adult incarceration for a broad range of offense categories. States such as Ohio and California have reduced re-offense rates through the use of alternative sentencing. In Illinois, the Adult Redeploy program has shown promise in reducing prison sentences and spending, while addressing the physical and mental health challenges faced by many. However, these efforts often do not go far enough. They are normally deployed only after someone has been to prison rather than when earlier signs

of trouble appear, such as at the point of arrest. They are also rarely extended to nonviolent, non-serious, and nonsexual offense categories.

24. A parallel effort to this is Chicago Beyond, https://www.chicagobeyond.org.

25. Brett Cyrgalis, "LeBron James Pledges $87M for Hometown Kids to Attend College," *New York Post*, August 14, 2015, http://nypost.com/2015/08/14/lebron -james-pledges-87m-for-hometown-kids-to-attend-college.

26. Chip Mitchell, "The Cost of Jobs," *Every Other Hour*, WBEZ, July 6, 2017, http://interactive.wbez.org/everyotherhour/the-cost-of-jobs/. For the history and current work of Manufacturing Renaissance, see http://mfgren.org.

27. For more on the role of human capital in economic development, see Jacob Mincer, "Human Capital and Economic Growth," NBER Working Paper No. 803, National Bureau of Economic Research, Cambridge, MA, November 1981; Jess Benhabib and Mark M. Spiegel, "The Role of Human Capital in Economic Development: Evidence from Aggregate Cross-Country Data," *Journal of Monetary Economics* 34 (1994): 143–73.

28. Collective impact efforts such as the Strive Together Network are well positioned to play leading roles in helping align and coordinate efforts in high-incarceration neighborhoods in urban places across the country.

29. Public safety is rarely taken up as a sphere of concern in either urban planning or public health, mostly because of professional territory rather than the actual importance of safety or its relationship to other major urban concerns. But public safety is foundational to nearly all aspects of urban life. It clearly affects matters of education, housing, the labor market, municipal finance, community development, and more.

30. See County Health Rankings, http://www.countyhealthrankings.org.

31. For an excellent review of restorative policymaking, see the work of the Illinois Justice Project, http://www.iljp.org/policy-and-legislation.

32. Part of this belief system is about which institutions are empowered to work toward safety. Importantly, private prisons are not allowed in the state of Illinois. But in many states, the role of corporate-run penal institutions is an additional hurdle to be overcome.

33. For an international example of a more enlightened system, see Christina Sterbenz, "Why Norway's Prison System Is So Successful," *Business Insider*, December 11, 2014.

INDEX